DRIVEN B

W

THE CO. ...IVE

John Newton	Salvatore d'Bergamasco
Deane Smith	Novella d'Bergamasco
Tony Flood	Anton d'Bergamasco
Karen Glennon	Isabella d'Bergamasco
Richard Rewell	Giuseppe d'Bergamasco
Tim Purcell	Frank Howard Bernstein
Francis Wait	Francisco D'Angelo
Sean Darcy	Cesare Pancucci

First published as a Paperback in The United Kingdom by Next Century Books in September 2023

Cover Design and Layout by
Tannishtha Chakraborty

I have a passion for design and want always to design and present good book covers. I specialise in anything print related and the challenge of bringing uniqueness to each design or book cover I work on.
tan.printdesigner@gmail.com.

All characters in this book are from the Authors' imaginations.

Printed and bound in The UK by

P2D Books
Milton Keynes MK45 5LD

ISBN 979-8-8651923-9-8

The Collective Authors

JOHN NEWTON – John, aged 88 is our oldest member, but you'd never guess it. Educated in Germany, John has travelled much of the world, has lived in five countries, and speaks four languages. Leaving The Kenya Police, he moved into business in Nairobi and became Regional Director for Schweppes in East and West Africa, Arabia, and India. Returning to Britain after twenty years he built up a very successful foods importing business. In a busy writing and broadcasting life he has written twelve successful books one of which continues to sell worldwide. The idea for 'Driven By Desire', his thirteenth, came when waking up on Christmas Eve 2022.

TIM PURCELL - In a media career spanning six decades Tim has been a screenwriter, investigative journalist for the UK national press, published author, publisher, director and producer of corporate and music videos, documentaries, TV series and feature films in the UK and Mauritius, where he helped to bring in the Film Incentive Scheme in 2013. Since its launch Tim has co-produced nine international Films and TV series from the UK, Canada, South Africa, Israel, Japan, Hong Kong and China including the 2014 box office hit, 'Break-Up Guru.'

3

KAREN GLENNON – In the 1990's, having been sponsored to complete a foundation course in journalism, Karen wrote for The Maynooth Newsletter, County Kildare, Ireland. She was a member of the editorial committee, author of articles on local celebrated individuals, critiqued movies, wrote comical pieces and reported on local events. After leaving Ireland, having worked for 18 years as a legal secretary, Karen continued to raise her family in Spain, during which time she found employment as a coach tour guide. Karen moved to the UK in 2015 immersing herself in writing entertaining blogs about everyday life, *Karensmadworld*, and a children's book *Mumpy's Tired Eyes*.

TONY FLOOD - Tony spent most of his working life as a journalist, initially on local and regional papers and then on nationals. He was also editor of 'Football Monthly', Controller of Information at Sky Television and enjoyed a spell with 'The People' before retiring in 2010. In *'My Life With The Stars'*, Tony recalls: *"My work as a showbiz and leisure writer, critic and editor saw me take on a variety of challenges - learning to dance with Strictly Come Dancing star Erin Boag, becoming a stand-up comedian and playing football with the late George Best and Bobby Moore in charity matches."* Tony now spends much of his time writing books and theatre reviews.

RICHARD REWELL – As a Qualified Chartered Surveyor Richard worked in the construction industry for over 35 years. Employed by both international companies and private consultancies on UK and overseas projects. His responsibilities ranged from construction finance and

4

sales to the production of in-house journals. This gave him a passion for writing. Although comparatively new to the craft, Richard has had one short story, '*The Fish Gutter's Journey*', and is currently working on his debut solo novel, '*Whisper Not The True King's Name*', a thriller to be published in 2024.

FRANCIS WAIT – Most of 84-year-old Francis's working life has been in the building industry, running his own company since 1970, his final business years spent in Belgium. Harbouring his ambitions to be a writer, to provide for his family, until he retired in 2004. Since then, Francis has won the Anderida Short Story Competition three times. self-published a number of books which are still available on Amazon, 'The Survivalists' 2019, 'Android Affair' 2020, and the fantasy novel, 'The Magical Pendant of Perdania', under the pen name, Frances Jaycee. Francis is also Membership Secretary and Treasurer of the Anderida Writing Group. He shows no sign of slowing down, having several new novels in the pipeline in addition to his own contribution to 'Driven by Desire'

DEANE SMITH – A trained Wigmaker who became interested in Alternative and Complementary Therapies in the 1980's and qualified as a Spiritual and Reiki Healer. Deane became a Practitioner of the Metamorphic Prenatal Technique and had two articles published in a national magazine. This led to an interest in creative writing, poems, and short stories. She joined Eastbourne Anderida Writers Club in 2019, where she met John

Newton who asked her to join his Collective group of writers for the book `Driven by Desire.'

Authors Previous Books

By John Newton

White Sunrise
Kitchen Gangster
The Assassination Diaries Comprising: -
The Bishop
The Mandarin
The Oligarch written with Tim Purcell
The Judges Part One
The Judges Part Two
The Judges Part Three
The Kenya Police Trilogy

By Tim Purcell

Wartime Wanderers
The Oligarch written with John Newton
Silent Coup

By Tony Flood

Triple Tease
Stitch Up! - Killer Or Victim?
Fall Guy - Who Really Killed His Wife?
My Life With The Stars – Sizzling Secrets Spilled
Secret Potion - Fantasy Adventure
Laughs And Tears Galore - Stories And Poems

By Francis Wait

The Magical Pendant of Perdania
Android Affair
The Survivalists

Acknowledgement

John Silverton For His Early Work On This Book

Chapter 1

The Bergamasci- Salvatore

Late that evening in the year 1922, Salvatore leaned forward, squinting through the bright new electric lights of his studio, to re-examine every line of the final design of this exciting ultra-modern automobile. Fingers tracing the sweep of carefully drawn lines, his heart thumped. He almost wept at the perfect shape and his advanced original, ideas kept completely secret from even his family.

Hardly any other manufacturer kept out the weather with glass side windows or installed a quiet exhaust system or a hidden spare wheel. No other manufacturer fitted special safe locks to doors that hinged forward to stop them opening in the wind when driving fast.

Beauty, safety, speed, and comfort.

Salvatore glanced up at his papà's photograph staring down from the wall, holding one of the cigarettes that killed him.

'What do you think of this papà? Would you approve? And will my argumentative family at next week's Board Meeting?'

His loved and admired papà left his birth town, Avellino, in the unstable mountains behind Naples at the age of sixteen. He never said why.

He went north and settled in Bergamo on the edge of the Lombardy plain where he took work in a family automobile repair shop and changed his surname to d' Bergamasco. He never said why, and no one ever knew his birth name.

Poorly educated and shy, at the age of twenty he bought the elderly repair shop owner out and in the next fifty years turned it into Motori Bergamasco, a small successful hand-built automobile manufacturer, which allowed the family to live well. When papà died, his Will left the business to his children in equal shares, on the condition that they continued to work in the business. Mama died, almost certainly of a broken heart, two months later. Her devastated children pulled themselves together and followed papà's wishes to keep the business going.

'But you wouldn't have succeeded much longer papà,' whispered Salvatore to his father's stern eyes. 'You refused to modernise. Like Henry Ford you became complacent at the money rolling in, but he woke up and saved his business. You didn't. I can already see early illness in our company. We'll be gone sooner than we can imagine without change. Do you see my brilliant new design from heaven papà? If so help me persuade my brothers and sisters.'

Salvatore opened a large flat especially secure drawer, slid in the dozen precious drawings, and set the three extra-safe locks to which only he knew the combinations and went home.

The next morning, he dictated a strict instruction to all board members, calling an important Board Meeting 'To Discuss the Future of Our Beloved Company Motori Bergamasco,' insisting that everyone attend.

His secretary raised an eyebrow and asked, 'How do I get this to Professor Paolo?'

'Ignore him. He is up the Amazon studying insects. If the message got that far he'd never read it.'

Chapter 2

The Board Meeting – Salvatore

Salvatore looked at his brothers and sisters sitting along one side of the shining oak board table, whispering to each other, obviously puzzled at the tall metal easel on the other side facing them. A large plain curtain hung from the easel top to the polished wooden floor, hiding whatever may be behind.

Anton, Marketing Director, big, bluff exuding his usual over-confidence. Giuseppe, Financial Director, quiet and watchful as ever. The beautiful Isabella nicknamed Creative Genius, because of her bright mind and ability to see solutions other people miss. And Novella, pretty, quiet, retiring, and shy. No board title at the moment. Salvatore always thought she is hiding a keen brain, but deep shyness prevents her from displaying or using it. She never spoke at meetings.

Salvatore took a deep breath and said, 'I'll now tell you why I called you here.'

Whipping the easel curtain up and over in the most dramatic fashion he could muster, he stood aside and pointed with his metal wand at the large artistic depiction of his newly completed automobile design.

Every face changed from puzzlement to surprise. Before anyone could speak, he began a broad description of this pride and joy new design, ending with, 'I have been working on this for the past year in complete secrecy.'

Anton said, 'Wow. This looks fantastic but why didn't you tell us about it earlier?'

Salvatore said, 'I had to keep it to myself, Anton. I couldn't risk word getting out. I've been working on the design by myself late every night in the office. My wife thought I must be having an affair and gave me hell every time I came home around midnight.'

Anton laughed. 'Perchance you were doing that as well with a nice little piece on the side.'

Salvatore chuckled and said, 'Your dirty mind would think like that. This morning I explained part of the project to her, and she burst into tears of joy at being the only woman in my life.'

In an excited shout typical of him, Anton, bellowed, 'The bloody car looks great. Tell us more. Quick. Don't keep us in suspense. Get on and tell us.'

Salvatore flicked the first design page back to display the second again for only a few seconds. 'I've designed this model with an eight-cylinder engine augmented by two superchargers. But the engine cavity is designed to take any size of power plant, large or small for different markets and different models.'

'Brilliant,' whispered one of his brothers so softly, Salvatore could not tell which one.

Isabella spoke up. Her quick mind had taken in and retained all six design drawings. In her gently intelligent voice, she asked, 'Will we have several models of the prototype in production for the brochure? I'm thinking of a long-distance tourer, racing machine, etc?'

'Why do you ask? Have you any ideas?' asked Salvatore.

'Of course,' she said. 'Given the choice I suggest launching the racing car first.'

'Why?'

'On the other hand,' said Isabella, 'The less affluent among our customers would be thrilled to afford a more economical version with many of the futuristic features you have designed. We can make this basic design into anything because all the components are interchangeable. It can be the tourer, a racing machine, a town car, even a military armoured car or anything else that will make us money. And all from the same production line. It could become the most successful motor autovettura project in the history of driving machines: in the history of our industry.'

A collective gasp passed round the table. Looking around the table at the shock or delight on everyone's face, depending on their speed of thought, Salvatore felt a surge of pride.

Anton leapt to his feet in excitement. 'I'll be able to sell this all over the world,' he shouted, knocking over his chair, 'When do I start? Have you printed a brochure?'

'Sit down and shut up,' said Salvatore. 'We have no brochure. There will be nothing in print before we are ready to start production. Before you leave this room, you will all sign a legal document swearing you to secrecy. If any one of you lets even a syllable slip out, you'll be instantly kicked out of Motori Bergamasco and our family. Cut off completely. No salary, no pension. Your shareholding will be taken away and you will have no inheritance.'

Giuseppe raised a hand. 'But you said you told your wife.'

'I told her I am designing a new factory.'

Giuseppe said, 'I oppose the introduction of a new model at this time of great unrest in society, the fascist revolution and rise of Communism could lead to civil war.'

'Our workers are content,' said Salvatore.

'Only for the moment,' said Giuseppe.

Isabella laughed. 'Oh, be quiet Giuseppe. You're always such a glum devil. But Salvatore, what a brilliant mind you have. This is just what the company needs to give us an edge in this competitive motor industry. However, do we have enough money in the coffers for these progressive design proposals or will we need investors? If so, have you any in mind?'

'We don't want outside investors,' said Salvatore. 'They would be in on the secret and probably insecure. What is your opinion, Giuseppe? You are our financial wizard.'

Before Giuseppe could speak, Isabella raised a hand and said, 'I agree with Agnelli, chairman of FIAT. if we allow the unsettling direction politics is taking to stop Italy moving forward in business, the economy will grind to a halt.'

Isabella noted a scowl appear on Giuseppe's face as he glanced in her direction, obviously resentful of her support for Salvatore's arguments.

Giuseppe frowned and said, 'The manufacture of a new model would necessitate increased production capacity which is not possible at our current premises. We need to maintain current production levels to preserve our income stream and protect the profits of which you all share. We are a family organisation; a new factory would require outside financing from investors who would naturally wish to acquire a share and seat on the board. Our family would lose total control. He who holds the purse strings could put a noose around our necks. And take all our secrets. This is why I am against this project.'

'Oh Giuseppe, you're being a glum devil again. Just go out and find the money. You usually manage when we get short. Be positive for once. As the creative genius you call me, my thoughts are that in order to get out ahead of the competition, we need to go all out with the official launch of this innovative project. How much more pzazz could we create than involving the glitz and glamour of the movie industry. Maybe a silent screen star, like, say, Rudolph Valentino, becoming the face of the campaign?'

The words are out of Isabella's mouth before she can stop them. With bated breath she waits for a reaction from her peers. 'Oh God. Am I pushing too hard?

Anton piped up to say, 'Great idea.'

Isabella relaxed.

Giuseppe turned to Salvatore and said, 'I suppose you are presenting a good project, dear brother.'

Salvatore said, 'I think it will make our fortune and take us to being one of the most important motor manufacturers in the world.'

Giuseppe creased his face into an expression of doubt. 'I appreciate the modular design has great possibilities for various models and applications, but it's the wrong time to invest in expansion in the current unstable political climate. If the board approves this expansion, we'll need a new factory, Salvatore. What plans do you have for that?'

'I did not lie to my wife. I have already designed a new factory and production line and surveyed a large greenfield site near Brescia. I told the owner we need a large food producing factory.'

Giuseppe chuckled and conceded, 'For once you are ahead of me, Salvatore. I am still against the project on financial grounds and will vote against. But call a vote now so the project becomes official.'

Before Salvatore could call the vote, Novella at the bottom of the table, raised a shy hand.

'Yes Novella. You have something to say?'

'Yes please. If I am allowed.'

Salvatore saw every head along the table turn towards Novella, probably all feeling the same surprise. So shy, she never spoke at Board Meetings and always voted in favour of every motion.

Novella took a deep breath and said in her little nervous voice, 'How exciting. A brand-new car design. I'm all in favour of that.'

'Well done, Novella,' shouted Anton. 'Come on Salvatore. Get on with the vote.'

'Wait,' said Novella in a surprisingly more confident tone. 'I have some great ideas for the prototype. Do hear me out please.'

Everyone fell silent and turned towards this new phenomenon of Novella asserting herself. Salvatore took his seat for the first time since starting the meeting, elbows on the table, chin in hands.

With increasing confidence, Novella began to reel off a series of suggestions. 'Autumn represents change a time for letting go of old ideas and preparing for the new to come in. Therefore, I'd like to see warm feminine autumn colours for the upholstery.

'For the interior of the vehicle, I suggest the colour of burnt orange for the upholstery to match with a chestnut dashboard in either leather or quality vinyl the interior of doors in peach, with one white lily to represent the flower of our beloved country.

'The outside of the car the colour of gold. On the two back wheel arches we can add a row of the red Bergamo Sedum Palmeri flowers. Another key feature, an electrically raised flag symbolising the white lily, easily adapted for the buyer's own personal country or needs.

'We could also include adjustable head rests made in soft durable woven material to match the door panels and help avoid whiplash if the car is hit from behind.

'For extra money future colours and materials can be easily adapted to suit a buyers' own needs.'

She paused and gulped.

Completely taken aback, Anton whispered, 'Wonderful. I could sell that by the millions to lady drivers.'

Isabella broke the short silence that followed, by tapping her palms together in a quiet clap that rippled around the board table as everyone joined in. 'Brilliant, Novella, my quiet little sister. Absolutely brilliant.'

Novella burst into tears.

Isabella jumped up and ran to hug her.

Novella recovered enough to say, 'And we could place a large silver medallion depicting a winged woman with long flowing hair at the top of the radiator presenting the warm feminine personality. Perhaps you could use it in advertising and the promotion of Motori Bergamasco, Anton.'

Salvatore stood and held his arms up to command attention.

'Amazing,' he said. 'Absolutely amazing. Novella, you have never had a job on this company board. You have now. From this instant you are our Materials and Colour Co-ordinator. Raise hands all who agree.'

Everyone raised hands.

From Isabella's warm embrace, Novella began to weep again, but managed to say, 'And can we please give my name to the new automobile. Can we call it Novella, which could appear in silver across the rear of the car, and my name in the centre of the winged woman at the front?'

Before Salvatore could put it to the Board, every hand in the room shot up in favour.

Except Giuseppe's.

He frowned and said, 'This meeting is not yet over. I still remain unconvinced by your argument, Salvatore. I appreciate the style and modular design has great possibilities for various models and applications, but it's the wrong time to invest in expansion in the current unstable political climate and with rising inflation. The fascist revolution and rise of communism could lead to civil war. We have already witnessed the workers seize the FIAT plant and raise the red flag of communism. As you know, Giovanni Agnelli, chairman of FIAT, has been forced to quit the company.'

'Yes, I had lunch with Gianni last week. He intends to regain control. If he can't, Mussolini will send in the Blackshirts. They'll sort the bastards out.'

Giuseppe growled, 'FIAT is big enough to weather the political turbulence. We may not be. The manufacture of a new model would necessitate increased production capacity which is not possible at our current premises. We need to maintain current model production to preserve our income stream and protect the profits of which we all share.'

Salvatore laughed and said, 'I'm not stupid, Giuseppe. I have a costing plan to be discussed in due course.'

'Why not discuss it now? We are a family organisation; a new factory would require outside financing from investors who would naturally wish to acquire a share and seat on the board. Our family would lose total control.'

'Not necessarily,' said Salvatore. 'Very well, I'll explain. We need long term investors. I think we should find money in a different way. We can issue shares through the Roma stock exchange, marketed at the man-in-the-street using millions of small investors to minimise the risk to everyone. Anton will organise an advertising campaign to attract investors. Some bank funding may be necessary to show security and the family board members would remain in control.'

'An interesting idea dear brother. You realise we are talking of raising capital in the region of two billion lire to fund this project in the first year. A small production unit, of say, 100,000 square metres would be in the order of 800,000 lire just for the building: land, machinery with additional marketing costs would be additional. We would not make a profit for several years. In any case, you're neither an accountant nor financier. What the hell do you know about money?' snapped Giuseppe.

'More than you think, *dear brother*. You're not the only one who can count. I have a legal group advising me on how to protect the core business and the family. The new venture is planned as a separate company with clear limited liability both legally and financially. Have you, the big clever finance man thought of that? I'll bet you haven't. If so tell me.'

Giuseppe looked down at the table, his face consumed in fury. He remained silent, appearing unable to respond.

Salvatore saw his family sitting watchful and silent. appearing content to allow the two angry brothers to fight it out. He studied Giuseppe's facial expression. It showed he knew he had lost and seemed reluctantly ready to concede that Salvatore had prepared his counter arguments well.

After a brief silence Giuseppe said, 'Very well. If the Board approves this expansion I will approach my good friend Giorgio Calvini, Chairman of Banco Ambrosiano, with a view to funding the project. The bank owns land outside the city which I've heard they are keen to develop for industrial use. However, there are few construction projects in Napoli that do not involve the Mafia, either through financing, construction materials or controlled labour. We don't want to attract unwanted attention from the Mafia. They may try to take us over.'

Salvatore shook his head and, glaring at his brother, snapped,' 'That's why I'm proposing my funding model to expand into this new project. Everybody knows that Calvini and his bank belong to the Cosa Nostra. We don't want to get into bed with them. We also know of some of your doubtful friendships and want nothing to do with those people.'

'Quite right,' agreed Isabella 'Luckily the Mafia has fewer connections here in the north than in the south, if this proposal becomes as big a success as it has the potential to, we'll need to do the utmost protect our interests.'

'Rather presumptuous of you to assume the board will approve the project,' said Giuseppe. My reservations, mainly because of the amount of money involved and the timing and the political uncertainty, remain unchanged. But if the board approves the project I will abide by their decision, and, if you allow me, as Finance Director, to meet your advisers I'll work with them on the share issue and if necessary, help arrange loans from one or more of the banks.'

Salvatore nodded. 'Ok Signore e signorini. Raise your hand if you approve the motion. Motion carried, with one against. I suggest we adjourn to Pavlov's Bar to celebrate. But remember, strict secrecy.

Giuseppe grunted and said, 'You all go ahead; I have a previous appointment this evening.'

'He's off to see his mistress,' Isabella whispered to Novella 'Every Thursday, "working late at the office." Poor Francesca . . . bastard.'

Novella murmured, 'Does Francesca know?'

'I expect so. Everyone else does.'

'I didn't.'

Chapter 3

Giuseppe and Rosalina

Giuseppe gave a sigh as he sat behind the wheel, a resigned sigh of the inevitable workload to come from Salvatore's new enterprise. But as he chugged out of the factory gates his face creased with a smile of pleasure; a short drive towards the town centre and he would be enveloped in the welcoming arms of his lover, the gorgeous Rosalina D'Innella.

With his marriage in the doldrums, he'd bought the one-bedroom flat as a bolt hole and investment two years ago and kept the acquisition from Francesca. The intention was to rent it out but during the renovations he had met and fallen in love with Rosalina, the flat now their venue for much needed romance and sex neither experienced in their marriages. Two, sometimes three evenings a week, he would use the 'working late at the office' excuse to Francesca. As for Rosalina, well, he never knew her conjured excuses to husband Giorgio, but she was always there waiting for him.

He smelled the delicious Bolognese sauce as he entered, saw the laid table with two candles flickering romantically. She hastened into his arms, they kissed and kissed.

'You look harassed,' she said concerned, removing his coat. 'Bad day at work?'

'Yes, problems,' he replied dolefully. 'A new venture proposed by Salvo. I was outvoted. It's madness to expand in the present uncertain political situation. It will mean much more work over the next few months and financial exposure to the company.'

'We will eat and then I will make you forget all your troubles,' she said enthusiastically.

He smiled in response to her suggestion. 'Let's eat later.'

Francesca was still awake when he arrived home. After a warm bath he wearily climbed into bed. She casually asked about his day, and he related the board meeting and decision that had gone against him. 'The extra work will involve more late office working,' he warned.

'Salvo always seems to get what he wants. You're the eldest, you control the finances, your vote should hold more sway,' she said in a disgruntled tone.

'And what did you do with your day dear?' he enquired, although not really interested.

'I had tea with Angelica this afternoon and dinner with my parents. My father said he had seen you entering a building in Seregino Road. What were you doing there? You said you were working at the office.'

'Oh, yes, I had to see one of our suppliers. Problems with production due to a workers' sit-in.'

'But it's all residential around there; there are no factories.'

'He was from Milano, visiting a relative, so I took the opportunity to meet him and sign a new contract. Now let's sleep, I've had a very tiring day.'

The next morning at the office Giuseppe gathered together the deeds and valuations of the company's freehold properties and, briefcase in hand, entered the waiting horse drawn taxi which cantered off to the local branch of the Bank of Ambrosiana. He had an appointment with manager Giorgio D'Innella to ascertain the bank's lending against the freeholds as securities and to discuss a share rights issue.

He had known Giorgio since his appointment as manager two years ago, meeting his wife Rosalina at a reception organised by the bank for local businesses. The moment their eyes met, Giuseppe and Rosalina realised there was inevitability to an affair of the heart. Giuseppe couldn't understand what she had seen in Giorgio to commit to marriage, the guy had no charisma, no warmth, an almost negative personality. She had sold herself into wealth, the comfortable lifestyle of a palatial villa on the outskirts of Bergamo. But with Giuseppe she had added love into her otherwise loveless life.

Giuseppe outlined the need for an initial loan of one billion lire without giving away any detail, save that it was for an additional production facility to expand their range. He eyed the man studying the property valuations and felt the surge of a delicious excitement when he thought that he had been bedding the guy's lovely wife for two years. How would Giorgio react if he told him? He regretted the affair had to remain secret.

Giorgio's scan of the deeds and valuations was annoyingly perfunctory, and he sensed a lack of enthusiasm, even of hostility, from the manager as he declined to offer finance, blaming the uncertain political situation. Did Giorgio know of their affair, but to preserve his marriage and social status pretended not to? Was his decision to refuse to finance Salvo's expansion in part an act of revenge?

Whatever the reason, Giuseppe felt affronted. 'Motori Bergamasco has banked at this branch for over thirty years, ever since my father began the business. We are a successful company with a loyal customer base, but we must innovate with new models as are FIAT and Ford if we are to keep and extend our market share. Expansion is not possible at our existing factory.'

'Obviously Motori Bergamasco is a respected company and valued customer, but the Bank's current policy is not to lend on speculative projects due to the civil unrest throughout the country. I think you will find other banks will take a similar stance.'

'Yes, but we are offering bricks and mortar security,' protested Giuseppe.

'With the rise of communism, we predict property prices will tumble,' countered Giorgio. 'And if Mussolini's fascists take control the whole country takes a leap into the unknown. I'm sorry, my hands are tied; that is the bank's present policy.'

'Maybe another bank will be more accommodating if rewarded with our account. I see loyalty carries no weight here.'

'Of course, we would be sorry to lose your account and the bank's policy is kept under review. In a few months the social situation may have resolved, and we will be able to help. But with the prospect of civil war, caution would appear to be prudent don't you think?'

Giuseppe inwardly agreed but wasn't going to reveal his thoughts to Giorgio.

'Now if you will excuse me, I have another appointment waiting,' said Giorgio, looking at his waistcoat pocket watch. 'In time I'm sure we will be able to help you.' He handed back the documents. Giuseppe avoided the handshake.

He was not entirely disappointed nor totally surprised the bank's response was aligned with his own concerns; he felt heartened by the vindication. He would report to Salvatore the need to look elsewhere for funding: other banks, companies looking for investment opportunities, or private financiers, not necessarily restricted to Italy. America seemed to be experiencing an exceptional boom time, 'The Roaring Twenties' he'd heard it called. Could Anton look into the potential for an American investor during his trip to New York?

Chapter 4

Isabella After The Board Meeting

Isabella sat on her bed sipping a last cup of cappuccino of the day, thinking of the board meeting. *Finally, someone is seeing sense. Salvatore's new secretly designed car is brilliant and will keep our fading company solvent for ever. Salvatore. Our parents must have seen the future and rightly named you as our true Saviour. Glory be to God!*

She smiled fondly thinking how mama would have scolded her for being dramatic, saying, 'Isabella. Always a drama, can you not calm yourself?'

It occurred to her now how boring that calm would be, and she doubted how she'd be able to maintain such a facade with Italian blood running through her veins. Isabella realised as a young schoolgirl that she saw the world in more colour than most people she knew, including her family. It brought life to the mundane, metaphorically rainy days. Too much life it may seem. She could still hear her mama's voice, fondly reprimanding 'Isabella, must you be so loud, perhaps you could tone it down a little, be more ladylike.'

Papa had loved Isabella's melodramatic side; he regularly pointed out how she took after one of his sisters, though always evasive when she urged him to elaborate a little.

Dear papà, *how I miss him.* A sudden sense of loss assaulted her. *Always such a closed book when it came to his past, but I felt he had written new chapters, for what reason he never explained, so I never asked why?*

Isabella recalled how papà had enjoyed the entertainment, explaining how she, his eldest daughter exuded an energy which drew people to her, and he regularly voiced how this would carry her through life, more than her stunning good looks ever could.

Looking in the mirror she saw the requisite long dark hair, a tangle of knots more than a mane of soft shiny curls. Twinkly dark eyes looked back at her as she scrunched her face with distaste.

Who must I thank for this rather large nose? Does that come from papà's sister, too? He never showed me a picture, so I have no idea.

A frown crept across her small mouth with its full ruby red lips, oblivious of the beauty her olive skinned, pixie shaped face reflected.

Isabella's protective brothers have always enjoyed the mischief she brought to an occasion. However, she feared her siblings may not take too kindly to the plans she has for a career outside the family business.

Without realising, Isabella spoke aloud to her image in the mirror. 'I so want to be on stage,'

She giggled nervously at herself for telling the truth, even to a mirror.

'It's like a drug that pulls me back again and again. What none of you know, dear brothers and sister is that, secretly, I've been performing in an amateur way, but having recently been spotted by a talent scout from Rome, an exciting opportunity might soon present itself.'

'My whole being comes alive when I'm acting,' she told the mirror. 'My head fills with joy when I think about it. I'll feel suffocated if I can't be out there regularly performing in front of an audience. No-one needs to know who I am; I'll be in character, and I can use a stage name. I feel like I'll die if I can't do this. I would be like a trapped bird. Maybe one day I'll star on the screen in a passionate movie with an organ playing romantic music while I swoon in Rudolph Valentino's arms.'

Until then, she felt her priorities should lie with Salvatore's new project, a swish, well-designed creation that she recognised as pure genius. Innovative and exciting news in a country on its knees economically, after the War, Isabella felt convinced a select clientele would be thrilled to see this project come into production. Thus, in her opinion, the company would be revitalised in more than a financial way, becoming leaders in their field. Ford Motors would need to look out. Isabella could see The Bergamasci taking to the world stage, with one particular family member going one step further, as far as the big screen. *Mama Mia.*

Chapter 5

Anton's Dilemma

Anton had much on his mind and his thoughts centred mainly on an offer he had been made to join a rival company.

Former college pal Bernard Myers, now working for his millionaire father at an American car manufacturer, had telegraphed to tell him that they were expanding into Europe with a new subsidiary called Comet Cars. They needed an experienced marketing director and Bernard had been in touch again to say that he was offering the job to Anton at almost double his present salary.

Myers' words kept buzzing in Anton's head. 'There's going to be rapid developments in the automotive industry, and we'll be at the forefront of that. This is too good a chance to pass up, buddy.'

But Salvatore's master plan meant Anton could have an exciting sales and marketing empire by simply staying put! The Italian family company Motori Bergamasco would no longer be in danger of going bust – instead it could eventually become a major player worldwide.

This is going to be a difficult choice. Do I accept the offer from Bernard to join a company giving me loads of money now or do I back Salvatore's 'master plan' for the future?

Anton had agreed to travel to New York to see Bernard and his father, so now he could kill two birds with one sailing by also checking out the American car industry for Motori Bergamasco.

The offer he had received from Myers must be kept

secret, but he needed to inform Salvatore about his trip to the States and took the opportunity to do so over lunch with his brother the next day in the up-market Queens restaurant.

After ordering the freshly caught lobster, Anton tactfully brought up the subject of his travel plan. He said: 'The USA is an ideal market for our Tourer and Town Car – they could both become very popular there. It will mean competing with the best that Ford have to offer but the time will soon be right for us to do so.'

'Sounds great,' responded Salvatore.

'I intend to sail to the States next week and spend most of my time in New York, finding out the best way to deliver and sell our cars. It might be possible for us to set up dealerships and I also need to talk to advertising agencies about projecting our image. Do you want me to try to sell our existing cars in the States or wait until the new models are ready in a year's time?'

His brother stroked his chin as he pondered the question. 'It will depend upon what response you get during your visit. Meanwhile, we'll be busy planning a new factory capable of producing the Town Car and the Tourer I've designed. You can arrange for your sister Novella to go to New York with you because she needs to see what the States can offer in seat coverings and other materials for the new cars.

'I've checked and there is a big textiles show on in Boston while you're there. You can send Novella up by train for a couple of days and even if the textiles are not suitable for motor vehicles, she'll come back with plenty of ideas we can manufacture outside of Italy to begin with. And there are a couple of textile shows in New York before you come home. Buy her a couple of tickets for those.'

Anton smiled with delight. *What luck. Novella will be fully occupied while I have my job interview.*

'You're a clever devil Salvatore,' he said. 'It'll direct Novella's energy and give her purpose.'

Anton finished his lobster and patted his ample stomach. He then sat back with a contented smile on his face, but it faded when Salvatore shared his thoughts on how they might promote the new cars.

'We could give a batch of them away to Mussolini and those who help him run the country,' he suggested. 'The ministers would love them, and we'd get great publicity.'

'We'd also get bad publicity,' pointed out Anton. 'There's a limit to how many cars we can afford to give away, and those ministers in opposition would be livid at not receiving one. They'd make allegations of a bribes scandal. No, Salvatore, that's not a good idea. It would be better to do a deal with one or two Italian film stars – if they were seen driving our cars most of the population would want one.'

'Just a souped-up Tourer for Mussolini, then,' said Salvatore, 'In special colours personal to him. And you'll be able to personally hand cars over to a couple of beautiful film stars. Do you know any?'

'A few,' said Anton, with a smile and a long wink.

Over coffee, Anton listened to Salvatore expand at length on his plans for the new cars. When his brother eventually paused for breath, he leaned across the table in close eye to eye contact and said: 'Don't you think we should also produce a high-powered racing car?'

Salvatore scoffed. 'There are so few Grand Prix cars or races it wouldn't sell.'

Anton's prominent, appealing features creased into

a grin. 'No. We wouldn't need to sell it. We'd only make two and form our own racing team simply to compete in the Grand Prix races. If we meet with even moderate success, it will put Motori Bergamasco on the world stage and encourage members of the public to buy similar models. Our new Town Car and Tourer would sell like hot cakes.'

Relaxed by wine and good food, Salvatore said, 'Yes, I think we could do that.'

He signed the bill and the two brothers walked from the restaurant happy at an excellent lunch and a productive discussion which could benefit them both in different ways.

Chapter 6

Novella After the Board Meeting

Novella left the Board Room feeling elated. She'd definitely been recognised as having a brain with intelligence. She quite surprised herself with the suggestions of colour for Salvatore's new design prototype. And also, delighted when everyone agreed that her name be used to represent the new trademark of Motori Bergamasco.

Knowing nothing of the automobile business, finance, and cylinder engines, she initially became scared to speak out. Yet beneath her fears something deep within came alive and Novella felt exhilarated when she stood and faced her elder siblings to talk about colours. What a buzz. What an experience. She loved it.

All she had ever felt was being an empty-headed silly girl, nervous and shy who could only make up knitting ideas for her skinny dolls and suddenly, overnight, she had become one of the team with a title. A part owner of papà's company. It now made sense why he had insisted, she took her place on the board. She now had a role in helping the company survive. She'd been made to realise that an automobile is more than an engine on wheels.

Novella felt proud of herself having unexpectedly found her voice and the ability to give opinions. And how coincidental that so soon after Salvatore demonstrated his new prototype, Isabella believed that money could be made for Novella by making her skinny doll clothes into children's and grown-up sizes.

'You could sell your ideas all over the world,' she said.

Novella realised that she could also profit from the sales of patterns to allow women to make their own clothes. *And I could manufacture and sell ready-made clothes for women off the peg.*

She couldn't be sure her brothers would understand, except her favourite, Paolo. She had never forgotten his wise words, 'Time is never wasted, whatever we do Novella. Everything we do is a learning curve, a reason that will make sense later. So, just keep doing what you are doing for the time being, and let fate take its course.'

That is what dear Paolo believes and now Novella believed it, too.

She spent a night of restless sleep and next morning woke full of doubt and feeling insecure about everything. She knew her dear papà had been born shy and wondered if his personality changed so dramatically overnight in the same way as hers. It didn't help that heavy grey clouds were laying heavy over the roof that morning.

Then Novella remembered the words of Salvatore: 'You have to remember how well papà did to overcome his shyness and to leave us with a business we can all be proud of, dear sister. If he can conquer his fear, so can you.'

Salvatore must be right, because she found that by putting her doubts aside, she could sense a remnant of change in herself, never before experienced. Her tummy seemed as tight as usual, and she felt taller in some strange way. This may be a sign of growing up now she had taken on a new presence of importance.

Just before the board meeting had ended, Salvatore suggested that Novella take a trip to America and find out more about colours and materials.

'Such a visit will be good for you, Novella, and for our company. You'll bring back plenty of news on what is happening and developing that fast changing and expanding market. Meet me in the lounge for coffee tomorrow afternoon and we'll make some plans for your journey and what information we need.'

Chapter 7

Frank Howard Bernstein

Frank knew his mother christened him Francesco, in deference to his Italian heritage but only she ever called him by that name. To everyone else he has always been Frank. But that bloodline qualified him to be entered as an inaugural member of the Order of Sons of Italy in America, founded in 1922 by the physician, Doctor Vincenzo Sellaro – and a bunch of others. His barber had dragged him along.

At the age of only seventeen in 1876, his mother became pregnant with a young lover she wanted to spend the rest of her life with. But to avoid the shame this would bring, her family emigrated to America where she gave birth.

Within a year, she met and married a rich charming man who accepted her baby, Frank, and adopted him as his own. Until the tragic loss of her nephew, she had never mentioned the place or the relatives she had left behind. Now she told Frank all about the recent killing of his cousin, and her early life in Italy.

Not long after this Frank decided to travel to Avellino in southern Italy, his mother's hometown, and investigate the death of his young relative what seemed to be a gangland shootout.

Some, like her childhood friend, first sweetheart and Frank's true father, Umberto, changed their family name and relocated elsewhere in Italy or America.

But most, Frank among them, shared an inability, or reluctance, to sever their birth roots entirely. Which is why he decided to travel across the

Atlantic to Avellino and delve into the reasons behind the death of Cousin Carlo Ianillo.

Frank, arriving in Italy, knew he had no skill as a detective in the conventional sense, but as a forensic businessman and entrepreneur, with a nose for digging into a deal and all its details.

On that first morning in the offices of Falcone and Ianillo he saw, but without being introduced to, a strikingly handsome Italian client. Frank saw him again later that evening, going into the hotel room of a woman, clearly not his wife.

Extra marital affairs were not his business. However, Frank learned the following day, this man is Salvatore d'Bergamasco of the well-known motor vehicle manufacturing firm.

Having travelled so far from the heavy industrial area centred on Milan, and more specifically the ancient town of Bergamo, from which, perhaps, his original family name derived, tweaked Frank's imagination.

Falcone, a distant relative, told him, 'Salvatore is here in another famed industrial zone with ambitions to construct an innovative factory near Bergamo for the manufacture of tractors and agricultural machinery. This is a euphemism for munitions at a time when Mussolini's Blackshirts are definitely rising in alarming prominence and looking for guns and ammunition.'

Frank also recognised the woman as being in the employ of the Camorra; the Neapolitan branch of the Cosa Nostra – *the Mafia.*

Chapter 8

Colonello Cesare Pancucci

Colonel Cesare Pancucci pulled his uniform greatcoat closer against the freezing Alpine wind blowing into Bergamo from the mountains just to the north.

'Break step,' he ordered his party to avoid treacherous icy patches on the cobbles of the narrow streets. The six uniformed Carabinieri marching with him from the barracks kept a dutiful silence, knowing that he discouraged chit-chat whilst on duty.

His thoughts were on his situation. How much more could he take before buckling under the strain? The responsibility of upholding the law in the current turbulent political situation weighed heavily on his fifty-year-old shoulders.

He knew when he joined the Carabinieri he could be called on to serve on both Italy's borders and city streets. He had assumed cities would be less demanding, but now he felt not so sure. At least on the front line you knew your enemy, and that those you were protecting wouldn't turn on you.

Unfortunately, the War had not been kind to him, and fighting the Austrians in Trento had left him with an injured left arm preventing him from further front-line service.

He felt concerned that so many factories in northern Italy were taken over by armed employees. Now, two years later, the Fascists had fought back, and Mussolini looked likely to become leader of the country. Perhaps this might bring more stability, despite it being at the expense of violence on the streets, deaths, murders, and beatings. Meanwhile he felt completely exhausted by it all, and there seemed no way out.

Coming closer to their destination, he saw a figure hurrying towards them. As the man moved nearer, he recognised Giuseppe d'Bergamasco, one of the family that owned the bespoke motor carriage factory.

'Thank God, you got the message *Colonnello*. I did wonder if we had sent it to the right place.' He led Pancucci to the corner of the street and pointed to a group of men in working clothes gathered beneath the sign *Motori Bergamasco. Motor Carriages of Distinction.*

'Can you please do something about this group of communist thugs? I think they've come from Milan. They're trying to break in and encourage my men to take over our motor works. My manager has locked the front door, but I managed to sneak out from a door at the back.'

Cesare Pancucci felt an overwhelming sense of apprehension, knowing that such a situation could so easily escalate into confrontation. The communists all over Italy had substantial support and even a small group could soon send out runners to bring in any number of local agitators. This in turn could prompt the *fascisti* to turn out with the potential of a riot developing between these two violent groups. He did not need a three-sided stand-off between police, communists, and Fascists. He had experienced this before and knew that injury or even loss of life could result.

He knew he needed to find a way of defusing these volatile situations. 'What do your employees feel about this state of political affairs Signore d'Bergamasco?' he asked. 'Do you have any communist rabble-rousers in your factory?'

Giuseppe shrugged. 'I think that they just want to get on with their work. The family has always done its best to pay them fairly and listen to their point of view, so I think we have their support.'

'In that case, may I respectfully suggest, Signore, that you return inside, assemble your workers, and encourage them to elect three spokesmen. I am, of course, relying on your assessment that they will support you and not the communists. Meanwhile with my men, I will secure the front of the building to let your representatives get out and speak to the rabble. If your workers can convince them that your factory is already under their control and they need no help, then hopefully they will disperse.'

'That seems a good plan. Give me ten minutes.'

Pancucci watched d'Bergamasco disappear down a side street and stood out of sight and silent for ten minutes before ordering his file forward, with the order, 'Make plenty of noise by banging your boots hard on the ground.'

Marching his six policemen noisily to the back of the crowd drew only a limited response, so he drew his pistol and fired one bullet into the air. The single shot that echoed around the streets produced a shocked silence.

'Now I have your attention,' he bellowed at the startled faces turned towards him. 'Let me make the situation clear. I am the law and order in this town and have two hundred armed Carabinieri at my disposal in the town barracks.'

He paused to let the words sink in then made a show of replacing his pistol into its holster.

'But – I am also a citizen and support the rights of citizens. If, as you profess, you also uphold the rights of the working man then you must respect those of this establishment.'

As he spoke, he saw three men sneak from the door and stand in front of the building whilst the attention of the crowd was diverted in his direction. One of the factory workers placed a box on the ground for the oldest of the trio to climb on and prepare to address the mob.

Pancucci pointed towards the factory. 'Their representatives stand behind you now. So, I suggest you turn and listen to what they have to say.'

'Comrades,' the man on the box said, holding out his arms in a gesture of inclusion. 'Thank you for coming, but I fear your journey has been unnecessary. I stand before you as the representative of the workers committee of this establishment. We have already taken control of the means of production, so there is no need for your intervention. I suggest you return to your homes and allow the democratic process of this community to continue in a climate of comradeship and co-operation. Thank you.'

He stepped down and stood silent as the group muttered among themselves. From where the police stood there appeared to be an element of consent and the men began to wander off. A few continued mumbling amongst themselves, but then shrugged their shoulders and also drifted away.

Pancucci saw the factory door, now no longer under threat, slowly open', and a smiling Giuseppe beckons him and the three workmen to come inside.

'Thank you Enzo.' Giuseppe said the older man on the back. 'I owe you a debt of gratitude.'

Enzo responded with a grin, 'Under no circumstances will we allow a group of stupid *Milanese* to interfere in our town *capo,* but I am dismayed that I have discovered in myself the ability to lie so convincingly. There is no workers committee and no appetite among the men to take over the factory, but we have concerns regarding the work getting less. Some are becoming worried about their jobs.'

Pancucci listened as Giuseppe appeared to carefully consider his words before speaking. 'We too have been aware of this for some time, Enzo. We have plans to change things for the better, but these must I'm afraid remain undisclosed for the time being until they complete. I can say no more, but I am sure you can trust my word.'

Enzo nodded and led his men back to their work.

Giuseppe turned to Pancucci. 'Not only do I owe you a debt of gratitude *Colonnello* for your action today, but I am also greatly impressed with your ability to resolve an extremely difficult situation. These are attributes that we will need if our plans for the future reach fruition. Perhaps we should talk if that may be of interest. Here are my contact details.'

Slipping the card into his pocket, Pancucci snapped to attention and saluted.

'Thank you, Signore d'Bergamasco. Glad to have been of service. Should you wish to contact me this can be done, as you know, via the barracks.'

Turning smartly on his heels he returned outside and marched his men down the now deserted street with a sense of satisfaction.

Chapter 9

Novella's Visit to America

Novella joined her brother Anton travelling by train to Cherbourg and boarded the luxury white star liner, The Majestic, sailing to New York.

The voyage took several days so she packed one of her dolls and knitting equipment to pass the time.

On the train, Anton told his sister that whilst they were staying in the same hotel, he was going to be busy, and she would have to find her own way round. Seeing Novella's nervous reaction, he took her hands in his to reassure her.

'Don't worry, you'll be fine.'

'But Anton, I don't know anyone.'

'This trip will be good for you to spread your wings. You'll gain the confidence you lack and become independent. Salvatore is relying on us to do well.'

Novella tried to smile but she felt too anxious.

Anton continued: 'Our papà made you a company director so you must act like one. We're here to do a job so think about the family business and focus on what you are going to do to gain the knowledge on colour and car materials.'

Novella nodded in silence.

On board the ship, while taking the air on deck, she chatted to George, a pleasant, elderly, Englishman on his way to visit his daughter and American husband in Nashville. He asked Novella to partner him for daily games of whist. 'It's in the card room on Deck 6 at 2pm, next door to the library.'

Novella jumped at the opportunity. 'Thank you, George, I would like that.'

They soon became friends and got talking each day.

One afternoon he spoke in detail about his Ford car and the pleasure it still gave him. 'I was the first man to buy the Ford T Model. I had my photo in the paper. It runs as well now as it did when I first bought it.'

This gave Novella the opportunity to talk about her plans. 'I would like to learn more about motor companies George, could you suggest anywhere I could go in America?' she asked quite casually, surprising herself.

He nodded, 'You might like to take a train trip to Detroit if you're interested in the history of cars. There's Ford and G.M motor production plants in Michigan, not far from each other. I was fortunate to be shown Ford's assembly line. It was fascinating to watch.'

It sounds really great to be shown around Fords assembly line. Salvatore would be so pleased if I pick up new ideas he may not know.

The next day, Novella told George she would find the courage to go to Detroit.

He said, 'It's worth the visit, you'll find it interesting, and the Wayne Hotel is across the road from the station. Stay there, it has everything – good food and wonderful views over the river where steamships chug up and down all day.'

On leaving the ship, Novella and Anton made their way to the Chilton Plaza Hotel in Manhattan and spent the day settling in. The next day whilst her brother spent time being busy, she got to know the local area and checked the train times to Detroit, intending on staying a few nights before returning to New York.

Novella, upset by her brother's earlier lecture, decided to lead him to think that she intended to attend the trade fair in Boston. Little did he know she

44

would be travelling west instead of north. 'You have to spread your wings' he said. So, she'd spread them her own way and take a fifteen-hour journey over two days to Detroit, Michigan.

Early next morning whilst sitting on the train, Novella sensed her papà's presence and felt it a sign that she must be doing the right thing.

'Oh, papà I do miss you so,' she wept.

Settled comfortably in a first-class carriage with her book, Novella read and dozed most of trip, in between dining, until her late evening arrival in Detroit where she was met by a new moon and sky full of stars. She entered the Wayne Hotel, ordered room service, and retired to bed.

Next morning feeling refreshed and energised, she boarded the local train to Michigan. In a strange way she felt a sudden buzz of excitement at being a 'spy' and her confidence grew. She gazed at herself in the compact mirror, smiling at the make up on her face that Isabella gave her the night before leaving home. 'Use this to look more grown-up sis, it will make you appear a stronger woman.' Novella liked her new image. Using cosmetics for the first time certainly made a big difference to her self-esteem.

Climbing down from the train at Michigan central station she caught a whiff of fried beefburgers and onions. With her stomach leading the way she strode across to the young man selling from a small hut. 'I would like to try one of your burgers and onions please.'

'With pleasure Ma'am.'

Novella took a bite, enjoying the combined flavours and found it most delicious.

'I've not seen you around these parts. Are you visiting family?' he inquired.

'No, I've come to see Ford and GM Motor companies. Would you know the way please?'

'You need a bus ride to get to GM Motors. It doesn't take long, and the buses run frequently. Ford is not too far away. In those boots you can easily walk it. Just follow the road for about half a mile and take a left, you'll see it right there.'

As Novella approached the forecourt of the factory, she saw a smart, slender middle-aged man rubbing the bonnet of a car with his jacket sleeve. He looked up, smiled, and stepped forward to introduce himself.

'Good afternoon, I'm Henry Ford, the proud owner of this fine establishment. You caught me in a long-term habit I find difficult to break. I don't like dust and smears on my machines you see.'

'Good afternoon, Mr Ford. My name is Novella d'Bergamasco, and I am from Northern Italy. I'm here on vacation and have come to see the world's fastest car making factory if I am allowed. You see, Mr Ford, on the ship coming over I met an elderly Englishman. He told me he bought the very first T Model from you personally and had his photo taken for the newspapers. Is that true?'

'Well, I'll be darned, you're speaking of that son of a gun George Clayton. His daughter married an American from Nashville. So, the old fellow is still alive and well? Does he still have that first machine?'

'Yes, he has the same habit of using his sleeve to buff up the paint work.'

Henry laughed until he hardly had any breath left. 'Oh, my dear lady, you have made my day. It would be a pleasure to show you my assembly line and anything else you want to see.'

'A ride in one of your cars and a photograph of us two together would be an experience I will never forget, Mr Ford.'

'It would be my pleasure, Ma'am. Now call me Henry and I shall call you Novella, my new Italian friend.'

You may hear a lot more of my name on the racing circuit one day, Henry

'But first we shall look at the showroom so you can see the extent of my machines and then I'll show you the factory.'

Henry took Novella's arm and walked her along a line of automobiles, patting each bonnet. He paused to admire his fastest and most expensive vehicle. 'This is the Speedster, my pride and joy. Here is the Tourer for long distances and this one is the Standard. I built it for the middle-class American as an affordable way to travel. The price starts at just under three hundred dollars, making it a car anyone with a job can buy.

For a moment Novella saw the tough entrepreneur and businessman shine through. *Just like you papà,* she whispered to heaven.

'I can see you thinking Novella – a penny for your thoughts?'

'I am thinking of all the lucky people buying your cars, but why are most of them black and not in bright beautiful colours?'

'The black ones are for the cheap family cars and the coloured vehicles are the more expensive. Also, black paint dries fast, and black upholstery is easier to clean. We have other ways to save our buyers money by using horsehair seat padding covered in vinyl and leatherette upholstery in the cheaper cars and coconut fibres in the others. I am famous for saying: you can have any car you like provided it is black. People laughed but bought my all-black cars because of the price. I pass on every saving to my customers.'

'That sounds a very clever policy, Henry.'

'To me it is logical. The time will come when every manufacturer copies my production method. Now let's go into the factory and I will show you how it works. The assembly line is based on a simple process. This is the line which the car parts move along to the workers. Each man will do the same job all day long. The man who places a part does not fasten it. The man who puts in the bolt does not put on the nut; the man who puts on the nut does not tighten it. With this method cars roll off the assembly line every ninety-three minutes. If it doesn't, I want to know why!'

'How fascinating, Henry. But don't the workers find it boring?' she asked, horrified at the thought.

'Probably, but they have a job in these difficult times and food on the table. I'm sure they'd rather be bored than starving.'

Walking with Henry out of the factory, Novella asked, 'I would also like to visit GM Motors Henry, could you please tell me the way?'

'I'll do more than that, Novella; I will drive you there myself. Fortunately, I have a client to see nearby who is interested in buying my Speedster. I planned to go there tomorrow but I will make it today. You have a look around and I will pick you up when I've finished.'

Novella couldn't believe her luck. The salesman at General Motors gave her a lot of information to take back to her family.

As promised, Henry picked her up beaming with joy. 'Another cash buyer collecting the car tomorrow. You, Novella, are my lucky angel. I must reward you before you catch your train.'

Henry handed Novella a box filled with a mixture of items. Included were 20 painted miniature metal cars, nineteen of which were his previous alphabetical prototypes. The last one: the quadricycle he built in the shed behind his house. Also, Henry had added a variety of coloured card charts, swatches and leaflets showcasing Ford's selection that he offers to customers. 'Just a small token of thanks for your visit today.'

'Thank you for everything, Henry, I will never forget this day.'

Salvatore will be so pleased with me. I hope Anton has done well, too.

Novella jotted down notes, from start to finish, on her way back to New York, where she visited the textile fair in Manhattan. She collected more leaflets, brochures, and firm's business cards.

Her work done, she returned to the Chilton Plaza Hotel to meet up with Anton.

Passing through the lounge, she noticed him tucked in the corner, holding hands with a beautiful woman.

Still feeling slightly peeved with her brother, she stormed over to their table to interrupt the two lovebirds. Deliberately, Novella planted a kiss on Anton's cheek, leaving a smudge of lipstick.

'You don't seem to have missed me while I've been away, Anton.'

Novella saw him flush ruby red. The woman jumped up and snapped, 'You didn't tell me you had a wife.'

Novella giggled, as Anton, obviously deeply embarrassed, muttered 'I don't have a wife. This is my sister.'

They all laughed together at the misunderstanding and after proper introductions, Novella eventually departed, saying, 'I need to freshen up after my long train journey, so I'll leave you now.'

Collecting her key, she said to the concierge, 'Oh, Charlie. Tomorrow is my last day on land. I'll miss New York, I enjoyed it so much here.'

Next morning In the lobby, she saw Anton's arms entwined with Ginnie's. In order not to disturb them, she scribbled a note and gave it to a hotel porter to pass on to him saying 'I'll make my own way to the quayside.'

Standing on the deck waiting for the ship to depart, Novella caught sight of George boarding and waved. 'Good to see you again, Novella,' he called out. 'Will we meet later for a game of whist?'

'I look forward to it George.'

Chapter 10

Anton in New York

Anton found the eight-day journey from Bergamo to America tiring.

It meant going by train to Cherbourg and boarding the very big White Star liner, 'Majestic.' At least they could relax during the six-day crossing, but space was at a premium, the ship being fully booked. Novella spent most of her time reclining on a lounger, chatting to an elderly English gentleman whom she partnered at whist. Anton preferred an early morning stroll around upper deck and spent rest of his time playing cards and drinking at the first-class bar with three like-minded male passengers.

He almost made the mistake of ignoring a middle-aged American who tried to engage in a conversation with him. But Anton's ears pricked up when the Yank mentioned that he was a salesman for the Ford Motor Company, and from then on Anton made Herbie a bosom buddy and took the opportunity to pump him for information. It helped that Herbie was prone to boast. 'Yeah', volunteered the middle-aged, balding man, 'We're one of the big three with Chrysler and General Motors – but we're the best by far.'

'Why is that?' asked Anton.

'We beat our rivals hands down for price and quality. That's why Henry Ford's Model T tops the sales charts and accounts for forty-seven percent of new sales.'

Herbie's non-stop prattle became boring, and Anton began to switch off. But, to his delight, the man invited him to call at their New York showroom and meet Herbie's boss.

Upon finally arriving in New York, they made the short journey to their five-star hotel, the Chilton Plaza, in Manhattan, where Anton and Novella relaxed in their luxury rooms before setting out to discover

The next day they set about discovering what Americans truly liked in terms of transport, fashion, and designs by chatting to as many local residents and commuters as possible.

At dinner they discussed their separate schedules. 'Well, Sis. This is where we split up,' said Anton. 'What time are you leaving for the textiles show in Boston?'

'Probably tomorrow. I'm catching a train at ten. The textiles show is in the afternoon, but I'll stay in Boston overnight.'

Anton seized the opportunity to encourage her to remain longer. 'Take as long as you like, sis. I understand there are several car businesses in downtown Boston you may like to visit.'

'OK, Anton. I'll see how it goes stay over and see you in a couple of days.'

He waved Novella goodbye and enjoyed a drink in the hotel bar while reading the notes he had made for his interview with Bernard Myers and his millionaire father Joe at Comet Cars.

A smartly dressed brunette sitting at a nearby table writing, caught his attention, particularly her long legs in a knee-length skirt. He smiled at her and asked, 'Are you here on pleasure or business?'

'I work in the hotel as the guest relations manager,' she replied. 'My name's Ginnie. And you are?'

'Anton. I'm here for a few days combining pleasure with business. I'm a marketing director with an Italian car manufacturer.'

They shared a laugh when they both asked, almost simultaneously, if they worked in a family business.

'Yes,' said Anton. My brothers and sisters are all on the board at Motori Bergamasco. What about you?'

'My father owns the hotel,' she revealed. 'How else would a woman obtain a managerial position in this age of discrimination? But I'm very good at my job.' She rose to leave.

Anton treated her to another smile. 'You're giving me a taste of your excellent guest relations skills right now,' he acknowledged. 'But just to convince me, how about having a drink?'

'Sorry, I'm due to attend a meeting in a few minutes.'

'What about this evening, then?'

She agreed to meet him in the bar at six. And, before hurrying away, gave him directions to the office block he needed for his appointment at Comet Cars. His job interview went well, with Joe confirming that they were willing to double Anton's salary and give him a plush office based in Milan as part of their expansion into Europe.

'Will you be concentrating on increasing the production of your existing cars or bringing out a new model?' asked Anton.

'Both,' replied Joe. 'We're already catering very well for the needs of the average driver, so the next step is to go up market by producing a new luxury car to compete with the Cadillac and Mercedes. Think you can handle promoting that for us?'

'No problem!' declared Anton. 'It sounds like a marketing man's dream. When will the new car be ready?'

Bernard volunteered the information Anton was seeking: 'It's already designed and will be produced in a few months. But first we want to hit the European market with our existing models.'

'So, are you planning to open showrooms throughout Europe?'

'That's the intention,' replied Joe, smiling broadly. 'But we'll start with Italy, France and England.'

Anton picked up a few more useful details and statistics before departing, making a promise that he would give Joe and Bernard a firm answer on his job offer by the end of the week.

What a dilemma. Should he take this dream job or stay loyal to his family after feeding Salvatore the information he had obtained?

The next port of call for Anton was Herbie's Ford showroom. The amiable salesman introduced him to his boss Willie Wiseman, a more cautious man than Herbie but nevertheless willing to answer the Italian's many questions. First, he had one of his own. 'What brings you to the States?'

'I'm just here on holiday,' Anton lied. 'I work for a motor manufacture in Italy called Motori Bergamasco which is small fry compared to your company. We have a lot to learn so when Herbie invited me to pop in, I thought you might be willing to share some of your knowledge with me.'

Willie smiled. 'You mean help you to steal some of our customers?'

'I think Italian cars cater for a different market, Mr Wiseman. Herbie mentioned that Henry Ford's Model T accounts for almost fifty percent of new sales. He believes that's because you beat your rivals on both pricing and quality. Do you agree?'

'Yes. Customers like to get value for money. It's important to give them a good car at an affordable price. Probably those are the two factors that appeal most to men, while women are, perhaps, influenced more by the look of a car and how comfortable it is.'

'Are you planning to bring out a new model soon – maybe one appealing even more to women?'

'There's talk of it, but nothing's been confirmed. At the moment we're selling so many Model T cars we're spending all our time producing them.'

Anton nodded. 'As we both know, the car industry is growing fast, but there aren't that many showrooms. Do you think there's a need for more showrooms and dealerships?'

Willie nodded. 'Yeah, there'll have to be in order to meet customer demands. Many middle-class Americans are enjoying higher earnings, and a car is becoming a necessity rather than a luxury. But your Italian company will only prosper if it produces an attractive, reliable model at an affordable price. Dealerships would be a good idea, with you selling our cars as well as your own.'

This idea delighted Anton. *This is something worth discussing with Salvatore and the board.*

Anton was delighted to find new topics of conversation with Ginnie that evening when she agreed to join him for dinner.

He spent most of the time gazing at the lovely brunette as they discussed music, entertainment, fashion, and the vast changes taking place in both America and Europe. But it was not too long before Ginnie quizzed him about the car industry.

To his surprise, she was able to help him in his quest to discover more about what was most important to new drivers. She said, 'Some people are prepared to mortgage their houses in order to buy a top of the range car. But I think they're in the minority. Most of the people I know would rather opt for a good dependable car that they can afford. It should look good, too, without being luxurious.'

She was echoing the opinion of the Ford dealer – and suggesting that the vision of Joe Myers to go up market with a new luxury car might be flawed.

'What would you prefer?' he asked.

'I'd like to see a car come on to the market that combines style with value,' she said.

Perbacco. She's just given me the perfect slogan. Style and value.

Ginnie had another surprise in store for him. She allowed herself to be tempted to join him in his room. A few smouldering kisses led to them getting even more physical on the enormous bed and Ginnie providing him with the most satisfying sexual experience of his life.

They repeated the experience the next night and Anton was again consumed with desire which increased as he caressed her firm, shapely breasts, and legs.

Anton had lunch with the glamorous American the following day. They then sipped coffee in the far corner of the lounge and held hands while consumed in a world of their own.

But their romantic interlude was interrupted by the untimely arrival of Novella. She planted a kiss on Anton's cheek, and asked mischievously, 'You don't seem to have missed me while I've been away.'

Anton's face reddened. Ginnie glared at him. 'You didn't tell me you had a wife,' she snapped.

'I don't. This is my sister Novella.'

Ginnie's expression softened, the tension lifted and there were laughs all round.

The remainder of their stay in the States passed all too quickly for Anton.

Ginnie promised to visit him in Italy, but he was not convinced she would do so while saying an emotional goodbye before boarding the ocean liner to England. He was close to tears as Ginnie waved to him from the quayside.

When Anton arrived back home, he had a lot to tell Salvatore.

Anton said most of the feedback he'd received at all levels is that price would be the most vital factor when introducing their new car.

'Design is obviously important, but we must keep the cost down or we could price ourselves out of the market,' he stressed. 'If we deliver both style and good value and make our new car accessible by opening showrooms in Bergamo and Milan, then we should be on to a winner. It may be an advantage to create dealerships and also sell Ford's Model T.'

Salvatore was not convinced. 'Who gave you this feedback, Anton?'

'I spoke to senior sales staff at Fords, who have the biggest share of the market, as well as directors at other car manufacturers, potential new customers and various existing drivers of both sexes.'

Salvatore frowned and sat in silence, thinking over the news Anton brought back from America, before saying, 'The idea of two showrooms and selling other marques with our own might work. Perhaps they'll be a guide for a new selling policy. I'll bring it up at a Board Meeting next week and you can report and expand on your new ideas.'

Chapter 11

Novella's American Report

Salvatore reached across his desk and rang the bell for his secretary.

'Tell Novella to come and discuss her trip to America please.'

His sister entered the room feeling slightly nervous and handed her folder to her brother.

'Please don't be cross with me dear brother. I didn't exactly follow your instructions because my gut feeling drew me to Detroit Michigan where I visited General Motors and the Ford motor factory.'

Salvatore waved a dismissive hand. 'Don't worry about that, Novella. I knew I could trust you to do the right thing. You used your own initiative and that is good. I'm sure you brought back interesting things to tell me. Please relax and carry on.'

Balancing his chin on a triangle of forearms fists and elbows he stared at her eager face, ready to listen.

'I have so much information Salvatore. It's hard to know where to start.'

'Take a breath and start at the beginning. Where did you go first?'

'I went by train to Ford Motors. Guess who I met Salvatore?'

'I don't know, someone important I guess, a film star perhaps?'

'No. I met Henry Ford. The founder of the company. He personally showed me around his factory. It was truly fascinating, and afterwards he gave me a ride in his speedster to General Motors.'

'Good god. How did you manage that?'

'He was driving that way to sell a car.'

Salvatore frowned. 'I hope you didn't tell him we made motor vehicles. He wouldn't take kindly to having a competitor in his plant.'

'Of course, I didn't. I'm shy, not stupid. In fact, I made the perfect spy, asking ingenuous questions he didn't mind answering.'

This time Salvatore laughed. 'You women have so many ways to twist us round your fingers.'

Salvatore pulled out Novella's sketch of the factory and laid it across his desk.

'What am I looking at Novella?'

'It's a sketch I drew of the Ford manufacturing line. It's brilliant. Instead of half a dozen men building a car together, Henry builds on what he calls his production line on which the workers stay still, and the car moves along.'

She stood up and began to follow the working method with a pencil.

Salvatore said, 'Sit down sister. Give me the pencil and I'll go along your drawing with you telling me what happens at each place.'

'Let me tell you the most important thing he told me first. He pointed out that using a moving assembly line allows for the work to be built step by step as it passes an individual worker who puts in the bolt but does not put on the nut, then a man who puts on the nut but does not tighten it. These simple moves allow cars to roll off the production line every ninety-three minutes instead of twelve hours. That is how he sells cars so cheaply. He saw a vision in a dream.'

Salvatore ran the pencil slowly, stopping and asking questions, amazed Novella could clearly answer without difficulty. 'You have a marvellous memory, Novella. We have all misjudged you for years.'

He studied the sketch for over an hour, making notes in his tiny handwriting, sometimes stopping to concentrate hard on one section, muttering to himself, 'I can improve on this.'

Finally, he called for his secretary to bring coffee. Sitting back in his chair, staring at the ceiling, he remained deep in thought for two cups before snapping upright and saying, 'Fantastic work dear Novella. I'll make sure you are recognised for this. Now tell me who else you spied on.'

'General Motors, they are very progressive and run their own in-house finance company so customer can buy cars on credit. This is part of their marketing and selling strategy. To keep their production line working they make minor variations to their vehicles every year to keep motorists interested in changing their cars. Perhaps you should speak to Giuseppe about this idea.'

Salvatore scribbled a note. 'We can arrange with a bank or independent finance house to work with us and supply the cash. Giuseppe will work out how to do this.

Good. Any other thoughts from America to tell me?'

'Only about colours and materials.'

Salvatore laughed. 'Oh yes of course that's why I sent you.'

Novella reeled off a number of ideas she thought Motori Bergamasco could use. 'Both Fords and General Motors use vinyl and leatherette on the cheaper cars and leather, suede, velvet, and a combination of other textiles for two tone effects. They also used trims to break up plain colours. General Motors had a colour calculator to match light and dark and upholstery options. These colour cards I have here show all the materials. And I have all these swatches so you can feel their texture and quality. I have also found out they import from stockists in Italy, France and Germany that supply everything we need to prevent us waiting for shiploads to arrive from America. I have supplied the names of the Companies.'

'Anything else?'

'Yes. They use underfloor padding to cut out engine noise.'

Salvatore made another quick note.

'You could be making us a fortune by what you've dug out in such a short time. This is what good spies do.'

They both laughed. He stood up and escorted her to the door, saying, 'Who thought our shy Novella would come home with a treasure trove of information?'

She walked from his office in a state of pride and high excitement. Looking over her shoulder she winked at the picture of her father and whispered, 'What do you think of your shy little Novella now papà?'

Chapter 12

Anton's New York Report

Salvatore took a thick writing pad and pencil from his desk and relaxed in preparation for his discussion with Anton. He always saw his brother as a force of nature with a strong, but erratic mind and the ability to win his points in meetings with a mixture of clever logic and passionate debate delivered in a loud voice.

Without knocking, Anton marched into Salvatore's large wooden-panelled office carrying two neat files and handed him one.

'This is the detailed report of my trip to America,' he said. 'You may wish to discuss it with me after you've studied it or, if you prefer, I could highlight the main points now.'

Salvatore glanced briefly at the report's index before placing it on the table and replying. 'It would help if we talked through it item by item now. Please sit down, Anton.'

His brother pulled up a chair and said, 'Perhaps I should first tell you of a vital personal matter. Comet Cars in New York have offered me a job at twice my current salary.'

Salvatore's brow knotted into lines and wrinkles, dominated by a ferocious frown that spread fast as an earthquake. His family called it the watch-out moment because the unpredictable what-came-next could destroy relationships, careers and whole lifetimes of work and endeavour.

He gritted his teeth. 'Are you going to take it?' he growled.

Anton flinched and took a deep breath. 'I haven't decided yet, but it's very tempting. I have to consider it. Comet Cars are rich and successful in America. They plan a worldwide launch of a new car and I would be in charge of their marketing in Europe.'

'So, you'd be in direct competition with us?'

'Not exactly. They are designing a luxury model for the top end of the market. That's my only reservation – it could prove to be out of the price range of many motorists. My other concern is one of loyalty to you and our company. Perhaps you could help me decide by making me an offer of a higher salary?'

With a fierce shake of his head, Salvatore snapped, 'Not a hope. You know very well that the new car and new factory will take all our cash flow and capital for the next two years before we see any return. There's nothing to spare. And if you get a big pay rise the other directors – your family – will expect the same. How do we afford that?'

'Surely you can see it from my point of view, Salvatore?'

'No, I can't. And I won't,' snarled Salvatore. 'I don't want to hear any more. Forget it and get on with your report. That's what we're here to talk about. Not your personal life.'

Anton exploded in an almost uncontrollable shout.

'What if I tell you right here and now, I'm going to leave?'

'Are you telling me that?' Salvatore shouted back, banging hard fists on the table.

'No, brother, no. I said I have to consider it.'

Salvatore added a grim smile to the ferocious frown and growled, 'Then consider this. You know I never accept an ultimatum. Tell me as a fact right now that you are leaving. I'll immediately accept. Within five minutes you'll be out of this factory with nothing. Absolutely nothing.'

Several seconds of dead silence followed.

Salvatore watched Anton's face, red with anger, freeze into a pale mask and leaned forward to hiss, 'And consider papà's will. It is clear that not one of us is allowed to leave. The final clause instructs his lawyers that any of us who abandons Motori Bergamasco is immediately struck off.'

'But I'm planning to get married,' whispered Anton, overcome by an air of defeat.

'That is nothing to do with me, nor a reason to give you money we don't have.'

'You're a hard bastard.'

'I am my papà's son. Do you think he could have built this successful business and pass it on to us if he had been a weak puffball? If our new project succeeds, we all benefit with plenty of money, large salaries, great bonuses, and a high lifestyle. If it fails, we all sink together. That is how papà saw things, and so do I.'

Salvatore stared across the table at his brother's slumped shoulders, placed his hands flat on the table and pushed his chest into a broad, silent, aggressive pose.

He watched Anton crumble, reach across the desk, pick up the report, and begin to riffle through the pages. 'I found plenty to help us,' he whispered.

'Speak up. I can't hear you,' said Salvatore in the unkindest voice he could muster.

Anton cleared his throat and repeated, 'I found plenty to help us.'

'Go on.'

'Almost everyone I spoke to told me that, depending on the market we aim at, price is the most vital factor when introducing a new car. A good design is important, and I know we have that, but we must keep the cost down to ensure we don't go beyond what most people can afford.'

'The opposite of what your friends at Comet Cars plan on doing.'

His voice and confidence strengthening, Anton agreed.

'Yes, indeed. But they're adopting a different strategy aimed at those with large incomes. Henry Ford's Model T is more affordable and has proved to be a best seller. Like Ford, we need to make our new car accessible and appealing to everyone. I suggest we use a slogan along the lines of 'Style Combined With Quality And Value', or 'Style Quality And Value.' I'll discuss it with Gino at the Agency and develop a hard-hitting advertising and marketing campaign. We have plenty of time to make a tough, modern, pitch to the public.'

'Good idea. Start planning right away and make sure I am involved by regular up to date reports. And everyone at the Agency from the cleaners and coffee girls to the top man must sign a secrecy agreement with strict legal penalties.'

Anton said, 'I took the head of a group of nation-wide repair garages to dinner and watched him get drunk. The main thing he told me is how they initially made the mistake of not stocking sufficient Ford's Model T spare parts. It's vital we provide garages with a large stock of spares for when our cars need repairing, even if at first with high credit terms.'

Salvatore said, 'My cars don't break down.'

'All cars break down sooner or later. Remember yours did a few months ago.'

Salvatore nodded and almost smiled.

He pointed at the report, 'I see on page four you suggest we open vehicle showrooms. Explain please.'

'The bigger American manufacturers have started opening showrooms in cities near their manufacturing plants. I used the same dinner-and-drink trick with Willie Wiseman, head of Ford's showrooms in New York. After a few too many whiskies, he told me they are considering not just showing their machines but using smart well trained young men to turn interest into a sale. He believes that dealerships would work for us if we did the same, especially if we imported and sold Ford cars as well as our own.'

Salvatore scribbled a note and waved a hand for Anton to continue.

'We could experiment with selling from two showrooms, one in Bergamo and one in Milan. We could start immediately to see if it works and throw out Fords when your new vehicle is available for sale.'

Salvatore started a second, longer note. Anton waited until he finished and added, 'Willie also said, make sure you have plenty of spare parts available because Fords are always slow in making repairs. I think Henry sees spares in a warehouse as a pile of dead metal, not live cash flow to make more cars.'

'What do you think?'

'I think it may be an error to ignore servicing. It may be as important in earning money as selling a car. Looking after our customers efficiently could bring us a steady long term cash business.'

'Did you think of that?'

'Yes. For an hour Willie's been drinking about ten glasses of whiskey. In the same hour, I'm sipping one glass of wine. I never mentioned the thought to him.'

Salvatore clapped his hands. 'You've come up with a brilliant idea of not just opening showrooms in Italy but turning them into dealerships. Congratulations.'

Delighted with the compliment, Anton said, 'What do you think about the spares and servicing idea?'

'Equally brilliant. Your immediate task is to set up the showrooms and salesmen. When they are operating, I will set up official engineering shops nearby and stock them with spares. Meantime, keep friendly contact by letter with your pal, Willie, and once those two plans are under way, you will go back to America and negotiate the Italy Ford agency contract. Make sure you leave a clause that gets us out when we launch our new vehicles.

Anton laughed. 'It will be Clause 100 that cancels the previous 99 clauses.'

Salvatore grunted and said 'Right. You have a lot of work to do. Now get out of here and get started. By the way. When do you plan to get married?'

'Don't know. I haven't asked her yet.'

Chapter 13

Salvatore Returns To Avellino

Salvatore hopped off the train at Napoli Centrale station to find Falcone's smartly uniformed chauffeur waiting on the platform.

'Are you well, Sir?' he asked, taking Salvatore's small suitcase.

'Fine thank you. And you?'

'Fine also, Sir.'

That ended conversation until arrival through the mountain pass to Avellino.

'Hotel or Office, sir?'

'Office please.'

Falcone's pretty secretary led Salvatore into the architect's office just as the man finished shrugging his shoulders into an expensive looking plaid jacket. 'Welcome,' he thrust out a hand for a brisk handshake, 'Did you travel well?'

'Comfortably thank you. I always sleep well on our Italian trains. The beds are so cosy.'

Falcone said, 'Bring coffee and biscotti for our visitor please, Antonella. Or do you need something more substantial, Signor d'Bergamasco? A cream croissant perhaps; so famous in our lovely town.'

Salvatore shook his head. 'Coffee and a few biscotti will be fine, thank you.'

Falcone launched into ten minutes of casual small talk about snow in the mountains, 'Still high on the peaks,' and, 'The chestnut crop is very much affected this year,' and more, until Salvatore became bored. He broke in and said, 'You've reserved me for one night in the same hotel, I suppose.'

'Not the same hotel. I thought a change might be more comfortable.'

Salvatore felt there must be a reason but decided not to query, so he let the question die.

He said, 'As explained in the telegraph I sent, my plan is to return to Bergamo on the midnight train tomorrow. This allows us two full days of detailed discussion, because we have much to plan and consider including the structure of our contract with you.'

Falcone raised polite eyebrows as though talk of money so early may be something gentlemen avoid. 'Of course,' he said.' But not until I know more of your project and complete planning drawings.'

'Precisely, my dear Falcone. Already matters have moved since last we spoke.'

'Is that not always so,' said Falcone, lifting his tiny espresso cup in what must have been a toast to fate. 'So, shall we proceed?'

Without telling of Novella's spying mission, Salvatore spun a vague tale around Henry Ford's production method and said, 'Instead our need is not for a large shed as I first told you, but a long, more complicated building with many entry and exit points for people, machinery and the engines, chassis and everything that goes into a quality tractor. The factory is no longer a simple structure. It will be an expensive structure. Do you wish to continue? If not say so now and we will part as friends.'

Falcone leapt to his feet, threw off his jacket, held out an energetic hand and snapped, 'Yes. I absolutely accept. I don't want to lose you to Sicily. It is such a dangerous place. Shake my hand and let's get to work.'

Salvatore grasped and fought back against the crushing grip. 'It will be a pleasure to work together,

Signor Falcone. As we are now partners in an exciting project, please call me Salvatore. D'Bergamasco is such a mouthful. What is your first name?'

'I don't have one. Just call me Falcone.'

Salvatore spent all day in detailed debate on the size of the land purchased, where he thought the newly shaped building would fit, and possible usage of the large spare space remaining. Falcone's pencil flew across swathes of large planning paper, sketching plans, abandoned, and thrown on the floor, scribbled and discarded again a dozen times.

'The approach and service roads, drains and sewers and general water management are as important as the buildings and we must get the groundworks right. Especially as the main building is at the bottom of a dip,' he said. 'I need to visit the land soon for a quick survey with my own equipment to allow me to start the first draft of plans.'

Salvatore clapped him on the shoulder. 'I planned that you return with me tomorrow for exactly that reason. I just haven't asked yet.'

'Capital idea,' said Falcone and told his secretary to, 'Book me tickets on the night train tomorrow, with an open return. I'm not sure how long I'll be away.'

By early evening Salvatore said, 'I'm exhausted. Can we stop now and continue tomorrow?'

'Of course, my dear friend. But first I shall take you for a celebratory dinner to mark the beginning of this great project. First your hotel to freshen up, then to the best restaurant in the centre of Avellino.'

Salvatore stepped out of the building and, glancing up at the sky turning to dusk, took a deep breath of fresh mountain air. A relief after being cooped up all day. He would rather have a snack and go to bed but felt unable to deny Falcone his moment of triumph at this new enlarged contract.

Waiting on the kerb for Falcone to bring his car, he looked across the road at a brightly lit café filled with smart business executives taking end-of-day drinks before going home. Sitting alone on a small pavement table, legs crossed, he saw a smart somewhat older woman sipping a glass of white wine. In the near dark she looked familiar, but he couldn't be sure.

Falcone led him into a restaurant of true luxury. 'What a fantastic place,' said Salvatore.

'Ah yes. In the north you think we southern Italians are a different breed. You see us as savages. But we know how to live well, or even better than you in the north.' He laughed. 'Excepting your beautiful city of Bergamo, of course.'

Salvatore began eating a delightful dish of sliced fish and exquisitely prepared tiny potatoes pickled in a superb, lightly spiced sauce.

'What a magnificent dish,' he said, sitting back and for the first time, looking around the packed restaurant.

'Wait until you experience the main course,' said Falcone. 'It is truly remarkable.'

Salvatore's eye fell upon a very well dressed and bejewelled somewhat older woman across the room staring intently at him. She raised her glass in an almost imperceptible little toast. Salvatore abruptly remembered his comment to Novella about women twisting men around their fingers.

In a low voice he asked Falcone, 'That woman sitting alone by the wall seems to be looking at me. I think she did the same from the café opposite your office. Do you know her?'

Falcone accidentally brushed his napkin to the floor.

Bending to pick it up his lips passed close to Salvatore's ear and murmured, 'Cosa Nostra. Stay away.'

Next morning in his private compartment, Salvatore reached across to lock the door and told Falcone of his meeting with the woman, leaving out the coffee in her hotel. 'She struck up conversation with me. It must have been pre-planned, as must the café and restaurant last night. Somehow, she knew I'd be in your office and the café and trying to make contact. Why would this be? And how did she find out?'

Falcone frowned. 'I believe her to be a Mafia spy and recruiter. You are a handsome young industrialist. Her employers may have heard whispers of your plans and want to go into the tractor making business. Could it be that one of your colleagues may have passed on your movements.?'

'None of my family would give away our secrets.'

'You cannot be sure. Cosa Nostra have many ways of finding out what they need to know.'

'I have too many things to think about than an older woman trying to pick me up. Now we have much to do in the next few days and must sleep.'

Falcone shook hands. 'Buona Notta,' he said.

Salvatore placed his suitcase hard against the door and turned the security key three times and whispered to himself, 'I hope to heaven that her friends aren't travelling with us.'

Brushing the incident from his mind he slept deeply until the wakeup call an hour before arriving at Milan.

Chapter 14

Frank Bernstein Introduces Himself

Shortly after dawn, Salvatore is sitting alone in the breakfast carriage with his morning coffee when an effusive Frank Bernstein squeezes into the seat opposite. Speaking Italian with an American accent he said, 'Hope you don't mind – my train wagon is jammed with passengers.'

He thrusts out his hand in greeting, 'Frank Bernstein, American tourist', he added needlessly, his hand still outstretched waiting for acceptance. 'I'm from New York City.'

Salvatore slowly accepts the handshake as a connection to the city his siblings have recently visited. *Is this fellow in the motor manufacturing business?*

Frank continues without missing a beat, 'Are you familiar with the Southern Question?'

Salvatore shrugs, disinterested. *

'The north south divide? Seems it happens in every country and always for the same reasons. The battle between poor illiterate farmers and the intellectuals and elites who control the wealth, the property, the industry. Which is why masses fled from Avellino in the immediate aftermath of reunification in 1876.' 'Perhaps not everyone shares your obvious passion for history, Signore Bernstein.' 'America doesn't have so much history of its own, so we love to latch on to our European roots; usually Irish but Italy is also burnt into our culture. Criminal mainly.'

Salvatore raised any eyebrow. *What is this strange man talking about?'*

The conversation is interrupted with the arrival of Falcone, who says, 'I see you've met poor Carlo's cousin, Signore d'Bergamasco.'

Frank smiled, 'I've not mentioned that yet, Falcone. Didn't see the relevance.' He turned to Salvatore. 'My cousin Carlo Ianillo, died in a Mafia hit. Cosa Nostra to be precise. I am sure that's a fraternity you probably steer clear of.'

Salvatore fought to control the discomfort caused by the direction of this conversation, and Frank's unwelcome familiarity.

Falcone said, 'I thought the postmortem concluded that your dear Carlo died in an unexplained crossfire.'

'And who paid off the Justice heading the postmortem, my dear Falcone?'

Frank turned to Salvatore, 'The problem with Carlo, like so many of our gender, is that he struggled to keep his *pene* in his pants. He fell for a slightly older donna fatale; so elegant and well dressed and dripping with jewelry provided by her Mafia bosses, trying to extract information on his high-flying clients. Which is why I am now on this train with you, following the paper trail that always leads to Milan or Turin, just the same as in 1876.'

'You are a difficult man to follow, Signore Bernstein. You seem to make the most tenuous connections where there appear to be none that I or any normal person would see and understand,' Salvatore observed.

Frank laughed. 'You must understand, my dear Signore, that the principal causes of the Southern

Question were centered on Avellino, a seat of revolutionary riots. When the Left took power, this area came to be dominated by groups that stood for and defended the narrow local interests, but not the elite. This made ripe ground for the Mafia to flourish in, but a region the intellectuals and various elites had to flee from. Many went as far north as they could – changing their family name along the way. Others, like my mother's family, simply joined that mass emigration to the United States.'

'A fascinating history lesson, Signore Bernstein, but one of no interest to me or my business.'

'Oh, but it is. History impacts us all. Knowingly, or unknowingly. Ask yourself what's in a name? Your family name I presume comes from the town of your ancestors. Mine, is a corruption; a German Jewish name derived from Berenstein or Berenstain. But my ancestors were Studebakers who came into Italy with the first tide of German immigration in the 1700's from the steel town of Solingen in the Bergisches Land, which means mountainous, the same word root as Bergamo. Who knows? Perhaps we're related.'

He laughs.

'Aren't we all; if we go back far enough,' Falcone interjected in an obvious bid to change the subject, 'And if what you say is true, Frank, then Omertà is the order of the day. In other words, shut up.'

Frank grins and places a finger to sealed lips.

'If you'll leave us now, Frank. The train arrives in Milan shortly. Signore d'Bergamasco and I have private matters to discuss and conclude before we arrive.'

'Sure.' Frank slides out of the seat making way for Falcone. 'Nice meeting you Signore d'Bergamasco.'

Salvatore forces a smile but says nothing as Frank disappears through the crowded carriage.

'Are all Americans like that?'

'Italian American,' Falcone corrects.

For a moment Salvatore's mind is distracted from business, 'Did you know the man's mother? Carlo's cousin?'

'Second cousin. It was his mother she was friendly with and just sixteen, maybe seventeen when the family fled overnight. They simply disappeared, leaving no hint as to where or why they were going.'

'Did they ever let you know?'

'Not until recently. After Carlo's death Frank told me that someone from the Sons of Italy in America told Frank and he showed up in Avellino unannounced.'

'He unsettles me.'

'Why? If he's heard about you, he'll see that you're just an industrialist building automobiles. Beyond that, he is simply a young man seeking news of some tragic happening in his family. Why should that bother you?'

'He may be an industrial spy,' said Salvatore.

Falcone chuckles, 'Frank? An industrial spy? Not Frank. He wouldn't know how to spy.'

It happens,' said Salvatore, thinking of Novella worming her way into Henry Ford's factory only weeks ago, thinking, *my little sister is probably the most unlikely spy in history.*

Chapter 15

Isabella's Ambitions

In her ancient apartment in the Old Town of Bergamo with its stunning views from all aspects, looking out over the river and plain beyond, an excited Isabella took numerous items of clothing from her exquisite walnut wardrobe lined with Chippendale. Putting together various outfits, holding each in turn against her voluptuous body, the Italian beauty, aptly nicknamed Bella by her adoring papà, swished back and forth in front of the Victorian free-standing mirror, a firm favourite of her late mama.

Admiring the reflection gazing back, long slender fingers touching the end of newly shorn locks, Isabella felt chic and fashionable. For the first time her hair appeared shiny and lustrous. None of her siblings had seen this new look and she knew with certainty that they would be shocked, though not entirely surprised.

The suitcase on the elaborate gold coloured bedspread decorated with bright red roses, neatly covering the beautifully handcrafted walnut bedstead, looked dull and worn as it lay open, barely holding any garments as Isabella tossed each item of clothing, one by one, onto the balloon backed carved walnut armchair, with disdain. It would appear that she had nothing suitable for the upcoming auditions in Rome which were just three days away. They may be small parts, but nevertheless the first step towards stardom. The new hairstyle would need a suitable new set of outfits to complement it. None of her garments were *vivaci* enough for the part she'd be playing.

Isabella knew that women were gaining more rights in Italy now: even female lawyers passing the bar; doctors; engineers were appearing. Although she realised the movie industry is not on par with these careers, she saw it as glamorous and revered. Isabella loved to be adored. It made her feel complete and gave her life purpose.

Now that papà had gone, and with him the adoration of his constant admiration: 'You are my special one,' he would say, she felt just another member of the family. It wasn't lost on her that her need to be on stage is a way to find that adoration elsewhere, away from the stifling of family life. Not for this signorina a transient romantic relationship but a gradual accumulation of adoring fans, who would hang on her every word. If pictures with words and music come eventually to the cinema screen, they would literally do just that. A shopping trip to Milan would be needed for the *impertinente vestiti* Isabella sought to wear, ensuring she stood out in the competitive crowd. She would have to make do with a few garments to start with. She had no time for a lengthy visit.

Cleverly avoiding suspicion, Isabella had arranged to stay with Alfina, her closest friend from boarding school while in Rome, cloaking her real intentions by the suggestion that she would mix catching up with her *amica* with looking for creative ideas for our Motori Bergamasco marketing team during her visit. The title of creative director couldn't have suited Isabella better as her creativity with the truth was developing to suit her personal life. However, having a limited time frame to find ways to promote their exciting new project was actually to her advantage as she could mix business with pleasure – her personal type of pleasure.

A perfect opportunity presented itself yesterday when her Marketing Director brother, Anton, mentioned advertising. Isabella's position on the board covers a multitude and getting the designs of the cars out there to a wider market could give her a great reason to go to Rome regularly, if need be.

In the optimistic consideration of reaching a second audition, *per favore dio* the stay could be for a week. The plan that should she get the part, a concession to her family about her acting aspirations should be in order. They would be shocked, of course, but the stunning heiress looking at herself in the long mirror, felt in no doubt that the opportunities this trip might present, are just likely to be the beginning. She could use the advantages of connections in the movie industry as a way to recruit the top stars to receive and talk about the new extra modern automobile models that Salvatore planned for production.

Feeling a little guilty because Salvatore had such great ideas for the company and she felt so distracted by dreams of stardom, Isabella excitedly reassured herself that she could juggle it all. She'd explain to her siblings how important it is that everyone should follow their dreams. At some stage she'd reveal her plans to help Novella with hers. She just needed to get a head start with her own, without raising suspicion.

Deep down, Isabella knew that she would never desert the Motori Bergamasco. It is papà's legacy to his children and she would not abandon the family ship, even if they encountered rough seas. Without Salvatore's plans it could well sink in the present climate and the reality was it gave them all a good income. She felt certain they were on the cusp of revolutionising the motor industry and aside from the loyalty perspective, she would be a fool to walk away from such a fantastic project. While Salvatore is busy, she can lay down her own foundations and build a fantastic career, but she would always be a Bergamasci, even if hiding behind a stage name.

Rehearsing the few lines, she had to learn, Isabella again stood in front of the mirror, doing some warmup exercises. She rolled her neck slowly forward and backwards, side to side, around in one direction and then in the other. After working down through her body, she inhaled and exhaled slowly to relax her body, then massaged her cheek and jaw muscles. She knows that, right now, all is well in her world.

Chapter 16

Salvatore and Giuseppe

Giuseppe opened the shutters and sun streamed into his office. He stood for a moment on the Juliette balcony and surveyed the factory complex built by his father and extended by the brothers over the past twenty years. A shadow of apprehension crossed his face at the thought all this could be put at risk by Salvatore's drive for expansion, saddling the company with debt for years to come.

Despite seeing Salvatore's unbridled enthusiasm, Giuseppe maintained that with the country on the verge of possible civil war, this is no time to risk a large capital venture. If Mussolini's black shirts march on Rome to overthrow the government and perhaps the monarchy, as rumour has it may happen and if the King called upon the army to suppress the black shirts, civil war would be inevitable.

Giuseppe agreed Motori Bergamasco needed expansion and new models, and that innovation is essential to long term success, but in such uncertain times? He heaved a sigh of resignation. He had little option but to go along with the project. He sat at his desk and perused the morning post to help calm himself down before his brother arrived for what may be a difficult meeting.

Salvatore strode into Giuseppe's office, typically without knocking. 'How did you get on at the bank for financing the new factory?'

Giuseppe leaned back in his chair. 'Sit down brother. Because of the unstable political situation, they are not lending on large capital projects,' replied

Giuseppe dolefully, 'even though we could offer freehold properties as security. I thought that might be the case. It's the wrong time to expand Salvo, as I warned.'

'I don't agree. Who did you see at the bank?'

'Branch manager Giorgio D'Innella.'

'You told him we must innovate with a new model to keep abreast of the competition and need space to build it?'

'Of course.'

'Do you think the fact that you're sleeping with his wife influenced his decision?'

'That is a personal matter. How do you know?'

Giuseppe looked puzzled and frowned with annoyance.

'My dear brother, there's not much going on in Bergamo that I don't know about. But not to worry, your secret is safe with me.'

Giuseppe paused and breathed a deep sigh of distress.

'No, I don't think he knows. He is always polite and deferential when we meet. I saw no change. All banks are adopting the same cautious approach to speculative projects; confirmed by my own enquiries.'

'Don't waste time. Go over his head, get to see his General Manager, in Milano.'

'Give me some credit brother; I already have an appointment next week. I'm also seeing the director of Banco Medici.'

'Banco Medici are known to handle Mafioso funds. I don't want the risk of dealing with those criminals. Papà always remained honest and dealt with honest people and money.'

'I know, but they are probably the only bank lending on capital projects. I'll keep you informed of course. Our accountant, Signor Albinoni, is looking into issuing a share option. We have a good reputation. Our shares will be valued and sought after. Meanwhile I need to see the land you bought for the new factory.'

'We can go to Salò tomorrow if you wish. I can free some time.'

Giuseppe thumbed his desk diary. He clicked on the intercom and spoke. 'Maria, postpone my lunch appointment with Signor Christi of the Chamber of Commerce with my apologies. I will be away tomorrow with Salvatore.'

'Have you read Anton's report about his American adventures?' asked Salvatore.

'I have and suffered his grumbling over your response to his offer from Comet. He won't leave us, but I have a compromise suggestion about establishing dealerships in Italy. Rather than getting into bed with Ford, we could attempt a relationship with Comet. Ford already plans to go upmarket with an additional model that could be direct competition to our Novella, whereas Comet's luxury brand would not. There is also the possibility that Anton could work for both companies on the marketing side; Comet need a man with Anton's experience of the Italian market. The contract would include a get-out clause if an eventual conflict of interest occurred. And Anton would gain extra income without leaving us.'

'Hmm, interesting. Not a bad idea. I'll give it some thought,' mused Salvatore.

In the open field, the strong sun necessitated a hat and dark glasses as Giuseppe walked around the site accompanied by a running commentary from

Salvatore: 'Road and rail communications are good with water and electric power available close-by. The main building will be in that flat-bottomed dip. Come and see it.'

Salvatore led him down a slight slope into a fairly flat depression. When he reached the bottom, Giuseppe looked up the slope. 'It seems to be deeper looking up from here, than down from up there.'

'That makes it attractive,' said Salvatore. 'It is almost invisible to prying eyes. We are just over sixty-two kilometres from the main road and railway and ten from Salò. This means it we should experience little local resistance or building difficulties. In addition, we'll generate work and prosperity, so can expect political favour. I'll suggest that the local politician, whoever he is, persuaded me to bring jobs to this jobless area. Big help for him in the next election. He'll be on our side with permissions and licences.'

'Good idea. But what about flooding with the production plant deep in a depression?'

'Special drainage. I already checked with our architect.'

'I'm impressed. But what about cost?'

'That's your department, dear brother. I'm in charge of building. You're in charge of getting the money.'

'But this is a big project. I've told you no one is lending at the moment.'

'I trust you completely. I've seen you in operation. You'll bring in the cash. Let's go and have lunch and I'll tell you about our benefactor, the man who sold us the land.'

'But we haven't bought it yet.'

Salvatore drove to a small restaurant in Salò where, for privacy, they sat alone outside in the shade of a tree. 'Security', said Salvatore.

'You nearly broke my back driving across that rough farmland,' groaned Giuseppe.

'Not when we've built a road direct from the main highway.'

'A direct road? Do you know how much that will cost? Why not use the road to Salò already available and turn left a couple of kilometres before the village?'

'I'll be here with my architect next week. He'll tell me what to do.'

Giuseppe exploded in frustration. 'Will he tell you what to do about the money too?' he snapped. 'An architect's idea of money is his percentage of a big uncontrolled budget that grows like that wheat over there.'

'Don't shout. We're outside for security. You're telling the whole village our business.'

Giuseppe slumped his shoulders and groaned, 'You're giving me an impossible job. You've already broken my back driving across that land. Now you're going to break the company with this crazy deal.'

'Don't exaggerate,' said Salvatore with a grin. 'In two years, you'll wonder what to do with all the money you're earning.'

Chapter 17

Francisco D'Angelo– Local Politician

Francisco strode into his office with the self-satisfied stride of a handsome, imposing man, looking in the massive mirror almost covering one wall and set to see himself every time he entered. 'I may be controlling a small pond, but being the senior local politician in my Province of Brescia I am without doubt the biggest fish,' he delighted telling his more junior political friends. 'Everyone does what I instruct, usually with considerable profit for you and me. We live in a fine world.'

They had to agree, as he certainly did wield an assured source of power, by cutting them in on the many applications for building and business licences that crossed his large powerful man's desk. He had plenty of other ways to dip his sticky fingers into many other small pies, giving a steady flow of relatively small change he distributed to friends, relatives, and young politicians on their way up who needed to be shown the ropes.

But, oh how valuable were those licences. Substantial chunks of cash extracted from often desperate applicants, needing to get a project going. He loved seeing their faces during fraught discussions when he dragged the proceedings out and they popped more money on the pile.

Friends would ask, 'Why don't you get elected in Milan? So much more money there.'

'Too full of crooks,' he laughed when the subject came up. 'You can't trust anyone in politics there. And they're always getting caught. I'm better off out here in the countryside where these things are much more relaxed and properly conducted, without corrupt police and those fiscal guys sniffing around. Some are quite honest you know, and you could end up in jail.'

The door opened and his assistant walked in carrying a sheaf of papers. A tall statuesque woman, hair carefully bobbed in the most up to date style, she had served him in many ways for many years. To keep her under control and constantly available, he paid her far above anyone else in such a position of trust and gave her a share of bribes received to keep her on side and silent about his illegal activities.

And she had one feature that favourable interested him greatly. She allowed him to touch, kiss and play-fiddle around when he felt in the mood.

When giving these sexual favours she looked over his shoulder, or across his desk and used the time to plan her family's dinner that evening. He knew because she told him, 'To keep you from thinking you're a great lover,' she laughed, as though joking.

Of course, he didn't believe her, convinced he knew how to satisfy a woman better than most men, even Rudolph Valentino.

She placed the sheaf of documents on his desk and waited for him to peruse them. He shuffled through and said, 'Doesn't seem much going on here does there Carla?'

She replied, 'I think you should look at that application from Salò, it's for change of use from farmland to industrial. Someone wants to start building a factory there to produce agricultural machinery like tractors and such like; they are going to need a whole raft of licences from all the utilities to roads and sewage. Even the building they are putting up has to be modern as possible.'

'Hmm, Francisco,' muttered. That's seems like it will be worth looking into.' He looked up, 'And find out who is selling this land and what the name of the buyer is,'

'I already know the name of the buyer,' she smirked. 'You missed it, it's on page three of that application,'

He frowned, not liking the implication that he was not studying the documents as closely as her.

'It's your job to look out for things like that and bring it to my attention.' He snapped. 'Who is it?'

'Salvatore Bergamasco,'

'Who the hell is he and what has he got to do with producing farm machinery?'

She knew the best way to get into his good books, 'I'll find out and let you know as soon as I do,'

He held up the document in question and said nastily, 'Why doesn't the name of the seller appear here?'

She shrugged, 'Apparently it's a private sale but it will be easy to find out the name of the seller as that has to be disclosed to the lawyers handling the affair.'

He shook his head, already smelling something amiss with the application. 'Something's not quite right with this, I want you to make further enquiries and let me know what's going on. Mussolini has already been intimating they want us to prepare for conflict and it would be very easy to change the use of a tractor factory to making vehicles for other purposes. There's a great deal of money to be made in any conflict whether it's here or elsewhere; and I want my fingers in that particular pie.'

He grinned lasciviously, 'As to that other little item, come in about two prepared for a private time with me. I want to show you a few tricks I picked up when I went on vacation to Spain.'

He would have been surprised when she left the room to see the look of disgust on her face. *'Someday I'm going to let him know how useless he is with his tiny prick,'*

D'Angelo sat at his desk for much longer than normal studying the documents from Salò; he noticed there was no mention of a sale price just a note saying to be agreed. 'Odd, very odd,' he thought. 'Who buys land without agreeing a price? Something's going on, and I'd better get to the bottom of it before anybody else does. I can smell a profit already.'

Chapter 18

Falcone Visits Salò

Falcone pushed open the car door and stumbled on the rough turf and hummocks of Salvatore's newly acquired land. He grabbed the door handle to save himself from falling.

Laughing he said, 'I'm used to mountains, not small hummocks.'

Salvatore chuckled and said, 'This field will soon be flat concrete. You'll feel even more out of place.'

'Where shall we start?'

'After that big lunch in Salò we'll take a gentle walk around the land, so you get the idea of the size and shape. You'll then be able to think about what you see and make your first sketches tomorrow.'

'Who is that ferocious fellow staring at you in the restaurant?' asked Falcone.

Salvatore paused before replying, 'Some crooked local politician.'

'I'll ask no more.'

'Best not to.'

Salvatore led the architect around the pegged-out boundaries, pointing at his new sketch of the factory layout and explaining his ideas. Falcone listened in deep concentration, making few comments although asking, 'At our first meeting in Avellino you wanted a large shed, which I took to square. You are now asking for a long narrower building. Is there a reason for the change?'

'I'll tell you in good time.'

Falcone nodded and asked no more questions, concentrating on what Salvatore said what he needed in buildings, approach roads, closed and open storage area. 'You'll have a land surveyor in Bergamo I can brief,' he asked.

'He'll be here tomorrow.'

Falcone nodded. 'I see you have everything worked out in your head. Well done.'

Salvatore smiled. 'We've worked most of the day. I'm getting cold and hungry. We should stop now and go to our hotel to shower and eat dinner. We can start early in the morning and complete our planning by mid-afternoon, get you back to your night train to Avellino after dinner up in the Old Town.'

'Good idea. Let's get back to Salò for a relaxing evening and kill this job tomorrow.'

Entering the dining room, Salvatore joined Falcone at a corner table and said, 'You were quick.'

'I'm probably, hungrier than you. By the way, don't turn round, but your crooked politician is here and staring at the back of your neck.'

'That's all he's going to see,' growled Salvatore.

Next morning around ten, Salvatore and Falcone were at the bottom of the dip, with Falcone explaining the French Drain system, 'No, my friend, it doesn't matter how heavily it rains, the combination of a wide deep channel filled with a bed of gravel, covered by earth under thick grass takes all the water flowing from the roof and carries it away into a deep sink about fifty metres away.'

'So, no pools of standing water forms puddles against the building to damage the wall?'

'None. Despite being in this dip in the land, your building is safe.'

'Clever those French,' said Salvatore with a chuckle. 'No. An American called Henry French invented the system. He practically invented the fine art of farmland drainage, mainly to remove waste-contaminated water from animal feeding areas to help prevent disease.'

The noise of a vehicle engine caused Salvatore to turn. At the crown of the dip, he saw the crooked Brescia politician clamber from an official government car.

Ignoring Falcone, Salvatore ran up the slope and hissed 'What are you doing here? This is private land, Get off it now.'

'D'Angelo whispered, 'Keep your voice down. This is private business. You haven't sent my car yet.'

'It's being built, you idiot.'

'I want it by the end of this week.'

'End of next week, now...' with the foulest of foul language for which Italy is famous, he again told the man to leave.

D'Angelo climbed back into the car and told his chauffer to go.

Falcone said with a wry grin, 'Again, I won't ask.'

That evening at the railway station, they shook hands and Falcone said, 'I'll have the planning drawings of the long factory ready in a couple of weeks. I'll place the offices, stores, and ancillary buildings where you want, but may make a few changes because of the lay of the land.'

'I'll follow your advice,' said Salvatore.

Before Falcone climbed into the train he turned and whispered, 'Be careful of that man. If he becomes too much, I have certain friends who will take care of him.'

'I'm not sure about that,' said Salvatore.

Smiling, Falcone held out his hand in final farewell, and said, 'I think you handle such problems differently here in the north.'

Chapter 19

Giuseppe's Finance Proposal

During the past few days, Giuseppe had applied his mind to conjuring a financial scheme that would get around most banks reticence to speculate on large capital projects. They tried to avoid exposure to the uncertainties of current political unrest and escalating inflation.

He outlined his innovative scheme to the General Manager of Banco Ambrosiano in Milano yesterday, but it fell upon deaf ears. Today, he returned to Milan by train and sat in the back of a taxi heading to the Piazza Cavour for an appointment with a director of Banco Medici.

He felt sure that the Medici name had been purloined as the historic middle-aged banking and political dynasty of the House of Medici long gone after a reign of three centuries. During this time, he had read in University, they created the largest banking empire in Europe aided by patronage and coercive control of the papacy and other political posts.

The Medici ruled by tyranny and corruption; much as the Mafia do today. The Medici dynasty ended without a male heir, their banking empire ravaged and pillaged by a Europe torn apart by wars and political conflict.

Today, the Bank's rumoured Mafia connections were a worrying aspect, but no bank could be guaranteed free of Cosa Nostra influence and that Mafia funds were being channelled into legitimate businesses to launder ill-gotten gains.

The taxi drew up outside a grand grey stone Palladian style building with a colonnade of Corinthian pillars supporting an open portico. A smartly liveried doorman ushered him into the banking hall; the marble floor, medieval religious paintings and glittering chandeliers imposed an air of confidence, solidity, and respectability.

Luciano Buracci welcomed Giuseppe with a warm handshake and ordered coffee via an obedient secretary. Reluctantly they both watched her leave the office.

Giuseppe handed Buracci a manila folder. The banker placed a pair of gold wired spectacles on his nose and twisted the earpieces into place and perused the papers inside, with an occasional approving nod. 'I had my assistant carry out a few background checks on your family company,' he said reassuringly. 'Everything seemed in order.'

'I would expect nothing less,' replied Giuseppe.

The coffee arrived. The shapely body inside the black dress seemed as fluid as the noir nectar. 'So, what can I do for you, and why not Banco Ambrosiano, your bankers of many years standing?'

'Ambrosiano and others are reluctant to engage with large capital projects at present. I heard on the grapevine that Banco Medici may be in a position to lend funds from private investors looking for a safe haven for their funds. So, I have an innovative proposal to offer which should be in both our interests.'

'It is true we do have a portfolio of clients looking to invest in manufacturing and infra-structure projects. What do you have in mind?'

'My company has acquired land for a new factory with a view to diversifying production into tractors and associated agricultural machinery.'

'A rather radical departure from your core business,' Buracci replied, with a sceptical frown. 'Fiat Trattori have been making gasoline propelled tractors since 1918 and Ford is established in the same market. That's serious competition. I would be more confident of your venture were it to be a new model of saloon or sports car. Do you have research data, a business plan, cash-flow, and income projections to support your scheme?'

'In the traditional sense, no, because I'm talking about an investment partnership without the traditional exposure risk,' replied Giuseppe.

'But the Bank will need . . . '

'Mi scusi, but please hear me out,' interrupted Giuseppe, raising his hand. 'The bank will not be exposed to financial loss if the new venture fails to be profitable, the bank's participation will be secured against the bricks-and-mortar of freehold property, details of which I have here.'

He reached into his briefcase and extracted a sheath of documents. 'The properties and land owned by Bergamasco are valued at four million Lire. The company needs finance of three million Lire, held by the bank to be drawn down as and when required. The Freehold titles would be temporarily transferred to the bank as security and the company would become a tenant paying rent in lieu of interest. This would afford stability, avoiding the turmoil of the financial markets and soaring inflation. Contractually, the bank would allow the company the option, in perpetuity, to buy-back the freeholds, in whole or in parts, redeeming the loans.'

'Hmm,' mused Buracci, stroking his beard, 'an interesting concept. But if property values decline, and your venture fails, the bank could be exposed to losses if forced to sell.'

'The bank's margin is protected by lending against only 75% of market value, and your asset would include the Bergamo car factory, which has been profitable for the past twenty years. We are confident that we can meet the rental liability from the profits of current production and sales.'

After a further questions-and-answers debate of the broad details of Giuseppe's scheme, Buracci conceded a cautious interest. 'I will need to put it to a board meeting,' he said. 'If you can let me have an outlined proposal in writing by Friday, I'll list it for discussion at next week's meeting.'

They shook hands and when Giuseppe stepped out into the sunshine, he removed his tie and strode to the Galleria Vittorio to seek refreshment, convinced he had made a breakthrough in the struggle for finance. Back in Bergamo that evening he would celebrate in the arms of Rosalina.

Chapter 20

Anton's Two Big Decisions

Anton lay awake most of night in his king-size bed, his mind in complete turmoil, trying to come to a decision. Should he accept or reject the offer of a new job at American car manufacturer, Comet Cars?

He felt sorely tempted to take this exciting new opportunity that would pay him greatly in excess of his current earnings. But if he did, Salvatore would make absolutely certain he would lose his share of papà's will and be forever banned from Motori Bergamasco. Should he blame papà for setting up such harsh rules, or blame Salvatore for ruthlessly applying them?

I'm damned if I'm simply going to cave into Salvatore's threats. But can I be disloyal and turn my back on my brothers and sisters at a time when they most need me? And it is Salvatore's fault or papà's for this awful dilemma?

Finally, at just after three am, he realised that family loyalty counted for more than cash and decided to stay. Exhaustion took over and he at last fell asleep for fewer than five hours. At eight, he left his rumpled bed and went out for a breakfast of black coffee and his favourite small cream pastries, feeling, at first, guilty at letting down his old friend Bernard Myers the son of Comet's owner Joe.

Then an idea struck him. Perhaps he still had something to offer Comet by suggesting a deal that might benefit everyone. He hurried to his office and sent Bernard in New York a telegraph saying: 'Sorry. I can't walk out on my dear family, so after much deliberation, I have to turn down your kind offer of a job with Comet. But I can help you develop sales of your new luxury automobile in Europe by recommending that Motori Bergamasco sell your top range new vehicle alongside our own cars in showrooms we plan to shortly open in Italy. If successful, we expect to spread retail outlets all over the continent of Europe. This means we can jointly promote our vehicles in a joint campaign of great benefit to the benefit of both our companies.'

If Bernard and Joe liked his plan, he felt sure he could convince Salvatore we would be better joining with a small company like Comet, than with the enormous Ford, who may swallow us whole once they saw the possibilities of overseas expansion.

Consumed with excitement, Anton began drafting a formal proposal to Salvatore for discussion with the Motori Bergamasco board of directors.

At three in the afternoon, he called in his secretary. 'Type this with enough copies for the full board and one addressed directly to Signor Salvatore. It is highly secret and must not be shown to anyone until after I have discussed it with him.'

He sat back, his heart beating hard again, thinking of what he now planned – another bold proposal, another transatlantic telegraph.

Anton hurried to the main Bergamo post office and crouched at a desk in the corner, his back to the crowded hall, he wrote and rewrote several times a second important transatlantic telegraph, this time to Ginnie.

'Can't stop thinking about you. I would like to invite you to Italy. Perhaps we could then discuss you considering joining me in a merger switching from

bachelor rovers to marriage united stop all love stop
Anton.'

Chapter 21

Frank Starts Digging In

Frank had never believed in threats, physical coercion, or outright violence to achieve his aims. Money had always been his chosen weapon of choice.

Much of this methodology he owed to his mother. When her cousin's son, Carlo, was murdered by the Mafia it ignited old memories. But not an urge for vengeance. The society she fled from in that tumultuous year was made up of three social strata's, the disorganised, scattered mass of peasantry, the intellectuals of the lower and middle strata and the great landowners. She fell into that middle order, her young lover, Umberto the first. This made for an uneasy alliance that both families opposed.

The forced separation at that time of Unification should have been the end of it.

Umberto had always been a bagman for the Mafia, performing illicit deliveries and running errands for his criminal bosses, many of whom were embedded in the landed gentry of which the Ianillo family were a part. They became critics of the emerging Government that who that in turn set its sights on eradicating organised crime.

The rift was inevitable. Umberto fled north, vowing never to forsake his homeland, whilst Frank's mother's family had more grandiose ambitions. Rapidly achieved with the arranged wedding to the millionaire, Howard Bernstein, within weeks of setting foot on American soil.

Whilst disputes over the ownership of the Ianillo estate rumbled on, well into the 20th century.

On the eve of Frank's departure for Italy his mother gave him a faded, creased black and white photograph of Umberto that she had clung to all her adult life. A shiver ran down his neck and across his shoulders as their eyes connected. Not dissimilar to the physical reflex he had upon meeting Salvatore d'Bergamasco for the first time.

His mother never did anything without an ulterior motive. Which she never verbally revealed.

Frank had often wondered why he was an only child. He put it down to his father being considerably older than his mother. Questions about his true paternity was a taboo subject. Why shouldn't it be? On his father's death he was the benefactor of such a vast legacy to ensure his silence. Yet nagging doubts had crept in. His mother had covertly sent him not on a quest to uncover a murderer, but to track down the man who was the father of her only son.

In those first weeks in Italy Frank found few clear answers, only more questions. There was no urgency. Frank was a patient man. Another commodity inherited with his wealth he found useful as a patient man Frank felt no urgency.

He felt also willing to wait for Falcone, his new business partner, acquired as part of Carlo's legacy, to divulge his reasons for accompanying Salvatore north. Since when Falcone had become very withdrawn, almost introverted. He absorbed himself in his work, spending extended hours locked away. Presumably working on the outline plans for the Bergamasco factory, which he shared with no-one. Sworn to some code of *Omerta*, obligated to never, under any circumstances, to divulge one word about his assignment until Salvatore allowed.

As a very silent partner in the architectural firm Falcone and Ianillo, Frank felt happy for Falcone to quietly run with it. He had other ways to get under the family's skin. On a fleeting trip to Florence Frank had secretly sent a gift of Gucci luggage to Isabella marked, *"From a distant admirer."*

Chapter 22

Isabella Auditions

Disembarking from the train at Roma's Stazione Termini, Isabella scoured the crowd for the beautiful Alfina. She didn't have long to wait as excited screams reached her ears from across the heads of the bustling crowds, faster than the speed of light.

'Bella, mia amica'

Smiling widely, Isabella briefly beckoned a porter to take her fashionable new Gucci luggage, a glamorous replacement for the tired baggage she had discarded after her trip to Milan. It was a timely gift from an eager admirer who had recently visited Florence. She remained stationary, arms outstretched, as seconds later a beautiful, animated young woman reached her, lunging forward as they wrapped each other in a warm embrace.

Short dark locks entangled long blonde strands, hair intertwining in unison with their bodies, affection permeating the surrounding air. Passers-by found themselves compelled to stop and admire the gorgeous vision the contrasting beauties created, Isabella's olive skin complementing the pale complexion and sparkling blue eyes looking back at her as they pulled apart, each admiring the other.

'Che bella, how you have changed, in such a short time, your hair, it is chic, no longer unruly, though I think it belies your true nature.'

The words tumbled from Alfina's full red lips as she continued. 'You are a true actress for no-one could possibly know what lies beneath that glamorous facade. Ah but *I* do and when you're a famous actress,

I will never give away your secrets. I'll take them to my grave.'

Alfina dramatically placed her hands, one on top of the other, palms down, on her small but firm breasts and both girls laughed raucously.

'I could have some competition if you were to decide to audition for the same parts,' Bella snorted to which her amica quickly reassured her 'Oh no, I will keep my dramatic side for the courtroom. I want my career in law to be as entertaining as I hope it will be successful.'

Isabella had been happy to congratulate Alfina on recently passing her final exams to become a barrister and Isabella knew that one day she would be very successful in her chosen field. The aspiring actress felt so proud of her clever bosom buddy rising against all of the odds to follow her chosen career path. What an act to follow.

Two days later, an excited Isabella burst through the front door of Alfina's beautiful home in the exclusive Aventino neighbourhood of Rome, shouting 'They liked me, they really liked me.'

She felt her audition for a stage production had gone well and she had been informed that there were three serious contenders for the part of which she is one. That excitement quickly dissipated when no offer ensued but with two more auditions lined up, Isabella cleverly used her dismay as a baseline for one of the parts for which she would be auditioning. Needing to play a sulky, tipsy twenty-two-year-old, proved to be easier as she had lost her sparkle, through sheer disappointment at losing out on the first audition.

'The part is yours,' said the producer. 'I'll send the contract tomorrow morning.'

Arriving home in a state of high excitement Isabella told Alfina, 'I'm tempted to avoid another ego bashing, I think I'll skip the third audition,'

'No darling. You must go. Never discard opportunities that give you choices. Please go and win a choice of two parts.'

'But what if I fail?'

'It is your duty to the women of Italy in these changing times to court success in your chosen field,' the flaxen haired beauty advised her talented amica.

The third audition involved Isabella using her natural musical talent as a flapper dancer.

'This is just for me,' she told herself, fitting easily into in the chorus of a big musical production, that brought her love of the spotlight to the fore.

She and Alfina had practised over and over again the previous night, taking the whole business very seriously, for ladies who loved to laugh. While in her absolute element rehearsing, Isabella nevertheless had a niggling feeling that her brothers would not be at all amused when she announced her aspirations for a stage career with the part of a chorus girl. The sulky debutante would be an easier pill for them to swallow.

Fate had other things in store, however. Isabella's great sense of rhythm and easy smile dazzled the casting director.

On her last evening in Rome, the two visions of beauty decorated a window of the revered Ristorante dei Castello de Cesari on Via Santa Prisca with its stunning views of the Aventine as they dined in style to celebrate Isabella's newly acquired stage role as a wild living outrageous flapper girl.

Chapter 23

Novella's Destiny

Life had become dull and mundane for Novella since her wonderful experience in America. She missed the excitement that travel had given her and loved the self-discovery of her newfound capabilities. She realised she had been closeted to the home for far too long and needed a new challenge.

She turned to her hobby. The one thing she'd never become bored with is her knitting and creating clothes for her dolls.

Sitting cross legged on her bed wearing a sloppy purple joe T-shirt, pink track suit bottoms and purple ankle socks she flicked back her long dark hair hanging loosely over her shoulders. She smiled, happy to see her sister Isabella standing in the doorway. She usually popped in for a chat on her way out for the day. She looked very elegant wearing a navy over-the-knee skirt with a pretty frilly blouse. 'Buongiorno sorella, that looks interesting, what have you knitted?'

'It's a bolero jacket I've designed for my Sophia doll. Do you like it?'

'Wow! I love it. Be a darling and make me one in that same colour. It would go perfectly with what I'm wearing today. I'll buy the wool.'

Novella had no idea how to recreate dolls clothes for women and immediately dismissed her sister's idea.

'Sorry Isabella, I only know how to knit for my dolls.'

Novella saw Isabella glance across the bedroom to the shelves of dolls wearing designs she had intuitively created. 'Listen to me Novella, you have an amazing talent you can profit from if only they were all knitted in women's sizes. There's an open market waiting to be exploited out there in the wider world. The gift you have for designing knitwear will take you far if you allow it. Believe me when I say women will wear the same clothes your dolls are wearing. I already see garments I would be proud to wear if you would knit them for me.'

Novella felt doubtful but her sister continued convincing her. 'Women knitters will want to knit their own from a pattern. Non knitters will buy them ready made. Factories with knitting machines will buy your patterns. Your dolls will set a new fashion trend. Use me and yourself to experiment on. Once you have created a variety of patterns you could travel the globe selling them. You'll be established on the world stage. You've got the taste for travelling now, haven't you? I'll leave you to think about it. I must go now; I'm meeting a friend and I don't want to be late. Arrivederci.'

Novella stared at her dolls with new meaning. Isabella had inspired her to look beyond what she had achieved as a hobby. Whether she had the ability to become a businesswoman only time would tell. The thought of travelling seemed very appealing and triggered her feet to itch. A new buzz of excitement registered in her brain as she recalled words of wisdom from her brothers Paolo and Salvatore.

Paolo said, just before he left for the Amazon when she still dreamt of being a hairdresser, *'Carry on with what you are doing. It's all worthwhile experience you are gaining for the future.'*

And dear Salvatore wanting to reassure her before she set sail for America. *'You have to remember how well papà did to overcome his shyness to leave us with a business we can all be proud of. If he could conquer his fears, then so can you.'*

With her two brothers words ringing in her ears, Novella found the courage to change direction. With great enthusiasm she quickly plaited her hair to stop the breeze blowing it into her face having decided she would ride downtown to Franny's Craft Shop. She took the scenic cycle path passing fields of cattle and sheep, a beautiful, thatched farm cottage with chickens foraging the floor bed before entering a local park close to a small shopping centre.

She parked her bike at one of the cycle stands outside Lorretta's hair salon. As she gazed through the panoramic window, her childhood longing at becoming a top hair stylist had faded. Her dream now focussed on travelling, rather than standing for long hours each day in one spot on the floor. She awakened to a new reality. Hairdressing would limit her travelling time and restrict her movements. She felt no guilt, but a sense of relief empowered her. She must follow her new destiny.

Inside Franny's shop amongst the pretty coloured wools, she felt at home. *If I can design knitwear for dolls I can surely design for people.*

Novella hurried round the shop gathering everything she needed, eager to start her new project, keen to get home and knit.

'Unusual for you to buy extra skeins of the same colour Novella. Are you planning on knitting something special?' Franny quizzed.

'It's a surprise for Isabella. I will bring it down to show you when I've finished, Franny.'

After leaving the shop she threw her purchases into her bicycle basket and quickly pulled it out of the cycle stand forgetting to look behind to see if anyone was passing.

'Ouch. Watch where you're going.'

Startled, Novella half turned to see a young man lying on the ground. She panicked, re-parked and promptly turned to help but he had already picked himself up. Before she could say a word, their eyes met. Held in wonderment. The first flush of womanhood awakened. Cupid's arrow pierced her heart. Unexplainable shivers rushed through her, opening up an aura of pleasure she had never felt before.

She felt vulnerable. In her weakness she lost her balance and fell into his arms. He held her close. The tenderness of his touch and the scent of his aftershave bewitched her. She nestled her head into his neck and there they stayed embraced for how long she didn't know and didn't care. She had never felt so alive. She felt suddenly awkward and embarrassed and forced herself to break away.

'I'm so sorry, I don't know what came over me. Are you hurt?'

'No bones broken, Signorina,' he grinned.

Their eyes met again. Afraid of being lost to her deepest feelings she stared at his head noticing everything. How his black hair parted on the right; those mass of waves swept across to the left and that attractive curl falling on to his forehead brought out the latent hairdresser in her. She felt almost tempted to run her hand through those amazing locks. Emotionally out of her depth, she needed to escape to prevent further embarrassment; inwardly running away from her fluttering fledgling feelings.

He broke the silence. His soft sultry vocal tones showed genuine care and concern. 'Are you OK now?'

He asked as he softly touched her hand. She felt he was talking about collapsing into his strong inviting arms. She looked again into his eyes, her resolve weakening. Feeling she may make a fool of herself she must leave immediately but first she must answer his question.

'Yes, I'm better now thank you,' She lied, 'I must go. I have to get home.'

He moved aside to allow her to reverse her bike. Exchanging one last smile they parted. She began to pedal away. He ran and caught up, trotting beside her. She dare not stop.

'What is your name?'

'Novella, What is yours?'

'Luca, pleased to meet you Novella,'

Words failed her, he stopped running.

Her flushed cheeks burning, she pedalled hard until she arrived home to see Isabella walking just ahead of her on the drive, in front of the villa. *Good, I can stop thinking of Luca now.* 'Isabella wait for me,' she called.

She is sure to see my flushed cheeks, and the joy bouncing off me.

Her sister stopped walking.

'What's all the hurry? You look as if you've cycled a marathon. Where have you been?'

'I've been to Franny's craft shop to get some more wool. I'm going to try and design your bolero today. I told Franny I am knitting you a surprise and I would take it to show her once I've made it. I'll get a pattern printed and ask her if I can add it to the patterns of the women's knitwear she already has,'

'Great idea, well done. You'll be a successful businesswoman in no time.'

111

Chapter 24

Mussolini's March on Rome

Leaving through the stage door of Teatro Salone Margherita in Rome, a theatre which had been dedicated to Queen Margaret, wife of King Umberto 1st of Rome in 1898, Isabella felt the warmth of the balmy late October evening as she stepped into Via dei Due Macelli. Intrigued yet frightened, the fully fledged flapper girl could feel the magnetism of curiosity beseech her to watch what was unfolding before her very eyes.

Throngs of people were marching on Rome, in a demonstration organised by Benito Mussolini, the leader of the National Fascist Party. Alarmingly she found herself immediately swallowed up by the crowds of thousands of Fascist demonstrators, the atmosphere both exhilarating and threatening at the same time. Serious change had been afoot for some time, with violent consequences for opposing factions.

How has it come to this, Isabella pondered, albeit fleetingly. *I have been so caught up in my own world, only contending with the political changes when they have been discussed at our board meetings and only then in the context of how they would influence our business going forward. Yet, this is affecting the whole country on all sorts of levels.*

Though the dramatic side of Isabella's personality revelled in the intensity of the atmosphere surrounding her, the reality felt daunting, and she found herself listening to the voices chanting a song she'd never heard before:

'Come on, comrades in strong ranks,

Let's march toward the future.
We're audacious and fierce phalanxes,
Ready to dare, ready to dare.'

I have an affinity with these people, for I too have a sense of adventure and I'm ready to dare to be who I feel I should be. Though, I'm not as brave as they who are openly, publicly declaring their support for fascism without fear of criticism or being struck down. Maybe the time has come for me to do the same, in my personal life, tell my family about my stage career, be brave and own who I really am.

Abruptly knocked out of her reverie Isabella found herself being shoved forward by the throng and to all intents and purposes appeared to be one of them. She could feel the sense of camaraderie, though veiled with more than a hint of menace. The Blackshirts were everywhere among the masses of working men marching through the city of Rome, some carrying banners, others singing or chanting, interspersed with political rallying cries from the mob.

There were no other women in sight and Isabella found herself being jostled roughly as the crowd marched closer together at a faster pace. To her horror she felt herself falling forward, the fear of being trampled paralysing her body to such an extent that she didn't put her arms out to break her fall. Miraculously she never hit the ground, instead she felt strong arms grab her upper shoulders and around her slim waist that carried her to the edge of the crowd down a narrow lane, out of harm's way.

'This is no place for a woman,' Isabella heard a deep male voice reprimand her just as he released his grip and placed her down against a wall. With a tip of his cap, the tall, burly demonstrator with a thick head of curiously sandy hair, took his leave and instantly disappeared into the fast-moving mob as it surged forward like a giant predator.

Shaking from head to toe, aware of what a close call she had just experienced, Isabella took time to catch her breath and steady herself. Reflecting on what had just happened, she scolded herself for the idiocy of her choice to leave the theatre at all. There had been rumours about the march on Rome and she could have stayed back after rehearsals, in the safety of the auditorium, with her friends.

My inquiring mind has often been my undoing, but I have just taken it to the extreme.

Isabella did however acknowledge to herself that the pure joy of recently performing in front of such appreciative audiences had been reflected in her enthusiasm within Motori Bergamasco where her proposal for marketing the Town Car to professional women with independent means had been applauded by her siblings.

'Your creativity comes as no surprise' Salvatore had said, 'Great idea. Of course, you are pointing out a whole new market. These ladies might never have driven before, having always been chauffeured and even if they have, their travel needs around the town, will be different now. Well done, Isabella.'

Taking time to regain her composure, the shaken young woman reflected on the double life she had been leading in recent weeks. Her excuses for visiting Alfina in Rome for such lengths of time were growing thin. Spending intervals with her clever friend, between the gruelling rehearsals and performances, though wonderful and endearing, had also led to intense discussions about the rise in Fascism in Italy and all it entailed. Isabella felt somewhat torn in the face of current politics as, though her friend was a firm anti-Fascist, her own mindset was developing slowly, and she craved more knowledge about the fast-growing movement. Admitting to herself that mixing regularly with working class people had opened her eyes to the lives of those less fortunate in Italy, Isabella felt her views shifting somewhat.

Before I involve myself more in all of this, I have to tell my family about my theatrical career. I am a performer and whether that be in the boardroom or on stage, it is in my blood. I want both, I want to be a director of Motori Bergamasco and also to have a stage career. What I must keep to myself however is that I may be a Fascist. I've yet to work out where my allegiances lie.

Chapter 25

Frank Finds Isabella

The Teatro Salone Margherita had started life as a *cafe chantant* in 1898. Somewhere to spend time before and after a show. One of very few theatres in Rome to still boast this peculiarity. Not just a theatre, but a meeting place. It was with this in mind that Frank had gone there, hoping to bump into Isabella d'Bergamasco between her afternoon rehearsals and the evening performance.

She hadn't shown.

By the time he'd found his way to the stage door he caught sight of her melding into the crowds thronging towards a mass rally of Fascists in the Piazza di Spagna.

He tried to keep her in his view but when she stumbled, he couldn't protect her. That duty fell to a stocky guy, thick locks of ginger hair tumbling across his brow. The man stopped her falling, then disappeared, leaving a stunned Isabella to roll with the people until she too vanished.

Frank had no desire to run with the pack to be blasted by Fascist rhetoric. He'd heard enough of that from the Italian community back home. For them Mussolini was very popular. Unnervingly, many Americans were drawn to Mussolini's Fascist movement too, but very few became supporters.

This seemed largely due to the conflicting descriptions of what Fascism really is. The American ambassador to Italy, stated: 'I am *greatly impressed by the efforts of Benito Mussolini to improve the conditions of the masses*' and found '*much evidence*' in support of the Fascist stance that *'they represent a true democracy in as much as the welfare of the people is their principal objective.'*

This played into the notion amongst the wealthy elite that the Fascists sought to eliminate the autonomy of large-scale capitalism and relegate it to the state. Ignoring the contrary notion that Fascism does support private property rights and the existence of a market economy and very wealthy individuals.

Frank knew from his own research that neither definition complied with the ideology created by the Italian philosopher, Geovanni Gentile, that Fascism is based on the principles of the 'Ethical State.'

'All things within the State.'

'Nothing outside the State.'

'Nothing against the State.'

'So, no property rights, no free market, only collectivism. Individuals have no rights. Fascism is profoundly anti-capitalism.'

'True capitalism needs true democracy', is Frank's conclusion. Something he saw could cause conflict for Isabella, being from a family of aspiring capitalists, but currently allowing herself to be devoured by the mob hysteria now seeping through every pore of Italian society.

The excited cacophony of those cramming into the public arena faded to a garbled background fuzz as Frank moved farther away, weaving through almost deserted backstreets until almost alone. Finding a discreet bar to while away the remaining daylight hours as he assessed where he had come; what he had achieved in so short a space of time and what courses lay open to him to find the answer his mother sought for her own piece of mind.

He would leave an anonymous gift in Isabella's dressing room before catching her evening performance.

Chapter 26

Isabella's Revelation

'A flapper dancer?' shouted Salvatore. 'Is this some kind of joke?'

He jumped to his feet, almost convulsing with shock and indignation. But not because Isabella had come clean. He had just seen the Avanti newspaper laying open on the solid wood Baroque dining table.

The headline '*A real Bergamasco flap*' seemed to taunt him above the photo of a chorus line of flapper girls, including Isabella, performing on stage at Teatro Salone Margherita in Rome. Her beautiful face clear to see and her smooth, firm body curves accentuated in dancing attire that didn't leave much to the imagination.

The article appeared more complimentary than derogatory and in truth Isabella felt thrilled with being thrust into the limelight. The producer of the musical had been delighted with the publicity and had even hinted at a bigger part for her. After the march on Rome, for reasons that were being kept secret, the lead dancer had made an abrupt exit. Rumours spread that her husband had suddenly been promoted within the ranks of the fascist army and was being generously compensated. This departure thus created a vacancy which every chorus girl vied for.

'I planned to tell you Salvatore, all of you,' she cast a pleading glance towards the other family members before returning to face her older brother. 'However, it's out now and I won't be bullied. I am a performer and I currently have a chance at the leading role in an excellent production. I intend to get it. I want this with every fibre of my being.'

'Isabella, darling, you are wonderful. I think that is absolutely incredible, my hearty congratulations,' Novella audibly gasped.

'*Nonsense*' bellowed Salvatore, 'you won't be taking any leading role, in fact you won't be returning to that *circus* at all.'

'Calm down Salvatore,' all eyes were on Anton, wide in amazement at his implied support of Isabella. 'We all need a passion in life, and this is Isabella's.'

Love has obviously softened Anton, Isabella speculated, aware of her brother's intense new American interest. *He's looking at the world with a fresh perspective. Whoever would have thought. Though,* she reflected, *I've never been in love. Who am I to question this?*

Emboldened by Anton's supportive words, Novella had some of her own.

'Yes, papà would have wanted us all to follow our passions.'

'Passions?'

Salvatore spat out the word.

'More like frivolities; you with your silly little doll's clothes and Isabella with this theatrical nonsense, prancing around in frilly knickers. Our passion should be Motori Bergamasco.'

'No,' Giuseppe interrupted firmly, 'That is *your* passion, Salvatore. You are consumed by making this company bigger and better, more successful than ever, at the risk of huge financial loss. Perhaps making us all poor and bankrupt. Why shouldn't Isabella and Novella follow their own dreams. They are fulfilling their obligations as directors of Motori Bergamasco. They are only needed for board meetings, every couple of months. These are changing, challenging times fratello. If we can't support one another as a family, what hope do we have against the forces that are ravaging Italy?'

Realising the meeting outnumbered him by four to one, Salvatore slumped in his seat and laid his head in his hands, looking bewildered.

'I don't accept these arguments but as they appear to be unanimous against me, I have no choice but to capitulate. However, passion can be a dangerous emotion, it can drive one crazy with desire, lead one down a dark pathway, eliciting immorality.'

'Immorality,' an indignant Isabella shrieked. 'Are you suggesting my dancing in a stage musical is immoral?'

'Indeed, I am not,' Salvatore denied in an unusually soft tone 'I am merely pointing out how passion can be detrimental, an emotion that, should you choose to embrace it, be prepared for sacrifices beyond anything you could have imagined. The challenges may be enormous. Think very carefully dear Isabella, before following this path.'

Salvatore saw how Isabella found herself caught off guard by his change of tone. With six years between them, she now twenty-nine, he thirty-five, together with the difference in genders, they had been reared dissimilarly. Nevertheless, she must have thought she knew him well enough.

He rarely showed a softer more malleable side since Papà had passed. Having no illusions about how fleeting this moment of vulnerability might be, he felt her probe a little further.

'Are you speaking from experience Salvatore? If so, you might enlighten us a bit more and, perhaps, convince me to heed your words of caution.'

Salvatore realised, from this new strength of voice and independence, he could do nothing to deter Isabella from this path now, especially with the chance of a leading role.

However, he knew she could see the anger melting from his face and realised she had seen right through him in this moment of rare defeat.

He caught a glimpse of the little girl who could easily manipulate papà with her dark eyes and silver tongue. He knew he had dropped his guard but recovered himself well enough to assume his usual more authoritative tone.

He replied, 'There is nothing more to tell, just a cautionary tale, dear girl. Heed it and follow your passion with care. I'll say no more, except good luck in your career. Become famous and a credit to your family.'

Chapter 27

Anton's Triumph

Two days went by without Anton hearing from Ginnie in reply to his shock marriage proposal.

'You fool,' he told himself. 'She presumably saw our sexual encounter in New York as merely a fling with a likeable hotel guest – not some big romance.'

But on the third day he received a telegraph from her. As he fumbled to open it, Anton wondered if he was about to read a curt rejection or an offer of a relationship.

It said: 'I've been thinking of you, too. I am willing to come to Italy so we can spend more time together. The idea of being wooed by a good-looking Italian is appealing. Then we can discover if this is a real love match.' It ended with three kisses.

Elated, Anton sat enjoying a celebratory drink of champagne, when a second telegraph arrived, this one from his friend Bernard Myers at Comet Cars, New York.

Not surprisingly, the message started with a critical note. 'My father and I were shocked by your decision to turn down our job offer which you had appeared to accept during your visit with us, but we appreciate loyalty to your family is normal. We will certainly consider your suggestion that you help develop sales of our new luxury car in Europe. Let us know how you propose promoting our product in a joint campaign with Motori Bergamasco.'

Great. Bernard and Joe are willing to consider my alternative proposal. I'm sure we could sell their luxury car, alongside our own new designs, in our planned showrooms.

Anton knew he now had to produce a startling marketing and advertising plan for Salvatore and the board. *Salvatore's new design should beat the hell out of our competitors and my campaign must do the same, but this joint venture can benefit Comet Cars as well.*

He eventually came up with two different advertising pitches, the first showing brightly coloured images of all three Motori Bergamasco cars, The Town Car for essential use around Italy's large cities, The Tourer for long distance driving, carrying smartly dressed businessmen, even the length of Italy, and The Speedster with its extra powerful engine for the young daredevil to hurtle over mountain passes, speed along winding valleys and splash through fast-flowing streams in clouds of spray.

Ideas flowed and he turned his mind to furiously scribbling a second set of Town Car advertisements to capture the attention of women drivers. These showed a series of fashionable ladies sitting at the driving wheel of Novella's elegantly decorated Town Car or displaying silk stockinged legs and an enigmatic smile while draped across the rear seats in an image of elegance and sophistication. They represented the modern young wife or girl-about-town.

Then Anton turned his intensity to seeking a few punchy words – a Banner Headline – to give weight to the advertising posters he had scribbled.

Almost immediately the phrase 'LEADING THE WAY IN STYLE, ELEGANCE AND PERFORMANCE flew into his imagination.

Because it appeared so easily, he mistrusted it. *Surely, finding the right words for something so important should be more difficult.*

He jotted ten alternative lines to grab The Town Car Ladies' attention before finally deciding his first attempt could not be beaten.

This new phrase – THE TOWN CAR LADIES – hit him in a hammer blow.

'Perfect,' he shouted, 'Absolutely perfect.'

Anton could see that beautiful Isabella would carry his determination for success across Italy, Europe; perhaps even the world, on posters, in magazines, newspapers, movies: her looks, personality and charm selling thousands of cars.

He knew she would clamour to make personal appearances and speeches everywhere in a big boost to her acting career.

While still hot with energy, he whipped off some punchy lines to support the Banner and, by now brimming with confidence, his mind brought up and immediately loved: 'TOWN CAR LADIES DRIVE IN LUXURY WITH THE SMOOTHEST RIDE EVER'

Knowing Salvatore wanted to launch with heavyweight marketing of The Town Car as the likely best seller of the three new vehicles, Anton decided that his presentation to Salvatore must lead with his Ladies campaign. Tourer and Speedster campaigns to men could follow. They could, perhaps, extend the Speedster name to Speedster Sport and smash into the young male sport driving market.

Finally tiring after four or five hours of extreme concentration and work, his vigour faded. With a long sigh, he settled back and shuffled through the pile of sketches and notes, looking for flaws and murmured to himself, 'No more I can do now. I'll take it to Salvatore tomorrow morning and hopes he likes it.'

At ten o'clock next day, when Anton started his presentation by telling Salvatore he felt they should run two different advertising campaigns, one male and one female that would also attract the attention of men he expected a hostile response. But his brother clapped his hands and said, 'Great thinking,' before turning his attention to ten minutes of silent shuffling through the advertising sketches and ideas Anton had spread in front of him.

'These look good to me. Who drew them?'

'Me. They are only scribbled thoughts, done in a hurry to get as many out as possible before they escaped. A good poster artist and advertising copywriter should be able to pick the best and give us a hard-hitting, colourful launch with a long-term follow-up campaign. It may mean us slightly amending the style of The Town Car, to make it more luxurious or something similar to show that we are building elegance and luxury for ladies.'

'No reason why not. Any additional cost should be minimal,' beamed Salvatore. 'Hopefully, most women will appreciate a car manufacturer pampering them in an age when they are seen as second-class citizens, even denied the vote and many other opportunities.'

'What next?' asked Anton.

Salvatore stood and shook his brother's hand. 'What next is easy. Take all these – every single one – to our advertising agency and give them a detailed brief. If they are not up to it, sack them and find an agency that is.'

'You really want me to go that far?'

'Anton. Be confident and tough. What you've given me here is the basis of an explosive launch campaign. It is brilliant, but basic. Add colour and sophistication and it cannot fail. I'll call a board meeting to settle agreement and finance. Now get out of here and get on with it.'

Encouraged, Anton raised a hand and said, 'Two more points, brother.'

'Go on.'

'Remember our plan to invite Ford to provide and sell their vehicles in the new showrooms I'm setting up?'

'I do,' said Salvatore in a cautious tone that brought a smile to Anton's face.

'Well, I've not yet contacted Ford and it strikes me we'd be better choosing a smaller company: one that will complement, rather than overshadow us. So, I suggest we start with Comet Cars. I know the owners and I've learned a lot about their plans to expand into Europe. I think our two companies would be a very good fit.'

Salvatore frowned in deep thought. Anton waited, tense and expecting a refusal.

His brother lifted his head and smiled. 'Excellent idea,' he said. 'And what else?'

'Can we definitely and finally agree that Isabella will be the face and name of our advertising?'

Salvatore laughed and clapped. 'My god, you're on song today, Anton. Of course, we can. I already see her great beauty over the whole of Italy, shining out on posters, in magazines and newspapers. And it'll be a tremendous boost to her acting career. She's such a show-off - she'll be tickled pink at seeing herself smiling and waving everywhere.'

'I thought exactly the same,' cried Anton. 'But we won't mention the show-off.'

Salvatore stood and, with a brisk handshake, sent Anton to his own room in a state of high excitement and triumph. But his priority now is to bring Ginnie from New York to Italy as soon as possible.

Chapter 28

Frank's Land Search

From studying Italian history at his American University, Frank knew that one of the better initiatives of the *Corsican Corporal*, more than a century earlier, was the introduction of the *Cadastre*, a comprehensive land registry administration, derived from the French system introduced in 1806 during Napoleon's first reign in Italy.

He knew that the registry is divided into two sections, urban and rural, with four main regional offices in Naples, Turin, Milan, and Rome. Whilst Falcone was on one of his silent trips north, presumably to survey the progress at the site of the new Motori Bergamasco factory, which Frank would have full details of in due course, he chose to visit Rome and investigate the dispute over the land that had resulted in Carlo's murder. It would also give him the opportunity to take in another of Isabella's performances, in the company of a rising Italian film producer.

Frank had checked in detail how the Land registry operated and discovered that, based on the personal data obtained from the deed itself and thereafter used to direct searches, all information is public, and any modification of cadastral maps must be introduced based on a *'Foglio di Notifica'*, a document produced by the office of Cadastre.

He followed through and found that this would also include a declaration of succession upon death and that the acquisition of inheritance rights requires either a formal act of acceptance or an explicit activity by which the beneficiary acts as owner of the asset. In this case a considerable tract of land on the slopes of the valley outside Avellino, facing Mount Vesuvius, producing two profitable crops of peaches and other fruits annually.

The original principal, listed as a Silvano Teresa, ancestor of a notorious family still residing in a nearby town that is dominated and run by the Mafia making it beyond governmental control. Another registered name, Umberto de Gennaro, possibly took his name from another regional town in the area. There were no further entries for either man since 1875, the date of assignment of Umberto's share.

Carlo Ianillo received the last share.

Frank felt in his element when delving into such research, inspired by that creation of Sir Arthur Conan Doyle. In his teens he found fascination when the Sherlock Holmes stories first appeared in American magazines in 1893 and rushed to buy the latest.

Frank knew that the declaration of succession must be presented by heirs or subjects holding rights to inheritance within twelve months of the person's death. As the legal beneficiary to the Ianillo portion of the land, Frank took the opportunity to commence the progress of succession for the entire deed. With the submission he would simultaneously request the related cadastral ownership changes. Such a claim of entitlement to the property would result in a cadastral land survey or, if the available cadastral information is not up to date, as in this case, land ownership could be claimed on a substitutive declaration containing the cadastral identification data of the real estate to which the claim is made.

The corresponding certificate of declared succession, together with a note, would be sent by the

Agency's Provincial Office to the local land registration service for its transcription with the effect of making it public.

If, as Frank suspected, the Teresa family had failed to make their own declaration of submission upon Silvano's demise Frank's own claim would rattle a few cages.

Satisfied that he had planted sufficient bait to ensnare his prey, and with full awareness that the engulfing town walls, whether they be physical or metaphorical, would not protect them from the wider law, Frank joined his producer friend, Leonardo Rinaldi, for early pre-show drinks at the Teatro Salone Margherita. He saw Isabella seated a few tables away, engrossed in a conversation with another attractive lady of similar age.

She paid him no attention. Why should she? Even if their eyes were to meet there would be no mutual recognition.

On this occasion he would leave no admirer's gift in her dressing room. He wanted Leonardo to appraise her performance and potential for an eventual switch to the silver screen whilst looks were still more important than resonance.

They were not disappointed. From the first dramatic entrance Isabella commanded the stage, holding the audience in her spell until the curtain descended to enthusiastic applause.

Three encores later Frank led Leonardo in threading their way through the crowds to the stage door where the obsequious doorman ushered the Producer towards the dressing rooms, maintaining a constant barrage of praise for his latest film. '*La belle Madame Herbert*', the old fellow kissed his fingertips,

'*Magnifique. The actress, Hesperia....*' he feigned a swoon.

'Until she opens her mouth,' he murmured to Frank, 'that will be her kiss of death if they move to sound with pictures.'

Pushing into Isabella's room he could see she still felt on a high when introduced to Leonardo, the emerging magnate of the silver screen.

'Of course, I know of you, Signor Rinaldi. Who doesn't? But who is your anonymous companion?'

She turned her shimmering gaze on Frank. 'Are you also in the pictures industry?'

'Not yet, but I could be a silent angel if a subject grabs me.'

'That accent - you must be...'

'American, yes,' Leonardo jumped in, 'with Italian heritage. Think of him as a talent scout. Frank insisted I catch your debut performance in a lead role. We needed to hear you, to absorb the emotion, the drama you could project that is fast becoming an essential skill for movies.'

'You nailed it,' said Frank, aware that Isabella had hardly diverted her eyes from him since they came in the room.

'I think I saw you in Florence. And I know I've seen you in this theatre before.'

'Scouting talent.'

Frank saw that as much as the bright and charming young actress seemed besotted with him from first sight, she simultaneously began to spin Leonardo into her aura.

'You have that rare and nebulous quality of a star,' said Leonardo, lifting and kissing the back of Isabella's hand.

She laughed, a tiny tinkling sound, and whispered, 'You men are so full of charm, but is it true or practised?'

Frank chuckled and Leonardo bowed, still holding her sweet little fingers, and said, 'You may or may not find out.'

Isabella snatched her hand away. 'I have a very clever lawyer friend – a woman – who spends her time out on the streets fiercely advocating rights for women through physical protest. I am not sure she is doing the right thing. I am growing to realise that a woman's femininity and guile can garner their desires and ambitions in more subtle and rewarding ways.'

'Such as being invited to dinner to persuade men such as we poor saps to push your career forward?' asked Frank.

With again the tinkling little laugh, Isabella, the actress, looked up at Frank, deep into his eyes from under lowered lashes and whispered 'Exactly.'

Both men laughed with her.

She took their arms and led the way across the street into a tiny, obviously expensive restaurant, where the theatre going diners rose to their feet, applauding, whistling, and calling, 'Brava, brava bella Isabella.'

She, smiled, bowed, and blew kisses before pulling her two men into a small room set up for private dining. 'A menage a trois dinner,' she giggled. 'What fun.'

Frank, enjoying his evening with this gorgeous woman, saw that Isabella savoured her new life of luxury and adulation. *She is, above all else, a d'Bergamasco driven by the genes of her father.*

Walking home through the crisp October evening, Leonardo said, 'I think she fancies you, rather than me. You could get a good ride out of her.'

'Don't be coarse,' said Frank. 'Do you think you'll take her on?

'Possibly. When she has more experience.'

'If I finance her with you saying nothing? I don't want my name involved.'

'What are you up to?'

'You'll never know.'

Chapter 29

Novella Had Much To Tell Isabella

Novella cast off the last stitch of a woman's bolero jacket she had attempted to design and knit. She felt slightly nervous sewing the pieces together, but she had nothing to fear. She'd accomplished the perfect garment and couldn't wait to see it on Isabella, now in Rome to audition for a stage show.

Eager to see what it looked like, Novella put it on and waltzed barefoot across her bedroom's plush carpet toward the oval Chippendale free standing mirror, prominently placed in the corner of the room away from the glare of sunlight piercing through the window.

I know it will be too big for me, but I simply must see what it looks like.

To Novella's amazement the chic bolero jacket fitted her beautifully. She is so pleased, her first attempt a success. Then she realises, *it's too small to fit Isabella.* She'll need to knit a larger size using more stitches.

She had run out of wool so must cycle down to Franny's craft shop to buy some more. With no time to lose, Novella went directly, forgetting she still wore the bolero jacket. She parked her bike in front of Lorretta's hair salon without a glance of envy. With that dream firmly in the past, she felt more enthused to get to Franny's shop. Novella pushed on the door to enter but found it locked.

Bewildered, she wondered why; the shop always opened on a Thursday. Disappointed, she turned away, then stopped as she heard the key turning in the lock and saw Franny changing the closed sign to open. Novella hadn't checked her watch before leaving home. Her rush to buy more wool, and what with the sun illuminating her room, the time seemed much later in the day.

'My, my, Novella, why the rush, and what a lovely garment you are wearing? It is so stylish and classy, turn around slowly so I can have a good look. Mama Mia. It is beautiful. Is this the surprise you have for Isabella?'

'Yes, Franny, it's a bolero jacket but it's too small for her, so this one will be mine,'

'And rightly so, do you need more wool?'

'Yes please, I will take three more skeins.'

'Now tell me; where did you get the idea of making this jacket?'

'It came from the idea of a design I created for my doll. I have a whole collection of dolls clothes I want to copy for women.'

Franny's eyes sparkled. She loved Novella like a daughter, not ever having any of her own children. She remembered Novella's mama with fondness, they were such close friends.

'You have your creative nature from your mama, Novella. She had the same creative ability, but it came to nothing. I would like to help you become a designer, will you let me help you?'

Novella rushed forward and hugged Franny. Tears began streaming down her cheeks as she sobbed.

'There, there Novella, you sweet child, let it out, you will feel so much better.'

Novella continued crying until her tears ran dry. She wiped the dampness from her cheeks and when the two women stepped apart, Novella could see sadness etched on the older woman's face.

'You miss her too don't you Franny?'

'Very much, we were so close, like sisters. She would often come sit with me of an evening when she felt lonely after your papà died.'

'That's so sad Franny but I am here if ever you need company.'

'Bless you dear, how about we have a nice cup of coffee and a tot of brandy; that should bring the sunshine back into our hearts.'

Novella had never tasted brandy but knew it as her papà's favourite drink. He had a store of it in the cellar. Dutch courage, he called it.

'I'll make it for us,' she ran into the kitchenette.

'Thank you dear, everything is on the work surface.'

A customer entered as Novella appeared with the drinks. The lady smiled and walked over to look through the patterns on display, but stopped and spoke in a soft voice, 'Buongiorno signorina, I am fascinated with the unusual jacket you are wearing. I can see its hand knitted. Do you sell the pattern here as I would really like to knit one myself?'

Before Novella could answer, Franny stepped forward to introduce the two women. 'Novella this is Margarete, a regular customer of mine.'

'Hello Margarete, I am pleased to meet you. I'm so glad you like my bolero. I have only just finished it for the purpose of designing a pattern. I am in the process of getting one printed and will give it to Franny.'

'I look forward to receiving it. It has been a pleasure meeting you.'

Margarete chose her wool 'paid her bill and left. For a moment Novella and Franny just stared at each other. Then clasped hands and danced around on the spot giggling like a couple of children.

'Your first customer' Novella, how does it make you feel?'

'I'm so excited, Franny, I can't wait to finish Isabella's so I can get the pattern produced.'

Franny laughed. 'Hey, I have an idea; let me try that jacket on to see if it fits me.'

Novella removed the jacket and handed it to Franny.

'It's a perfect fit, it's meant for you,'

'Lend it to me for a week. I will see how many customers become interested.'

'Keep it, the colour suits you.'

'I couldn't Novella, it's your very first one. You should treasure it to remind yourself of your new beginning into the world of business as a designer. Don't worry about knitting one for me, you have enough to do, I will enjoy making my own. Now keep an eye on the shop. I am going upstairs to get my camera so I can photograph you wearing it. You will need a picture to show your design on the front of the pattern.'

Having had her picture taken, paid for her wool, and said goodbye, Novella headed toward her bicycle, looking about her to see if Luca is anywhere in sight.

Still yearning for him to take her in his arms again.

Over the next week she kept busy knitting Isabella's bolero and designing the pattern. On her way to the printer good fortune smiled upon her again as she strolled along a parade of shops. She saw a window filled with all kinds of materials. Intrigued, she went inside and saw a beautiful selection of dress making fabrics. One bright flowery colour caught her attention. Her creative imagination opened to the idea of making a bolero jacket in this delightful fabric. *Oh, that would look so fashionable.*

With no pattern to guide her, she had to rely on imagination. She knew mama had an old sewing machine and a dressmaker's dummy at home. She would resurrect them and see what her creative abilities could conjure up.

After several attempts and alterations, she finished the bolero and tried it on. So impressed with the outcome and the thrill of the challenge it gave her Isabella decided that after each knitted dolls creation she would follow it with one of these beautiful new fabrics.

The next time Novella popped in to see Franny she is carrying a pile of bolero patterns. 'I've received thirty requests for your jacket pattern,' Franny excitedly told Novella.

'Thirty? That's amazing, I suggest you keep wearing it for longer, Franny.'

'Yes. Until I have finished making my own, then you can wear this one. We could then travel around Bergamo to other craft shops, both wearing the jacket to see if we get more interest.'

'What a good idea. In the meantime, I will continue adapting my dolls clothes, so we have more patterns to sell.'

Chapter 30

Frank's Land Inheritance

Returning from Rome to Avellino, Frank made a deviation that would take him to his inheritance. The trees were in full bloom, with the second harvest of the year still some way off. He saw a few farm workers tending the crop. On the terrace outside the main farmhouse, an elderly woman sat alone, dozing, with an open newspaper spread across her lap, a light breeze riffling through the pages.

He brought her awake by asking a question. She seemed unfazed by the appearance of a stranger speaking Italian with an odd accent.

'Is the owner here?'

The woman squinted up but said nothing.

'Signore Teresa?'

A slight, silent nod implied she is the owner.

'Silvano? Is he not here?' Frank knew the answer but wanted to hear it from her.

'My husband died.'

'I'm sorry to hear that,' he deliberately paused for effect, 'Recently?'

'What year is it?'

'1922.'

'Three, maybe four years ago, during the Albanian troubles.'

'He fought during the Italian-Albanian border war?' Frank asked, surprised. 'The Mafia had their own army; they had no need to join in and help the Italians.'

'Join in with the Government? NO. NEVER.'

With venom in the old woman's tone, accentuated

by spitting with unexpected force, she snarled, 'Those bastard Albanian gangsters tried to muscle in on our businesses.'

Frank silently absorbed the information. He knew the history of those turbulent times in Albania. Whilst most of the Western Armies were engaged in the French and Belgian trenches of the first World War, Italy's protectorate of Albania had been challenged by Austria and Hungary. For a brief period, they succeeded. But by the end of 1919 they had been all but kicked out.

Frank also knew that during this time a great deal of illicit money circulating, found its way into the Mafia's sphere of influence in Milan and Rome. The Albanian Mafia, tired of just being doormen and enforcers, for their Italian masters, expanded south to secure their own territory. Their pillars of influence being drugs, prostitution, gunrunning, and people trafficking. A turf war with the Teresa family became unavoidable, with casualties on both sides.

'And Carlo Ianillo?' Frank finally ventured.

The old lady looked as though ready to hawk a gob of spit again but, swallowed and controlled herself.

'Dead,' she now totally focused on Frank. Mesmerized, her eyes opening wider, as if seeing a ghost.

'You look familiar.'

'Do you recognize this man?' Frank thrust the old picture his mother had given him directly in front of the woman.

For a moment she squinted, peering closely, then looked up at Frank, back to the photograph for those few moments, lost in the past.

'Umberto de Gennaro', she whispered, as though saying the name aloud would summon the devil.

'Is he also dead?'

The old woman shrugged as she slowly relaxed back into her chair. 'Long gone. Umberto is long gone.'

Frank needed to clarify strange ambiguity in her expression. He needed certainty.

'Gone? ....as in....'

'Dead?', she finished the question for him, shrugging again. 'Another turbulent time. As a young man – too young for love – he made the mistake of starting a passionate affair with the daughter of a farmer.'

She shook her head, probably at the folly of youth.

'Neither family would bless a union. When they were caught together ......' she paused, unsure how to say it without resorting to vulgarity, '...in the act on hay in the farmer's barn...'

Frank and the old woman just looked at each other.

Little more needed to be said.

'Silvano saw to it. The girl and her family were packed off to America and Umberto banished. This is the first time I've even given them a second thought.'

Staring at Frank he saw understanding dawn in her eyes.

'You have his exact likeness.'

Frank knew then that the man in the picture his mother had given him must be without doubt, Umberto de Gennaro, his biological father.

Chapter 31

Salvatore and The Architect

In Milan Station, Salvatore kissed his wife goodbye and followed the uniformed porter into the train. 'Don't drink too much wine on your journey,' she called after him.

'This is a night train to Napoli, 'he called back. 'I'll be asleep soon after dinner.'

The porter shrugged and said, 'Women.'

Salvatore laughed. 'They worry about the wrong things.'

After a good dinner he smoked a cigar in the restaurant car, checked his notes for tomorrow's meeting, returned to his luxury sleeping car and went to bed.

Next morning a madly driven taxi took him through mountains and down steep valley roads to the town of Avellino. Relieved to arrive in one piece at a building marked by a large sign stating Falcone and Ianillo, Architects of Note, he said to his chauffeur, 'You should be a racing driver.'

'I was, but I crashed. Will you need a taxi to get you back to Napoli?'

'Not after that drive. I'll go by train.'

'Very slow,' said the driver, taking the fare and offering no change.

Salvatore smiled and entered the offices of Falcone and Ianillo, to be received by a pretty secretary and shown into a pleasing room with shining dark wood furniture and silver. A well-dressed middle-aged man lifted himself from his large office chair to shake hands and say, 'I am Falcone. Welcome to Avellino. What brings you all the way from Bergamo to see me?'

'I need a first-class architect and your reputation travels.'

Falcone smiled. 'Please sit down.'

Both men settled and looked at each other. Falcone said, 'Your reputation as a maker of automobile travels also. I am pleased to meet you but puzzled. You have first-class architects in Bergamo also. Why come this far south?'

'I could go farther south if you don't want our business. To Sicily, for instance. There are some excellent architects there also.'

Falcone smiled. 'True. Let us stop this jousting. I see you are carrying a plans storage tube. What do you have to show me?'

'Will your partner Signor Ianillo be joining us?'

'Regrettably no. He sadly passed away a few weeks ago.'

'Condolences. What took him?'

'Crossfire in a restaurant.'

A moment of silence fell on the room. Salvatore considered the implications and decided to ask no further questions.

'I need a first-class architect to design a quality factory. I am offering you the contract.'

Falcone stood and held out his hand. 'I accept,' he said.

Salvatore stood. took the man's strong grip and replied with his own, saying, 'This project must be kept top-secret.'

'Of course. Every project that comes into this establishment is top secret, Signor. Let's get down to work.'

Salvatore opened his storage tubes and emptied several large plans onto the leather topped desk, spreading, and smoothing them with care.

Falcone perched a set of gold spectacles on his nose, bent to place his face a few inches above the drawings and study them in concentrated silence. Salvatore relaxed in his chair, allowing Falcone all the time he needed to go through the draft pre-architect sketches.

The pretty secretary tiptoed in with a pot of coffee and a plate piled with small, sugared biscotti and tiny cream cakes. In exaggerated silence she poured two espresso cups almost to the brim and pushed the plate silently towards Salvatore. He nodded his thanks. She gave a sweet smile and allowed him to watch her creep from the room; tightly clad hips swaying for his pleasure.

Salvatore sipped his coffee and ate a couple of noiseless cakes, leaving the biscuits in case they crunched and disturbed Falcone's absorption.

After about ten minutes of wasting time studying Falcone's silver decorations balanced around the room on every shelf, cabinet, or cupboard, the man startled Salvatore by throwing himself upright and snapping, 'What we have here is a large shed. Why do you need me to draw such a thing. I am highly qualified and respected architect, not a draughtsman.'

'You are exactly right, my dear Signor. It is a large shed. But it is going to be a very complicated large shed. I am going to tell you something highly important to my company and highly confidential to my company. As a very successful automobile builder we are planning to move into the manufacture of agricultural machinery and equipment. Tractors, for instance. America and Russia are building hundreds of

144

thousands. Soon they will be producing and selling millions all over the world.'

'My dear Signor, this still remains a large shed.'

Salvatore jumped from his chair and looked down at the slightly smaller Falcone, and in a firm loud voice, said, 'No my *dear* Signor it is the beginning of a large manufacturing component planned to spread and spread across a large area I have purchased on the Plain of Lombardy towards Verona. I assure you, Signor, you will be designing and drawing complex plans linking buildings, towers, roads, and services for many years to come. If you are not interested, I shall pack my bag and travel on to Sicily.'

He stared straight at Falcone, adopting the fierce face he used on difficult workmen or suppliers and even his own family when they became argumentative. He also used the trick of clenching his jaw to make his face go red in a glare of fury. It always worked.

As it did this time.

For a moment Falcone looked shaken before relaxing and raising his hand to grasp Salvatore's in a hard manly grip. 'An unfortunate misuse of words, my dear Signor. I apologise. I am delighted that you have come to my humble establishment with such a grand and broad project. Shall we sit and proceed to deep discussion during which you fill me with detail.'

Salvatore spent the rest of the morning and afternoon until early evening explaining the large shed and the big agricultural project he had invented. To avoid errors, he repeated all his automobile plans, turning them into farm machinery, at the end even thinking, *Perhaps we could go into tractors. They're not that different to automobiles.*

With the sun sinking behind the mountains, he called a halt, 'I need to rest now, Signor Falcone. I must be up for the early train to Milan.' He refused Falcone's offer of dinner; accepted a lift to his hotel and Falcone's chauffeur for the drive to Napoli next morning, promising to invite the architect soon to Bergamo for more detailed discussions.

Sitting alone and eating a wonderful meal of fish caught that dawn from the Gulf of Napoli, Salvatore fell into conversation with a handsome somewhat older woman on the next table. 'I am staying in a different hotel across the square,' she told him. 'It is a pleasant evening. Shall we stroll across for coffee there?'

The next morning, he crossed the deserted pre-dawn square to his own hotel in time to shower and pack in readiness for Falcone's large limousine to collect and carry him to his train for Milan.

Over breakfast in the first-class dining car, watching the mountains pass by, Salvatore went back over yesterday and his success with Falcone and the woman. 'My God, she never told me her name and never asked for mine,' he whispered to himself.

This brought him to his no-name father. *Perhaps that is how it is in Cosa Nostra country. No names, no trouble. What had Falcone said about his partner? Crossfire in a restaurant? Or too well known? This is something to remember.*

Chapter 32

Kindred Spirits

Novella ate a full breakfast before pedalling down to Franny's shop for her midday appointment with Mr Beradi from the knitting factory. With her hair neatly plaited, she wore blue slacks and a long floral sleeved shirt.

She arrived at Franny's shop at eleven thirty, giving herself plenty of time to cool down from her ride, unsure what to expect from the meeting. This is her moment to make a good impression with Mr Berardi, but she felt too nervous to feel confident.

As time neared midday her throat became so dry, she struggled to swallow, worried her voice would fail. *If only I could run to Franny's kitchenette and sip a few drops of Franny's brandy, I'm sure I would feel so much better.*

Instead, she had to make do with a cool glass of water and a warm smile of reassurance from her dear friend.

'What's this man I'm meeting like?' Novella asked.

'Handsome and charming and I would think about thirty years old. I only saw him for a moment when he gave me his card.'

The door opened. Adriano Beradi Junior, oozing charismatic confidence stepped into the shop at precisely noon, smartly dressed in a lightweight grey suit, cream shirt, grey tie, and black shoes.

Franny introduced him. He smiled. staring into Novella's eyes, he surprised her by holding her gaze a few seconds longer than she would normally expect.

Novella immediately felt a friendly rapport with Adriano. Quite different to Luca who'd completely stolen her heart.

Adriano stepped forward and shook her hand, lingering before letting go.

'Hello Novella, I have been looking forward to meeting you. You are a very talented lady if you do not mind me saying. Would you do me the honour of having lunch with me, I know a very good restaurant around the corner? We could discuss our business there.'

Novella dropped her head in embarrassment as she looked down at the clothes she chose to wear and felt foolish. She was not adequately dressed to sit in a restaurant. If she had known, he wanted to dine out she would have worn more suitable clothes and asked the chauffer to drive her.

She'd even forgotten Isabella's advice, *'Wear makeup when talking business, it makes you look a stronger woman.'* 'Whatever must he think? Me, a twenty-six-year-old still wearing schoolgirl plaits to go to a meeting.'

Adriano smiled. 'I'm sorry, it's presumptuous of me to presume you would want to join me for lunch. We can talk here if you prefer.'

'No really, I would love to have lunch, but I am not suitably dressed for a restaurant.'

Adriano spontaneously whipped off his tie, opened his top shirt button, removed his jacket, and rolled up his sleeves, then stood before her, with a big grin, hands on hips.

'There, how do I look now?'

Novella giggled, 'Smart casual.'

'Ready for lunch then?'

'I'm ready.'

Novella looked into his twinkling eyes and noticed how relaxed and safe she felt in his company. A total stranger, now a friend with the same sense of humour that has got her laughing again.

Over lasagne and salad Adriano outlined his proposal. He explained that his company had facilities for designing her dolls patterns to any size. This meant she could profit from a collection of girls wear as well as women's. This would stop her having to spend hours and days knitting one garment to create a pattern.

A sense of relief washed over her. With someone else doing that task, she could at last get back out into the countryside on her bike.

Adriano also assured Novella, 'This will not prevent hand knitters using the same patterns you have designed. Your patterns will be circulated to all our company's wool stockists, and we will send copies to you should you wish to build your own contacts as well.' He then discussed contracts and legal agreements.

'You will need a good business lawyer to look after you every step of the way, he will advise you to write in a get-out clause should you decide one day to open your own company. We have no problem with that for none of us knows what's around the corner, therefore it's always best to be prepared.'

Hiding excitement at the way this meeting is going, Novella, nods. 'Thank you, Adriano. It's very kind of you to make me aware. I will get a business lawyer first thing, then maybe we could meet up at my home so you can see my whole collection. Please allow me to reciprocate and have lunch together.'

'I would like that very much; shall we say midday at yours the same time next week?'

'Perfect.'

'And over lunch, you can tell me how you started knitting and becoming so creative.'

Adriano escorted Novella back to Franny's shop and shook her hand. 'I look forward to seeing you next week.'

Novella told Franny her exciting news. 'I have to find a business lawyer Franny, where do I begin?'

'I can recommend Rossi and Russo; Russo is the best. He is my business lawyer. Come to the door, I will show you their offices.'

Franny pointed across the square. 'See that posh building. Russo's office is on the first floor. Pop over and make an appointment.'

After making the appointment for two days' time, Novella initially thought of contacting Giuseppe to go with her, but a strange thought stopped her.

Why? I don't need my brother. What did Franny say yesterday? 'You are an intelligent woman, not a child.'

She's right. I'll go alone and learn for myself. I can't always run to family for everything. I am planning an exciting independent business of my own. I do not want them interfering.

Chapter 33

Salvatore Meets the Crooked Politician

Francisco called his secretary in and asked, 'Have you collated all that information I asked you to put together for me?'

She nodded, 'All except the name of the seller, so for the time being it is impossible for put any pressure on him to get more information. There are several items that have started to cross your desk such as permissions for roads and all the ancillary items such as Electricity and Sewage.'

'Hmm,' Francisco muttered. 'Maybe I'll have enough to put some stress on this guy, what's his name?'

She laughed and leant across his desk affording him a view of her ample cleavage. 'Your memory is terrible. He is Salvatore d'Bergamasco. Try and remember when you meet him. If you put your suggestions to him in the best way, it could mean a great deal of money coming our way.'

Tearing his eyes away from her dress Francisco said, 'Arrange an appointment with him at the usual place. It's about time we got down to business.'

Two days later Francisco walked into a small, classy café in the centre of Brescia and to his surprise he found d'Bergamasco already there sipping an espresso. He had placed himself at the rear facing the entrance, a position Francisco liked to take himself as it afforded a view of the entire café and the world outside. All he would now see is the wall behind with a tiny picture of some local view.

d'Bergamasco stood as he approached and held his hand out, 'Hallo Signor D'Angelo,' he smiled. 'I am Salvatore d'Bergamasco, please call me Salvatore.'

Taken aback at this familiarity, Francisco had no option but to reply, 'Hallo, I'm Francisco.'

Salvatore sat down and signalled to the waiter. Formalities over, they sat and took stock of each other in a few minutes of small talk: The weather here is not too bad, how long did you did you take to reach Brescia, where is your office, until Salvatore broke off and asked, "Well since you asked for this meeting perhaps you can enlighten me as to its purpose.'

Francisco smiled, 'I see you don't waste much time on formalities Signor,'

'I think I know already the reason you have called this meeting as I have been expecting it and what we are going to discuss. Whenever I am asked to speak with a politician out of his office, the subject is always the same – money on the side – and I don't like this part of Italian business.'

Francisco grinned and nodded agreement. 'I see you know the game.' Reaching into his briefcase he drew out a sheaf of documents. Laying them on the table he said, 'I'm sure you know what these are, as they were submitted by your company. But to be sure, I'll tell you they are applications for change of use for farmland to industrial.'

'Yes, I know that' Salvatore snapped, 'Now tell me why are taking such detailed interest in the matter, or shall I guess?'

Francisco spread his hands expansively, 'By all means guess, Signor. You'll probably be right. You must recognise the way we do business in this district. It is necessary to offer a little grease to ease these applications through the planning system.'

He leant forward and whispered in a confidential tone, 'All these applications can be approved if I receive the right amount of grease.'

Salvatore placed his face very close to Francisco's, staring directly into his eyes. 'What you are saying sounds too much like blackmail. Maybe I should report you to the authorities?'

Francisco stared back. 'Try and do that if you wish but be assured that I *am* one of the authorities. I collect for a small group that splits the grease in various percentages, depending on their job in our local government. All very efficient fellows. They control such applications as yours with eagle eyes. Your complaint would go nowhere.'

Salvatore nodded, 'Just as I expected. What amount of grease do you have in mind, you criminal bastard?'

'A seat on your board and twenty percent of your company's profit.'

Salvatore broke into a harsh chuckle and spat on the table just missing Francisco's right hand. 'That's what I think of you and your group of dim-witted felons. As a politician you are too stupid to know that we are a family firm. As part of our legal framework nobody except family can be on the board, and as to twenty per cent of the profit, that's more than I get myself.'

He began to stand, 'This discussion will cease now. Don't contact me again, you arrogant shit. Even if I wished to bribe you, I'd never agree to such outrageous terms.'

Francisco laughed and grabbed Salvatore's arm, 'Please, dear Signor, sit down. Your insults don't bother me. Politicians hear far worse. We are in an opening gambit to test the lay of the land.'

Salvatore slammed back onto his chair. Pointing a fierce finger at Francisco, he snarled, 'I understand you people talk like this, so suppose I must listen. Get on and tell me a figure right now or our business ends right now.'

Francisco pointed back at Salvatore, 'I don't like people pointing fingers at me. It is offensive, so let us both put down our hands and settle this business.'

'Tell me,' he hissed, 'The best offer, for your co-operation. Remember I have powerful friends who could disrupt your little game with a well-aimed bullet.'

Salvatore ignored the threat, pondered a moment then said, 'No. You name a figure as I don't know what you consider suitable. Plus, two percent of future profit from the new factory.'

'That's far too much,' Salvatore snapped.

'Then give me your best suggestion,'

Salvatore named a figure somewhat lower than he planned in preparing for this encounter and said, 'But no profit percentage, however, I'll throw in a free car for you alone to have the satisfaction of you knowing you're screwing your friends.'

Francisco, secretly delighted, frowned, and said, 'I know you want to bring some industry to this small corner of Italy but appear to me to be willing to give only peanuts for the privilege. I have to spread this money a long way here, as the citizens involved are not paid at all well and need something to keep the wolf from the door.'

'That wolf is probably *you*, my friend, but it is my best and only offer for immediate acceptance. Should you refuse, I'll remain a landowner of some agricultural land near Salò and go to another region where I can be treated with respect.'

Francisco sat for a while thinking it over. He knew that even accepting a lower deal than intended, he would pocket a firm personal profit once he skimmed more than normal from the cash received. *And I'll have a car. I've always wanted one.*

Feigning reluctance, he finally he held out his hand and said, 'I accept.'

Ignoring the proffered hand, Salvatore stood. 'My office will be in touch. But do not try to contact me again. I have no wish to socialise with blackmailers.'

Nodding Francisco stood also. 'I am sure our paths will cross again Signor, especially if you build a factory here.'

Salvatore ignored this last exchange and walked out of the Café leaving Francisco to foot the bill.

Francisco nodded to the waiter to bring him another espresso and sat for while thinking of the conversation, knowing, and resenting he had been bested.

Now his thoughts turned to revenge and how to carry it out.

I'll get you d'Bergamasco. Nobody crosses me without paying. On the other hand, I screwed a new car out of him.

Chapter 34

Novella's Dreams and Nightmares

Novella began to have dreams. She saw images of papà watching her driving a gold two-seater handmade sports car out of his Bergamo factory. It had a long bonnet with a soft top folding roof. She looked very happy, her hair blowing in the breeze. She loved to wake up recalling that image, wondering how to make it a reality.

One night Novella had a nightmare. She felt papà urging her from the grave to pay more attention to Salvatore's plans of expanding the company with a bigger factory in the Salò area of Brescia.

He must be filling my mind with messages of concern about Salvatore putting the family in danger. I must vote against his plans.

She woke up sweating, fighting for breath, unable to move. Papà's voice clear and commanding. 'Somebody is waking a sleeping giant in Avellino. Be prepared for the consequences.'

Novella shuddered; She wiped the sweat from her neck with the top of her negligee.

A frightening premonition that one day the family may be at risk of losing what papà had worked so hard for all his life.

Trying to get back to sleep, another message came through. '*Rats will spring out from the woodwork. Old scores to settle. Too close for comfort.*'

Novella is terrified.

Had papa done something wrong in his distant past that's coming to haunt his offspring?

Another message from papà. *Salvatore is going out on a limb with a gamble too irresistible for him to turn his back on, purely to achieve his desires.*

Another message. *Salvatore should heed Giuseppe's warnings, but he is pushing him too hard for immediate capital, too impatient to wait. Mistakes will be made.*

Novella always felt that Giuseppe struggled with the worry of having to pluck loans out of thin air to keep the company solvent.

She felt angry with herself because she hadn't supported Giuseppe in the voting, preferring always to vote for her favourite brother Salvatore. *I don't like the personality he portrays at board meetings. So fierce and demanding, not the calm, funny, caring man I loved so much growing up.*

'I don't like attending board meetings,' she'd told Isabella. 'Salvatore scares me, he reminds me of the boy at school who bullied me.'

Isabella agreed. 'I suppose that's just the way he deals with business, because he's not like that normally, is he?'

Novella felt since arriving home with her news from America telling Salvatore about Ford's assembly line system, he has developed ambitions to become the Henry Ford of Europe. He thinks selling mass produced vehicles will save us all and make our fortune. He'll stop at nothing to reach his goal, treading on toes, and pushing anyone aside who gets in his way.

Had Giuseppe already signed a deal with the devil? Did he go to a mafia bank using papà's factory and other family assets as collateral. Had papà warning come too late?

Persistent thoughts of future family discord flooded her exhausted mind. How can I convince the family of papà's warning, especially with Salvatore such a driven man.

Her brothers, all powerful men, want to succeed in their own way, but the family, being glued together by papà Will makes it difficult.

How can I convince the family to take me seriously papà?

Chapter 35

Ginnie's Welcome

Amidst the hustle and bustle of Southampton docks, Anton managed to become deep in thought as he waited for Ginnie's ocean liner to arrive from New York.

He'd enjoyed his share of affairs but had never been in love before. *I've finally met the girl of my dreams, but am I the man of her dreams? Have I been too impulsive in expecting this whirlwind romance to have a happy ending?*

With his mind still full of worries, he finally saw the beautiful brunette emerge from a host of arrivals. Casting all his doubts away, he rushed forward and swept her into his arms.

The warmth of her body and passionate kiss were reassuring.

As they left the docks, Ginnie told him about the trauma of preparing and packing for her six-day crossing. 'Never mind, darling,' he assured her. 'You'll be able to relax now and explore Italy with me.'

But after exchanging their latest news, he noticed a few awkward silences during their ferry crossing to France, and their train journey from Calais to Milan.

She put into words his concerns. 'It may take time for us to pick up our relationship where we left off in New York, Anton. We'll have to be patient while we get to know each other.'

'You're right, my darling,' he agreed. 'Hopefully meeting my family won't make things more difficult. They drive me crazy at times, but they mean well.'

'Mine, too. All families can be a pain.'

Fortunately, his brothers and sisters greeted Ginnie warmly and Salvatore showed great charm in his welcome. He wanted to know all about the Chilton Plaza in Manhattan and Ginnie's role in helping her father run the business.

She explained what she did as the guest relations manager at a five-star hotel, and how much she enjoyed her job.

'You would no doubt find it hard to give it up and move to Italy,' Salvatore challenged in a harsher tone, no longer coming across as Mr Charming.

Anton answered for her. 'Being put on the spot by you as soon as Ginnie arrives isn't going to help,' he snapped.

Concerns that they might find it difficult to fully resume their relationship were allayed by some steamy romps in the spacious bedroom of his luxury flat.

Their second night together was ecstatic and after she slipped seductively out of her flowing negligee to give herself to him, Anton gushed: 'You are a true sex, Goddess.'

Later in the week they visited the impressive Galleria Vittorio Emanuele II shopping arcade, where he bought Ginnie an expensive three-row, long cultured pearl necklace with a diamond clasp. She showed her full appreciation when they dined in the flat that evening by coming to the table topless, apart from the necklace which dangled over her pert breasts.

'Do you like them?' she asked, tantalisingly.

'The pearls or the breasts?'

'Both, darling. Perhaps you would like to bring me a glass of wine and then you can inspect them.'

When he handed her the wine, she tipped a few

drops of it over her breasts and invited him to lick it off.

As he did so, Ginnie teased: 'Perhaps we should eat later.'

The necklace again became the centre of attention when Ginnie wore it the following day on a visit to the family home to which Novella had invited them to tea.

Novella and Isabella both said how lovely the pearls were.

'Yes,' Ginnie replied. 'It was so kind of Anton to buy them for me. They really are beautiful.'

Anton accepted praise from the three women but noticed his sisters exchange glances that seemed to suggest they thought he'd been too generous in splashing out on such an expensive gift.

He changed the subject by asking: 'What do you think of the old family home, Ginnie? I used to live here until I bought myself a flat a couple of years ago.'

'It's delightful. I love traditional old properties with character. That's what we lack in the States. How many of the family live here now?'

'Only me,' replied Novella. 'The others moved out to enjoy their privacy or get married. This old villa is too big for me really, but I love it's wonderful high ceilings and beautiful old fireplace.'

They then sat down to enjoy a large afternoon tea. 'It's a shame my brothers couldn't come, but neither could get away from the office,' said Isabella. 'Working in a family business is so time consuming. Was it hard for you to leave your work at the hotel in New York, Ginnie?'

'Yes, but my father has got someone in to cover for me for at least a month. Then we will take it from there.'

After tea, Anton and Ginnie looked round the large, landscaped garden. They then lingered in the covered courtyard leading back to the villa and overheard a conversation between the two sisters in the lounge.

Novella was telling Isabella: 'Goodness knows how much Anton spent on that necklace. Ginnie is a lucky girl. I do hope she loves him and isn't simply attracted by the prospect of marrying into a wealthy Italian family. Status and money are so important to Americans.'

Ginnie, clearly embarrassed as she entered the lounge, gasped: 'Is that what you think of me?'

'Sorry,' muttered Novella.

'That remark was completely out of order,' Anton chastised his sister. 'And you're way off the mark. Ginnie's father actually owns a chain of hotels, so her family is probably richer than ours!'

Anton decided it a good idea to spend less time with his family and concentrate on showing his cherished guest the many attractions of Milan, the mountains, and lakes. They started by spending a couple of days in a luxurious hotel beside Lake Maggiore, with beautiful views towards Switzerland.

'You've not seen anything yet,' boasted Anton. He then rented a horse-drawn carriage for a three-day tour of Milan. The elderly driver, a font of historical knowledge, took them to the majestic Duomo Cathedral, the dazzling La Scala Opera house, the medieval Sforzesco Castle and the Santa Maria delle Grazie convent, housing Leonardo da Vinci's mural of The Last Supper.

Cars were not uppermost in Anton's mind, but he found time to send another message to Bernard Myers and his millionaire father Joe at Comet Cars. He assured them they would benefit from having their new luxury model promoted by him in Italy and displayed at Motori Bergamasco's newly built modern showrooms.

Chapter 36

D'Angelo Makes New Demands

Francisco D'Angelo stared at the documents lying on his desk. 'Is this all of them?' he asked his assistant.

She shrugged and he watched her magnificent breasts quiver. 'That's all that came through from the civil servants.'

He took a closer look at them and frowned. 'These drawings are for a factory to produce tractors,' he said, 'it seems to be a bit out of the way to build heavy machinery, doesn't it?'

She shrugged again.

He shook his head, 'You never seem to know when I'm asking a rhetorical question do you?' he said sarcastically. 'Now I want you to set up a meeting with this Salvatore again, I want him to know that this isn't the way we do business here. And this time he's going to find that I'm going to be calling the shots. First, he's going to discover that nothing goes out of the council offices without my approval. And even then, he'll be in for a shock because I'll stop him getting permission to have the plans approved. Then I'll stop him from building anything here until I get my little cut, only this time it's going to be bigger than his last offer. That only gave permission to change the use of that land from agricultural to commercial, and approval for the infrastructure like roads and sewage. Or my friends will have something to say, and if they get involved it'll cost him far more than he's willing to pay. Call d'Bergamasco to meet me in the same café as before, but outside.'

A few days later D'Angelo sat in soft late September sun, determined to be settled before d'Bergamasco arrived. A few minutes later, a harmless old couple shuffled to a nearby table – the last available at this busy morning. The husband pulled out a watercolour set and his wife a small pad of writing paper. 'You paint, darling,' she whispered to her husband, 'While I write to Agnese.'

'That's why we came here, you silly woman,' he said, rolling his eyes. 'Can't you remember anything?'

D'Angelo turned away to watch d'Bergamasco stride through the café into the garden and join him on the opposite side of the table. Salvatore scowled at his opponent and said, 'Well, D'Angelo. What is so important that you've dragged me here at such short notice?'

D'Angelo deliberately pondered the question in aggressive silence with a deep frown, before growling, 'You seem to think you can come into an area and go roughshod over any opposition to your illegal plans. Well, that comes to a stop right now; I conceded last time because I wanted you to commit to coming here.'

Salvatore raised a hand, 'We made a firm deal. I have nothing else to discuss with you. There is no more in the pot. You have five minutes before I leave, so give me reason to stay even that long. Remember other areas are interested in my project and have offered finance to move in with them.'

'That's not true about the pot, is it? Nor about other areas. Now, in September, with your factory only a few months from completion and machinery beginning to arrive, you're in far too deep to pull out now. We both know you're bluffing. Your costs so far must be substantial and unrecoverable. If you abandon this project now, you'll break your company. Be sensible and discuss the future cost of my personal services right now.'

He leaned forward and, in a confidential tone said, 'Which, incidentally, will also be substantial. Now are we going to discuss what really is going to happen or do we go on shilly-shallying around the subject wasting our time?'

Salvatore glared at the man opposite him in obvious hatred, 'I don't like you D'Angelo, and you will be making a big mistake if you think you can cross me without some very serious back-up.'

'Aha,' Francisco sneered. 'Now we come to the crux of the matter. I *do* have some very serious back-up as you put it.' He held up his hand, and counted off, 'One, every man in the council offices is looking to see some profit from this venture. Two, all the workers to build your tractors from Salò that I put forward for you to employ will want a piece of your pie, and I expect a percentage of their salaries. And finally, I can mention one organisation who will be asking me for a contribution to their funds. I'll name them when the time comes.'

Salvatore laughed, looked at the sky and asked, 'Is that all?'

D'Angelo smiled grimly. 'No. There's more. Where, for instance, is the car you promised me? You keep putting me off, probably hoping I'll forget about it.'

Salvatore groaned, 'It's not forgotten, you idiot. We only produce a certain number of vehicles each month and you'll have to wait your turn.'

'Well, you'd better get a move on, or I might go back on my word and withdraw all those permissions you've got so far.'

'If you do that, you'll regret it I can assure you.'

D'Angelo waved a hand in dismissal, 'Empty threats my friend. Empty threats, You're the one who'll regret things if you don't get round to my way.'

D'Angelo smiled at Salvatore, knowing he had the upper hand. 'Now shall we get down to business?' he asked.

'Get on with it will you,' Salvatore snapped. 'I do have more to do than sit here with a crook waiting to be blackmailed.'

'Incidentally, the lump sum of cash you promised when first we met has not yet arrived.'

Salvatore held his hand in the air, 'The amount you demanded takes time to gather. We are working on it. We hope to have it soon.'

'When is soon?'

'Early October.'

'Make sure it is no later, my friend.'

'That's the second time you have called me your friend and you can stop right now. I'm not your friend and never will be.'

D'Angelo shrugged, and said, 'My new demands are very simple.' He smiled, 'Something I mentioned before – a seat on the board and twenty percent of the turnover, after legitimate expenses of course. And I want you to build me a luxury villa in the countryside near Brescia. I've already had plans drawn.'

Salvatore leapt from his chair, 'That concludes our business for the day,' he shouted. Other café customers turn to look. The café owner started forward, but D'Angelo waved him away, laughing as though they were sharing a joke and said, 'For god's sake sit down and be quiet. The whole café will know our business.'

Salvatore spread his hands on the table and hissed, 'These demands are outrageous, and you have no hope of getting anything more out of me. You can take all your permissions and stuff them where the sun doesn't shine. I'll get on without your co-operation.'

He shook his finger under D'Angelo's nose. 'And stay away from me in future because the very sight of you makes me want to *vomito*.'

He bent, picked up the cup of coffee and threw it in D'Angelo's face. 'I'll order you another one on the way out,' he called over his shoulder.

Several young men drinking beer laughed. 'Has he been shafting your wife?' one called out.

D'Angelo sat there seething, dripping coffee down his jacket and shirtfront. *That stupid man doesn't know what's in store for him. If he refuses to deal with me, I know someone he'll be forced to deal with.*

The elderly couple, apparently shocked at the coffee throwing, hurriedly packed up and left.

'My colleague has an uncertain temper,' he called after them. 'It means nothing. We'll be friends again tomorrow.'

Chapter 37

Being Frank About Ginnie

In the packed bar of Rome's Teatro Adriano, Frank, in deep embrace with Ginnie, just before curtain opening time, caught sight over her shoulder of Anton's furious face forcing his way towards their table through the noisy throng of people.

Frank unwound from Ginnie, sat up and straightened his tie. 'I think your fiancé's here,' he hissed.

Ginnie jumped up to defuse an awkward situation.

'Anton, this is Frank. Frank Bernstein. A friend from the States.'

Frank reached out his hand, 'Actually, we're more than friends, we're sleeping partners really,' immediately regretting his poor choice of words and seeing the big hole he had immediately dug.

To avoid digging it deeper, he laughed, 'Not in a biblical sense, of course, I'm a silent partner in Ginnie's New York hotel business.'

'My father's hotel business,' corrected Ginnie.

'Of course,' said Frank.

Anton, begrudgingly accepting Frank's handshake. 'I understood it to be a fully family-owned operation.'

'It is. I just stepped in at a difficult time where no bank feared to tread and sort of stayed to help with expansion. When that's done, I'll step out again. Please sit down. Let me get you a drink.'

As neither expressed a preference Frank ordered a chilled bottle of champagne, 'To toast the happy couple.'

Frank could see that Anton, very angry, had difficulty containing himself yet could easily read his thoughts: *This man; this stranger, this so-called friend of Ginnie's is way too familiar*

Anton reluctantly sat and Ginnie explained, 'Frank joined in with my dad just after the War.'

'That's right,' said Frank. 'In the USA, the War saw our economy grow; even accelerate as we mobilised a big army and removed many of our male population. Government and business needed more office workers and factories took on more labour and the female workforce exploded to fill the jobs.'

Anton nodded, taking it all in.

Frank could see him begin to relax and continued, 'As fast as the economy grew during the war, it plummeted in the immediate aftermath. The downturn only lasted a few months; then a second recession hit and, by January 1920, being labelled a depression. We had eighteen months of severe inflation, causing financial devastation.'

'Something you don't seem to suffer from, Signore Bernstein.'

Frank smiled. 'The second-best course of action to protect against inflation, Anton, is to invest in a wonderful business.'

He gestured to Ginnie, who smiled. 'That's because no matter what happens with the value of the dollar, the business's product will still be in demand.'

'And the first best?'

'Have a mountain of assets.'

Ginnie broke in to say, 'Somewhat ironically the hospitality industry, especially restaurants, boomed during the war years,' then...' she hesitated...'the US Government rained on our parade',

Frank jumped in and used the waiter's arrival to point at the lively fizz being poured, and almost shout, 'Prohibition. What an absolutely insane law.'

For a moment Ginnie's own bubble deflated. 'The takings from our bars had kept us afloat through the down times. Prohibition nearly shut us down.'

Frank continued, 'Not that booze disappeared completely, but the supplier became the Mob, known here in Italy as the Mafia.' And their prices were extortionate. Even bankers went on the wagon.'

'The Mob had the monopoly,' Ginnie explained. 'If you didn't pay, or worse, refused to even order...', again her voice faded and this time tears well up and she couldn't finish.

'Ginnie's Pop needed protection from the racketeers.'

With a smug look, Frank raised his glass to indicate his part as saviour.

An uncomfortable silence followed.

A void, that Anton filled.

'How, exactly, were you able to do that Frank?'

'Family connections.'

'Family as in blood?'

'Kith and kin. That's what also brought me into the War. The allies needed translators. Italy still straddled the fence a year after it started. Negotiating with us for territory if victorious, and with the Central Powers to gain territory if neutral.'

'And Bernstein is a German name.'

'Touché.' Frank smiled. 'My mother's family are from a small town near Avellino.'

Frank saw this peaked Anton's interest.

'That's why I'm here. Visiting long lost cousins.'

'What a coincidence.'

Anton's softly spoken words were not lost to Frank. He said, 'I did see your brother there very briefly. Not long enough to be properly introduced.'

'And now you're here in Rome for my sister's Premiere.'

'Thanks for the prompt.' Frank jumped to his feet, 'Better grab my seat whilst I still can.'

He downed his last drop of champagne, 'If your papà can't make it from America for your big day, Ginnie – or doesn't want to; I will happily walk you down the aisle.'

He kissed her on both cheeks and left with a fleeting shoulder tap for Anton.

Chapter 38

Isabella's Big Break

Reaching for a pen to sign the contract for her starring role in Leonardo Rinaldi's new movie, Isabella discreetly pinched her outer thigh under the rosewood desk in the office of her lawyer, Lidia Poet.

Is this really happening? It's been such a short time since I got my first part on stage and here I am taking the leading role in a famous producer's new movie. Perhaps, if I am truly successful in this film, he may even move me from here in Rome to the new centre of world movie making in Hollywood, California.

As if reading her thoughts from across the desk, Lidia smiled and nodded, quietly acknowledging the moment.

'You have come so far in such a short time, dolcezza, thanks to your incredible talent. I've read the contract thoroughly, and as explained before, the changes we agreed will protect your autonomy should you wish to change studios in the future.'

Naively Isabella asked, 'Why would I want to change studios, Signor Rinaldi's work is revered in the movie industry?'

The older woman's dark eyes took on a more serious look as she explained.

'These are exciting but turbulent times Bella, and prone to change very quickly. You might even be tempted by Hollywood in the future. Regardless, my advice is to work hard, enjoy the feeling of achievement and of course, the adulation, but tread carefully. Though things are slowly changing, we are living in a man's world and while the movie industry

173

may seem progressive, men's attitudes are not. A beauty like you could very easily be taken advantage of. Beware the predators, those who will manipulate you into their bed or even pressurise you into sex with the promise of fame or the threat of exclusion. Being so gifted, you will always be in demand, but to put it bluntly, men will want to ravish you because of your allure. Those who watch you on screen can only fantasise about it, but the powerful ones often see it as their right.'

With a look of gratitude, Isabella gave her friend a grateful half smile. Her use of the word 'ravish' inadvertently brought Frank Bernstein to mind.

Oh, to be ravished by HIM, she imagined, recalling that first and only encounter. Those mysterious deep blue eyes carried her mind into The Blue Danube Waltz. With soft violins playing in her heart, she imagined herself spinning around a dancefloor, enfolded in those strong arms.

Is this love? Isabella had pondered that night.

I've heard how it can take you by surprise but surely not at first sight. Her world had fallen away at that moment. It took all her intellectual strength to bring herself back to earth and tune in to what the producer had to say.

For an ambitious actress on the brink of success, I totally let my guard slip.

But Frank had seemed to approve of her too.

Isabella remembered being aware of this, and smiling, now conjured up his image.

Oh, his wide mouth, I can only imagine how it would feel to kiss him, have his tongue slip inside my lips.

The music became faster in her mind. She felt blood rush to her head and envisioned being whirled faster around the dancefloor as the tempo increased.

A knock on the door of Lidia's office interrupted Isabella's daydream, followed by a young woman popping her head in, apologising for needing to speak to the lawyer briefly on a pressing matter. Pushing her chair back, Lidia slowly, stiffly rose from the chair. Now in her seventies, with no intention of retiring any time soon, having worked all her life to be recognised in her profession, excused herself for a few moments and left Isabella gazing at the contract.

Instead of reading the words in front of her, Isabella found her mind returning to the night she met Frank Bernstein.

Leonardo Rinaldi had extended an invitation. 'I thought you might like to come to the studio and see what it's all about. A movie is a whole different concept to being on stage, but I really believe you're made for the big screen.'

Recollecting her reaction, Isabella smiled. The actress in her had hidden the excitement that had welled up inside. *The big screen, this is what I've always wanted.*

Though still acutely aware of Frank's presence, Isabella had regained her composure and turned her attention to Signor Rinaldi speaking of screen tests, contracts, production dates, suggesting she give notice immediately at the theatre. She now recalled her inner voice screaming with excitement, but her expression gave none of that away.

Smoking a Toscano cigar after the trio had shared a delicious meal, Frank suggested they move on to an American style nightclub he knew, designed as a Prohibition gin joint. Isabella had been trying to avert her gaze from Frank throughout dinner and the thought of being in a dark smoky venue with jazz music playing in the background, creating a sultry atmosphere, had been almost more than she could bear. The instant physical attraction she felt for this man she had never experienced before.

In fact, she hadn't had the strength to resist the temptation to spend more time with him. Trying to convince herself that the true reason for extending the evening is the importance of being in the presence of Signor Rinaldi, she gave in to her feelings. Why try to escape the reality of the situation?

Rinaldi led the way down a set of elegant stairs to a large room designed as an American gin joint, where a pretty waitress brought delicious Italian cocktails served in specially designed glassware.

Isabella held herself like a star, gracing her audience with the delight of her style and presence. A cleverly designed aura of prohibition and secrecy filled the room, adding a quiver of excitement.

The rasping voice of a beautiful black jazz singer, dressed in silver sequined flapper attire with matching rhinestone pearl headband, flooded through the smoky underground venue, which felt to Isabella like another world. Regularly recognised as the talented performer she had become, she stood for a moment, smiling at those around her, cigarette smouldering in its holder between her long, slender fingers, taking her best theatrical pose.

A round of applause rose from the patrons seated at various tables, lit only by dim lamps and Isabella nodded appreciation as in the background the singer continued uninterrupted, as though none of this was unfolding in front of her eyes.

Inwardly, Isabella had been beaming at how this must look to both Frank and the producer. *This appreciation and recognition are a definite testament to my talent and at last I like what I see in the mirror, or is it the fine wine I've enjoyed this evening?*

Luckily the screen test she had since undertaken had proved just as favourable, confirming the experienced producer's keen eye and he had even complimented her voice as he pointed out that one day it could be just as important as her looks and talent. She understood to what he meant. Talking pictures were rumoured to be the next big thing and in fact, if she got in at the beginning, that could seal the deal as far as her career went.

With no sign of Lidia returning to the room, Isabella resisted the impulse to sign the movie contract right now but held back and allowed her mind to return to *that* night.

Seated at the best table in the house, Frank had ordered a Negroni. The strong flavour of Campari in the cocktail endeared his companions when they had a taste, so they too ordered one each.

'It's really good to see you tonight, Signorina d'Bergamasco,' the smitten cocktail waitress purred, taking in the two handsome men in the beautiful actress's company. 'Drinks are on the house,' she continued, nodding towards the bar to indicate the owner of the joint standing there, smiling and tipping his glass of champagne in a toast. Surrounding him were three men who looked as though they may be from Cosa Nostra. Isabella had an awareness of that Mafia persona.

She knew such men were becoming visible within nightclubs and fancy restaurants; easily identifiable, not necessarily by their cheap suits and short hairstyles but the egotistical stance that elicited a powerful energy. Being no fool, she knew they funded and 'protected' many of Rome's businesses and keeping on the right side of them appeared to be the best course of action. Embracing the moment, she gave her sweetest smile in return in a gesture of thanks. She couldn't remember the last time she had paid for a drink.

Lifting the cocktail glass to her ruby red lips, Isabella caught a glimpse of the beautiful micro mosaic bracelet on her wrist. Gifts had been left anonymously on occasion in the theatre dressing room by admirers, one of which she now wore. Catching Frank's gaze briefly fall on the piece of jewellery, she felt the need to explain where it had come from. He nodded, with a half-smile when she revealed its origin. Isabella couldn't help but notice something in his eyes which suggested he may have seen this bracelet before. Her heart skipped a beat.

Could he be my secret admirer? Or is that a stretch of my imagination? I need to compose myself, and not gush too much.

Continuing the conversation, careful to include Signor Rinaldi, Isabella knew that this could be her big break and she mustn't put it in jeopardy by something as fickle as casual romance with his friend.

Still waiting for Lidia to return and witness her signing of the contract, Isabella recalled how that night had ended. She felt the gentle touch of Frank's hand on her back as they ascended the staircase to the street. Electric shocks charged through her body that caused her to trip on the last step with the jolt his touch caused.

Stumbling over her words as well as her feet, she mumbled 'These shoes, I really shouldn't have worn them tonight, they are too high.' Frank took Isabella's arm to steady her. As soon as the trio reached street level Frank hailed a taxi, then turned and asked for Isabella's address.

Disappointment flooded through her as she climbed into the cab alone. Never having been tempted to sleep with a man she had just met, this feeling of wanton lust in her loins felt alien to her, along with the rejection that assaulted her as he leaned in and kissed her lightly on each cheek.

'I'm sure we'll meet again,' were the last words he uttered, closing the taxi door.

'Now, where were we?' Lidia boomed as she returned to her desk. 'Apologies for the interruption. Are you ready to sign this contract?'

Isabella smiled and once again lifted the silver-plated pen from the desk, those familiar colours of the mosaic bracelet catching the light as it dangled from her slim wrist.

Who needs romance? This is where my future lies, on the big screen, my big break is happening and nothing will hold me back now.

With a satisfied smile the rising star scratched her name firmly on the contract: *'ISABELLA D'BERGAMASCO.'*

Chapter 39

Salvatore Plans Revenge

Salvatore worked carefully on a detailed plan to ruin the arrogant corrupt politician D'Angelo.

First, he set his two elderly detectives to work on finding out the true extent of the man's power. After only a week they reported that he held a lowly elected position in Brescia's regional government, far from the tough and rich Milan-based political system that towered over Lombardy, ruling with strength and guile through a series of small civic bureaux, such as his.

'He talks big as though elected to the Milan government and everyone believes him because he shouts so loud and frightens everyone,' said Maria. 'He plays the big important government guy but lives in a dump near a slum area with his wife and four children.'

Flavio, her husband, took over. 'But those we spoke to who know of him told us he is a minor elected official, poorly paid and with a small office. No staff, only one secretary he sexually abuses regularly during working hours.'

Salvatore grunted. 'Why does she put up with it?'

'Money. Her husband is an almost illiterate agricultural labourer who got her pregnant at sixteen. To keep her in line, D'Angelo shares some of his bribes cash with her.

'He earns three or four times his salary through corruption and drops her a few Lire after every deal to keep her on side.'

'Do you think we'd be able to turn her to work for me, so she reports his crimes to me?'

The two old people looked at each other and nodded. 'Especially if you offer a regular salary and a job in your new tractor factory.'

'Get on with it then. No hurry. Find a way and bring her under my control.'

Next, he returned one early morning to the Brescia café shortly before opening time and sat with the owner, saying, 'I've come to apologise for the fuss I caused last week in your garden.'

The owner laughed and shook Salvatore's hand.

'The bastard deserved it. He's always touting for money in my café but there's nothing I can do. He has most of the poor souls he brings here by the balls including me, because he personally controls all Brescia licensing. He could make the lot of us bankrupt in seconds. He takes money and valuables from everyone in his grasp. Even those women opening shops and food stores have to lay back and offer him sex to order. We wish someone would shoot the dirty sod, but we'd probably get someone worse, so better the devil we know.'

'Did you see me give him a face full of hot coffee?'

'Sure did. I would have applauded if he hadn't been facing me.'

'About twenty people were in your garden. Did any of them comment to you?'

'Almost all. They wanted to know who you are so they could send congratulations. Can I have your name?'

'No point. I don't want to be famous. I only came to apologise.'

'Very well, but I'm not going to let you leave without a bottle of wine.'

181

Salvatore's elderly detectives returned three days later. 'We followed D'Angelo's secretary from the street market and offered to help carry her shopping,' said Flavio.

'She looked very exhausted, so I sympathised and suggested coffee and cake at a small place we'd scouted,' said Maria. 'Flavia left us to go to the bank and she soon opened up woman to woman on her terrible life and her disgusting boss. She told me how she had no friends because the man she works for is a crook and that nobody in Brescia speaks to her. When Flavia returned, we offered her help in finding an honest properly paid job in a big company.'

Maria said, 'I told her we'll speak to a friend and arranged to meet in the same café tomorrow. That's now where you come in, Signor d'Bergamasco. What do you want us to do?'

Salvatore said, 'Go and sit with my secretary for a few minutes. I'll call you back as soon as I've decided.'

He dropped his head, chin in hands, remaining completely silent for twelve minutes; his mind working in deep concentration. Calling them back in, he said, 'Tell her almost the truth that you are detectives employed investigating corruption for a rich client building a case for the police. Don't tell them either client or case. Say if she cooperates, she will avoid jail for being involved, and that your client needs mimeographed documents from your office on the biggest bribe D'Angelo is currently seeking. Tell her she may or may not need to give evidence in court at his trial. If she agrees, promise her that if she agrees, she will be paid a decent salary by your employer from the day she signs up and at the end of our investigation both she and her husband will be given suitable jobs, with her children moved from Brescia to a quality house in another town.'

'My god,' gasped Maria. 'I reckon she'll jump at that.'

'Threaten her with complete secrecy or prison. Make sure she understands I am completely ruthless.'

Flavia chuckled. 'I don't think we'll get that far,' he said. 'She'll jump at your offer long before we need to threaten. She hates her boss and would love to see him ruined.'

'Get her working on the mimeographs as soon as possible.'

'Yes Signor.'

As soon as they left, he called Giuseppe to come straight away, and told him, 'I want to meet the policeman who stopped that riot threatened by those Milanese communists a few months ago.'

'Why?'

'I'll tell you when we're on the way to his barracks. For the moment just let him know I need to speak with him sometime soon on an urgent matter.'

Giuseppe returned with good news. 'I received a warm welcome from Colonel Pancucci. I mentioned the occasion we last met when the Milanese communists tried to take over our factory.'

'Ah yes. I remember. You and he kicked them out back to Milan with one gunshot.'

'Well, he did Salvatore, by shooting a bullet into the sky while I hid in the background.

'Very wise.'

'He remembered that little incident and commented on how amazing it is that one loud bang worked so well. I told him you needed a meeting. He immediately agreed and asked us to lunch tomorrow.'

'Where? I need a private discussion between only the three of us.'

'He has already reserved a secret room in what he called a pleasant little restaurant the police use when a subject needs to be kept secure and confident to sing. And he recommended their wonderful Caprino Bergamasco.'

'My favourite cut of veal,' said Salvatore, 'Especially when served with thinly sliced sautéed potatoes fried in butter and oregano with long green beans.'

'That's how he described it, and I told him how we both loved that delicate dish. He then asked me to please bring my esteemed brother at noon tomorrow and we will enjoy a perfect lunch, while discussing how he can assist us.'

The next day Pancucci shook hands in his office and led his two guests across the road to enter a small luxurious restaurant and through a very heavy door into a small candlelit room.

'Completely soundproof,' said Pancucci.

'And beautifully furnished,' commented Salvatore.

'All traditional from the late Middle Ages,' replied Pancucci, pouring red wine into small glasses. 'This room has been used for clandestine business since the middle of the Venetian Empire. Those who enter are never recognised or talked about after they leave. so let us drop the subject and get to our own business.'

'Yes,' said Salvatore. 'I am having trouble with a local politician in Brescia called D'Angelo.'

Pancucci raised a hand. 'Asking for bribes?'

'Yes. Outrageous payoffs in cash and kind to authorise our new factory in Salò.'

'Do you have direct evidence?'

'Yes.'

Salvatore pulled a copy of Maria's statement from an inner jacket pocket. Pancucci placed reading glasses on his nose and held the paper to the nearest candle. Salvatore watched him study each word with deep concentration, before saying, 'I know of the man. He is subject to many complaints from small businessmen. I have opened a file on him.'

'You are already investigating him?' asked Giuseppe.

'No. It is a file of complaints from small people frightened of giving evidence in court, so we can do nothing.'

'Will this help?'

'It may, but wily Italian politicians rarely admit to having been anywhere that may lead to charges.'

'You need independent witnesses to his presence?'

'Yes. About forty, all entirely independent,' and with a completely straight face Salvatore told Pancucci of his coffee throwing incident, while watching the poor Pancucci struggling not to laugh.

'You may truly have him by the balls, my friend, but judges and politicians frequently belong to the same religious or legal lodges and in court may see the coffee attack as whimsical and this statement as contrived. Do you have something a jury can hold against a judge's beneficial summing up.'

'Yes. I expect strongly damning documents in my hand, signed by the criminal himself, very soon.'

'Such strong evidence will allow me to arrest and charge him straight away.'

'I would rather you set up a slow investigation covering several months, allowing him to realise he is being stalked.'

A slow smile crossed Panacci's face. 'I'll put my best stalker on the case.'

'Why did you ask him to do that?' asked Giuseppe.
'You'll see,' said Salvatore.

Chapter 40

Novella Fights Back

Anton arrived unexpectedly to take Novella to get her driving licence. The factory now built she knew it wouldn't be long before Salvatore's car would be operational and ready to drive. She needed her licence for the launch.

So excited to be playing a major role she'd been to Lorretta's hairdressing salon and got her hair coloured with streaks of orange highlights to match the interior of the new Town Car.

Thinking that's why Anton had surprised her, but he had other things he wanted to talk about.

A bittersweet moment she would never forget as Anton landed her with his bombshell announcement.

'We are soon to announce Salvatore's new design and the day of the launch.'

Novella bursting with joy told him about her hair. 'What do you think of my new hairstyle, I've had it highlighted to match the interior of the car especially for this occasion.'

Anton ignored his sisters excitement and came straight out with it, more excited about his own marketing campaign than her hair.

'Isabella is going to be the face of the new Town Car. Her face will be splashed across billboards, newspapers, and magazines. I've been busy drafting all the plans.'

Seconds passed as silence filled the air. Her brother's words were unimaginable to comprehend. Pain shot through her, a blade slicing into her soul, followed by a fire of pent-up rage hurtling towards

Anton. All she could think of is how much time and effort she had put into Salvatore's pet project. All the promises made at the board meeting. He'd made her the colour and material co-ordinator. She would be talking to prospective buyers. Her name printed on the car. She had inspired Salvatore with Henry Ford's assembly line.

Increasingly angered, her mind worked at high speed: *I had done all that hard work. Salvatore now would allow Isabella to steal all my glory. How could my brothers do this to me?*

'That's not true Anton, I don't believe you, I'm the face launching the Novella car. The car is all about me. The colours, the name, the interior materials. It's ridiculous that Isabella sits in the driving seat.'

'You can still talk to the buyers', he smirked. 'Anyway, she is a celebrity, she's famous, you're not.'

'We're not advertising a celebrity; we are advertising our Motori Bergamasco with its new prototype car design. I'm looking forward to driving it to the show. That's why I thought you had come today, to take me to get my driving licence.'

'I am going to take you to get your licence, but not for the reason you thought. Come on let's go, we can talk on the way.'

Novella obeyed as she'd always done all her life, whether with papà or her brothers. They made sure she knew her place. Novella's the baby of the family and the baby she would stay.

Anton did his best to change the subject to try and ease the tension, knowing nothing about her patterns.

'Are you still knitting for your dolls?'

'Let's keep to what we were talking about.' she snapped. 'Is it yours or Salvatore's idea to use Isabella?'

'Well, I mentioned it and Salvatore thought it a brilliant idea.'

Before Novella could respond Anton pulled into the Council office car park and pointed.

'Go through the main door over there and turn right to reception. They'll help you, I'll wait here, hurry up.'

Novella took her time walking, deciding that the days of taking orders from her brothers are over. As reality sunk in, she realised the real reason Anton came today is to get her used to the idea before the launch campaign and Isabella's advertisements appear, grinning at the world in her appealing way.

Isabella obviously knew of the plan and had kept if from her. *How could she? Certainly, she could. She is my sister. Always thriving on attention and adulation. She would expect to take priority over me. She always got her own way by twisting men around her little finger, even with papà. Stealing my glory is the icing on her cake.*

Novella knew Isabella loved her but would never allow the little sister win at anything. Her competitive streak is too strong. *So how can I blame her? She is who she is.*

She stamped her feet hard in bitter fury just before entering the Council offices.

I'm not a child anymore, I will not allow myself to be treated like a fool and be walked over She set up a plan to ease her pain and throw it at Anton whilst still in her outraged mood. Having completed the forms and received her driving licence, and climbed back into Anton's car, intending to shock.

'Listen dear brother. You can tell Salvatore from me, I do not want my name on that car, and I will not be at the launch. If you both want Isabella to launch

189

the car to glamourise yourselves then she can have her name on it. I want no part of your stupid plan and I want nothing to do with the new manufacturing plant. No car with my name will come off that assembly line. The way I am feeling I could easily walk away from this family right now, but I will allow my two devious brothers to redeem themselves. You will build me my own handmade car, in my own name, in honour of papà in his original factory by his loyal workers.'

Anton interrupted, 'Hold on Novella.'

'Shut up Anton. I'm speaking and telling you *exactly* what I want. I see the image regularly in dreams. Tell Salvatore I want a two-seater *sports* car, the colour of gold, with a long bonnet and a drop down soft top roof. He has to make it his priority, if not it's goodbye.'

Anton laughed. Then his expression turned serious. 'I am not going to be spoken to by my little sister in this manner. That is some threat. Salvatore will laugh as I have. It's a preposterous idea. The same as your dreams of warnings that Salvatore's putting the family in danger. Your ideas that papà's and mama's spirits are close by. How ridiculous. We're not going to pamper to your childish whims. You're just having a temper tantrum. Get over it and learn. This is what happens in business. Decisions are made to benefit the company not an individual. No more of this nonsense. It's time you grew up and acted like a woman and stopped playing with dolls.'

'Be it on your own head Anton and don't say I didn't warn you.'

She slammed his car door with one word, 'Goodbye.'

Turning away, she saw the expected shock in his face.

Chapter 41

Novella Grows Up

Novella realized how grown up she felt purely by lightly chatting over lunch with a man she did not know at all, about something as important as forming a business alliance with a knitting company. Her nerves did not waver a moment. She felt so proud of herself.

He is so suave and sophisticated. I had spent less than two hours with the man, yet he made me feel a woman of equal intelligence. Franny is so right. I must embrace being an adult if I am to become my own person for I have so much to give to the fashion industry. I must therefore face the challenges of the future head on. I have a new purpose now.

She slipped into bed that night and fell into a restful sleep, thoughts still on Franny and her wisdom. *Maybe the old wife's tale is true, Franny's belief that turning money over on a new moon accumulated money. How coincidental that he should appear in my life the very next day and we discuss business contracts.*

Novella laughed to herself, imagining images of her bank balance accumulating sums of money after she takes up the Beradi offer. *I can't wait for the legalities to be agreed so business can begin.*

Meeting Carlos Russo the business lawyer she understood why Franny chose him. A charming middle-aged man who soon put her at ease. He explained the formalities of his fees and the role he would play in their partnership now he worked for her

Russo looked up. 'I have read the comprehensive draft agreement from Berardi. I am quite impressed. With your permission I will meet with Signor Berardi personally to go through the finer details before I would advise you to sign.'

'Novella said, 'Yes please Signor Russo. Do meet with him and discuss anything you think may be of interest.'

'Do you have any more questions with which I can help you Signorina d'Bergamasco?'

'No thank you, I will wait until I hear from you.'

Novella left Signor Russo's office feeling extremely pleased with her first lawyer-client performance. It seems clear her new business deal is heading in the right direction. *'All I now need is for Adriano to like my dolls' clothes when I see him at home for lunch in three days' time.*

The days flew by and before she knew he is standing on her doorstep waiting to be invited in. Novella, riding high on natural adrenalin, is overjoyed to see him. *But not entirely sure if it is to do with the man himself or because he is the way forward to getting her closer to her dream of being a first-class fashion designer.*

'Hello Adriano. Please come in. I thought it would be good that I show you my dolls clothes whilst waiting for lunch then we can take our coffee into the garden.'

'I entirely agree. I am very eager to see your collection.'

Entering the room Novella watched Adriano walk over to the shelves of dolls and chose the ones that immediately drew him in.

'I have a lot more packed away in boxes so you will be making patterns for a very long time,' she laughed.

'This is extraordinary Novella. I really did not expect to see so many. You are right, we are going to be kept busy for a long time. I would like to take these five dressed dolls today so you can see what factory machining can do in transforming your designs into adult dresses. They'll be made in the next few days.'

Over lunch Adriano reminded Novella of his interest in knowing the story of her knitting passion.

'I can see it clearly. It is so funny remembering. It all began on my seventh birthday, being given my first Sophia doll, some knitting needles and wool. Mama tried to teach me to knit a scarf for my doll, but it did not go well. She cast on a few stitches, but I kept making extra ones. After much practice I took to knitting well.'

'When did you begin making dolls clothes?'

'Early one morning at dawn. I woke with a clear vision how to make my doll a skirt and top. From then on, my passion grew stronger and now I get flash ideas at any time. I only decided to transform them into women's garments after I had finished making a bolero jacket for my doll and showed it to my sister Isabella. She liked it so much she asked me to make one for her. With very little thought it came naturally. Franny, who owns the craft shop, saw me wearing it and suggested she model it when serving customers to see if they were interested. She had thirty requests in the first week.

He smiled.

'That is an amazing story. Thank you for sharing it with me.'

'You're welcome, would you like to see the garden now? I'll show you where I sit and knit.

Strolling toward the old willow tree Novella felt deep in her soul that she had known Adriano forever instead of just one week. She felt an unspoken bond of trust being cemented whereby she knew she could tell him anything and he would listen and understand.

Sitting on the bench she felt the warm breeze blow a quick gust, rustling the leaves. Novella sincerely believed it to be her mama and papà's spirits. The belief brought comfort to her.

'My soul feels completely at one with nature when I am here Adriano. It is where I feel my parents the strongest since their passing. They too enjoyed sitting here.

'I feel a magic to this special place too.

'It's not my imagination after all if you can also feel it,' Novella whispered.

'Definitely not imagination. I find a very calming and peaceful presence emanating throughout this whole area. I have a book you can borrow if you like reading. It is called Spirit of Trees. One of my treasured reads. Come, let me show you something. Place your back against the trunk and feel its pulse. Trees do not have a heart like us, but they do breathe. Not everyone can sense it but those who do are most fortunate.'

Closing her eyes, Novella rested her back onto the trunk. She giggled with joy as she could feel a trickling movement within the tree. 'This is truly magical. Thank you for sharing this experience and your knowledge with me.'

On returning to the bench, they agreed to sit a while in quiet meditation, as Novella often did. When finished they strolled back to the villa chatting about everything and nothing.

'Adriano, I wonder. I know you are a knitting company, but would you like to see my other ladies collection that I designed, using fabric.'

'Goodness me Novella, you are full of surprises. Do lead the way, I can't wait to see.'

It is clear to Novella, by his expression, that Adriano is impressed with the variety of fabric styles she had made.

'They are amazing. The colours so dazzling. It is clear to see you have a very fertile imagination that you respond so well to. What do you intend to do with them?

'I really do not know. I haven't thought about it, until just now, when I asked if you would like to look at them. I just enjoy designing new fashions.

'You could have your own fashion show. If you would allow me, I know several people in the industry. I may be able to direct you to the right people and places.

'I would be grateful, thank you.

'As I said just now, you are a woman of many talents.

'You flatter me. Thank you. What you say means a lot.'

The villa felt empty to her after Adriano left. Novella could see her maid Julia smiling while serving afternoon tea and cake

'You look happy Julia. Care to share your thoughts?' Novella said

'I happened to be admiring the garden when I saw you and Signor Berardi crossing the lawn and thought how good it is to see you laughing again.

'He is such easy company and a very good listener and makes me feel so good about myself. I have not yet told my family that I plan on going into business with his papà's company.

Chapter 42

Novella Wins

When reporting her anger to Salvatore, Anton laughed and said, 'I'm telling you; Novella has a fire in her you would never believe, I do think she means it. She's in such a state she'll walk away and to hell with the money from papà's will.'

Salvatore frowned.

'She'll come round, she's our kid sister. You know what this amounts to don't you?'

'No. What does it mean?'

'Emotional blackmail. Being defiant towards her elders. I'd like to slap her down and put her back in her place but can't because, you see, what she has done is given us the perfect design for your idea of a young man's car. It works two ways by attracting both men and women. Her suggestion is stunning. A long bonnet: very phallic, coloured gold with a beige soft folding top. Dazzling. I can easily build the cars individually in our traditional Bergamo factory. That would make Novella happy and stop her abandoning us. She'll see we are agreeing with everything she wants, because she is right, not because she has won an argument.'

'Do you know, I think you're right. But she'll still see it as a battle won.'

Salvatore nodded. 'Who cares? I'll accept that because I'm beginning to believe she's a gift. A prodigy. And more inventive than any of us. I can easily turn her amazing ideas into better vehicles. I'll speak to her this afternoon while it is all still in her mind and use her brilliance to our advantage.'

'Shall I tell her to stop her sulky mood?'

'No. I'll speak to her this afternoon without mentioning moods and tell her I'm impressed to hell with her new plans for a specialist Sports Car and to join me tomorrow morning at ten for a detailed discussion. I'll agree to everything and offer her a personal board meeting which she controls. No one else will speak. Novella can take the floor and in her own words without interruption show her design planning and genius.'

'Terrific idea, brother.'

'When Novella's plans are voted through, including the name of her car, specially renamed The Novella Gold with The Angel of Bergamo flying on the bonnet. The Angel can appear in our advertising too.'

'What about the Town Car?'

'We'll keep the Town Car with the brand 'Isabella' just as already planned. And our beautiful sister will be seen everywhere on all the posters as the face of the car and the company.'

'Spot on brother, let's shake on that. But what about these warning dreams of Novella's about you putting us in danger by building a factory in Salò. Are her dreams opening up past history?'

'I've been thinking about that,' said Salvatore, 'papà told me privately, he'd changed his name for personal reasons when he moved north. He could well have skeletons in the cupboard, which may bring danger to our family and future. When I speak to Novella this afternoon, I'll tell her she is not being ignored but promoted and that we all need to listen to her brilliant ideas at the special meeting.'

Chapter 43

Giuseppe's Confession

Giuseppe felt himself sliding down the sixty-degree slope of an ice-covered granite slab the size of a tennis court. No matter how hard he tried, Giuseppe had no grip to stop his skid towards tumbling over the edge into the valley a thousand metres below and death.

He twisted to try and see how close the slab's edge is, but instead his eyes were drawn to the terrified faces of his comrades, as they disappeared over the edge only fifty metres away, followed by their screams, knowing they were falling to their doom and, in a few seconds, he would follow.

One, two metres, and he flipped into the void shouting, 'God forgive me.'

'Giuseppe, Giuseppe. You're dreaming,' said Francesca. 'Sit up. There. Take my water.'

'Sorry. I had a bad dream about the war. I'll be fine,' he said taking the glass from his wife.

He sipped the water and watched Francesca lay down on her side, her back to him, and switched off her bedside lamp. *Only a few years ago she would have sat up with me until I had calmed down. She would hold me until I fell asleep. How I miss that affection from her*

Giuseppe remained sitting up in the darkness, listening to his wife's light breathing and the breeze blowing through the cypress trees outside their house.

Does she know about Rosalina? I've been a fool to get involved with that woman. I want my marriage. I want my Francesca and the kids. I don't want to be involved with Rosalina.

199

One way to hang on to my marriage is to be one hundred percent honest and to tell Francesca of my affair before she finds out. And after that I'll go and see Rosalina and tell her the affair is over, thought Giuseppe, before pondering the fact that Rosalina had not been the woman he thought when first they met. She became prone to unnecessary nasty asides aimed at Francesca, the kids, his brothers, and sisters, especially Isabella.

What an idiot, why did I let her get away with that? Why am I so gutless?

Then there is her repugnant attitude towards the workers at the factory and her most recent target, the Jews. Giuseppe sighed, *I'm a clown. Why, oh why. did I get mixed up with that woman? Idiot. I never felt love, only lust.*

By dawn, Giuseppe had not slept since waking from his nightmare. He rose and showered, deciding that once the kids were in bed that evening, he would tell Francesca of the affair.

Going to his dressing room, he pondered another problem with Rosalina. Her sympathetic comments about the fascists. But at least he had done something about that, and he would know more, later, by lunchtime when in the café for lunch with a two of his factory workers.

He had arranged for them to keep a distant watch on Rosalina for a few days. 'I'll mark you down as off sick. No problem boys. After all I am the bloody company financial director. Now, are you happy to do this for me? It will take you about a week to get an idea of what's going on. Naturally your pay packet will have a little extra in it this week,' said Giuseppe the week before, when he spoke to two of his most trusted employees, both former comrades from the War.

'It's not a problem, Padrone,' said Enzo.

'We are happy to help, Padrone,' said Claudio.

At one o'clock, Giuseppe met his two friends in the back room of Café Lentin, an establishment buried in the back streets of Bergamo, a short taxi ride from the Motori Bergamasco factory and famed for its homemade food. The three friends enjoyed a magnificent lasagna and were sipping some Oro Pila brandy when Giuseppe offered his friends a cigarette, reflecting on what Enzo and Claudio had reported to him about their surveillance of Rosalina.

They reported that she had hosted a meeting of seven people at Giuseppe's apartment on Seregino Street. Two of her guests were confirmed by Enzo and Claudio as known fascists. Three days later, Rosalina and her husband Giorgio D'Innella had held a small dinner party at their home, their guests being prominent fascists, including two ministers from Mussolini's government.

'She never mentioned using my apartment as a meeting place for these dreadful people. That's it then. Obviously, she's a bloody fascist,' said Giuseppe before taking a mouthful of brandy.

'Padrone, there is something else,' said Enzo.

'Go on,' said Giuseppe.

Enzo looked to Claudio and back to Giuseppe before saying, 'Rosalina's chauffeur is a good friend of ours, and over a drink last night he told us that in a few days she is off to Rome. To meet Mussolini himself.'

'Oh God,' said Giuseppe, taking another mouthful of brandy, swiftly followed by another.

He spent the afternoon back at his office struggling to concentrate on the day-to-day matters of his work, but not doing well. His mind being full of the pending confessional meeting with Francesca.

Somehow, he got through the time by concentrating on accounts in his office and attending a retirement presentation, then back to a complex price analysis of tenders for the new manufacturing equipment and an outrageous regional land tax demand signed by D'Angelo. *It'll be a good thing for Salvatore to get his police friend to sort that crooked leech out.*

He looked at his watch. Six-thirty and time to reluctantly go and make his confession. He lingered in the car park for a while, talking to some of the workers about football, Bergamo's football team, but decided that stalling for time did not help, so faced up to the inevitable and drove home.

'Please, Francesca. I would like to talk to you,' said Giuseppe in the lounge doorway watching his wife pour herself a substantial goblet of red wine.

'Go on.'

'Francesca, I've been a fool. An idiot. I'm deeply sorry but I've been having an affair. Francesca. I made a stupid, terrible mistake and I'll regret it for all of my life. But more to the point, I've hurt you. I've let you down and the kids too. I beg your forgiveness.'

'I know you bastard,' said Francesca hurling the goblet of wine at her husband and just missing.

'I guess that's the least I deserve,' said Giuseppe holding his head as wine oozed from between his fingers and dripped onto the cream Persian carpet.

'You're a lucky man. You have two loyal sisters. They would not let on when I questioned them. But I had my suspicions months ago, you absolute shit.'

Giuseppe took a step closer to Francesca. 'Darling Francesca, I am so sorry I you down. I want to save and rebuild our marriage. All I need is to be with you and the children. I am truly sorry. I swear I'll never do such a thing again. I love you. Please give me another chance.'

'Get out of my sight you dirty shit. Sleep in one of the guest rooms.'

Giuseppe stared at his wine-stained face in the mirror of the guest room's ensuite. He dabbed the mess on his forehead with a white hand towel and said to his reflection, 'Well, what in the name of God did do you expect?'

Chapter 44

Lust and Passion

Reaching across for a cigarette, Isabella carefully lifted the filter holder from the bedside table, before lighting up. Laying against carefully piled plumped up pillows with a white cotton sheet tucked around her waist, pale full breasts remained visible, their pink nipples hardened by the cool morning air. Dark curls matted against her crown, exuding a sexiness that could never be acquired in a hair salon.

A naked figure stirred beside her, half covered by the same sheet, his lithe figure covering the full length of the bed, feet dangling over the end as his body extended in a morning stretch. With blonde hair as straight as Isabella's is curly, he looked a pretty picture and indeed his performance the previous night had not disappointed. All that pent up sexual attraction Frank Bernstein had stirred in Isabella had not gone to waste, with no shortage of men willing to sate it, though few she would permit to try.

Alberto, a regular lover, having proved himself satisfying and with a great sense of fun into the bargain. As a Fascist through and through, Isabella found his stoic beliefs both interesting and alluring. Though she hadn't admitted it to any of her close friends or family, she found herself being swayed slightly to the right.

'I won't romanticise this, I'm an intelligent woman. I'll consider the pros and cons before allowing myself to become involved in any way,' were the words she chose when standing her ground in a rare serious moment when Alberto tried to convert her.

'Il mio amante, you are incorrigible,' she giggled now as the ever-ardent Alberto, tweaked one of her erect nipples and, taking the cigarette holder from her long fingers, placed it on the ashtray beside him. The moment his lips touched hers Isabella forgot everything else but the ride to delicious oblivion.

This is what I want, this euphoria, no complications, just physical love, joy, happiness, rising higher and higher, writhing in ecstasy. Sex is a drug to me now, nearly as important as fame.

Resting afterwards, while Alberto fell into a slightly snoring sleep, Isabella stayed awake, thinking how her rising celebrity status had gained new respect in the family. Enough for her brothers to have voted her as the face and figure of the new Town Car, dropping hints that dear Anton has developed a fantastic marketing campaign to be launched shortly throughout Italy and Europe. 'Not a word to anyone,' they had warned. 'We're just preparing you for more fame. Don't forget to share it with your family.'

But Isabella felt certain that her little sister Novella would be livid at being upstaged by her unthinking brothers' plans. They have never heard her whispered secrets for a full and successful life in warm summer nights in their little girl's bedroom. Carefully planned; carefully worked out and bursting to life at the board meeting when Salvatore presented his new range of stunning vehicles.

Of course, she had never heard of Salvatore's wonderful plans. None of us had. But Novella's speed of mind that only I knew of, even when presented openly at the board meeting, failed to impress, or be noticed by the others. To them she remains a shy little girl, who listens but rarely speaks.

But her performance at the board meeting made Isabella feel uneasy. *I've been her protective older sister since she came into the world and know both her secret intelligence and my little sister better than any man, including her brothers.*

She is far cleverer than her brothers know and may already be planning in that sly little head a form of cunning revenge on me, or even all of us.

Isabella couldn't help feeling aggrieved. *What did Novella expect? Hasn't she designed the interior and picked the colours in her moment of glory at the meeting? Yes, and she worked hard going to America and doing research but that was her role. I too have worked hard, and being a celebrity will help promote and sell the car. Novella hasn't got a famous face, a lovely one of course, but not famous. Why can't she just be content with her own business venture? According to Anton she has fire in her soul. What have I unleashed?*

I guess all will be revealed at the special meeting Salvatore has called. Anton seems to think she has been childishly temperamental. However, I must admit her proposal of a special sports car is quite exciting and the fact that Salvatore has agreed to it, almost unbelievable. This should all be very interesting.

However, even in the arms of an amazing lover who was doing unspeakably amazing things to her, Isabella felt an uneasy feeling creep over her.

Yes, I'm enjoying the limelight in the public domain, but it looks like my little sister might be about to draw attention away from me in the family business. I can't have that.

Realising these intrusive thoughts were dampening her libido, Isabella dismissed them.

I'll observe Novella at the meeting and consider for myself whether she's a cause for concern. After all, my movie career is far more important, let Novella have her tantrum. It's time she grew up.

Letting go, allowing her body to respond to Alberto's touch, she felt the blood rush to her head and reaching orgasm, her body shook as she simultaneously floated on a cloud of pure ecstasy.

Chapter 45

D'Angelo's Downfall

Salvatore rose at dawn on that chill October morning for this important drive to Salò, doing his best to avoid feeling excited at his secret mission.

With enough of the new factory complex completed and the car production line installed, he had, for several weeks, been training four hundred workers to assemble imaginary cars, using large maps and drawings of the Henry Ford production line system.

They thought it amusing that it limited one person to one task. Salvatore set up a training hall with the large diagrams on the walls and laughed with them during the early lectures, because this method of construction seemed so bizarre.

'Are you saying I stand in one position and push one bolt into one hole all day as a tractor chassis passes me Signor d'Bergamasco?'

'That is exactly what you do,' said Salvatore. 'Your four friends at each corner do the same and the next men in line place on the nuts which the next men tighten.'

His answer brought instant hilarity, from the trainee car workers. Salvatore smiled and said, 'Look,' pointing out the man's position on a wall drawing and explaining, 'The four men placing wheels on the chassis at the start do nothing else. Then four men push what is now a skeleton car along the line from start to finish. When it passes you and your three colleagues, each one shoves your bolt into the hole and picks up another to place in the following skeleton. The next four men secure the bolt and so on down the production line.'

'Will we do the same with the engine Signore?'

'Of course. It will be suspended above the skeleton and dropped into the engine cavity when the chassis passes by and bolted in place by the next men working in their positions and so on until the skeleton rolls off the end as a fully built and completed car.'

'It seems a slow job for so many men doing simple jobs,' said one of the workers. 'How long does it take to finish one car?'

Salvatore pointed to his factory manager, sitting at the back. 'Stand up and tell us how long it takes a team of twelve men to complete one car in our Bergamo factory, please.'

'About twelve hours, Signore,'

'Did you all hear that? asked Salvatore. 'Twelve hours. Are you sure?'

'Yes, Signore.'

'Using this new system, we plan that a whole car is built in one hour and forty minutes.'

A murmur of disbelief went round the room followed by the word, 'Impossible.'

'It is already being done in America.'

Salvatore laughed. 'Hands up those who will bet against me when I say we *will* do it.'

No one moved. Salvatore realised that these men, new to employment after years of no work, would not argue with their boss.

'Don't worry. You will be fully trained over the next three months. By the time you build your first car, you'll be faster and better than those Yankees.'

'Of course, we will, Signor d'Bergamasco,' shouted his factory manager. 'Won't we boys?'

Every man in the room rose, cheering, whistling, stamping heavy boots, and waving enthusiastic arms in the air.

Those several weeks had passed in a swift blur and this group of Salò farmworkers had grasped the idea of how they would work from tracing fingers along the maps and drawings and listening to continual lectures.

Today Salvatore, swearing them to silence with threats of instant dismissal, told them, 'You will be building a new modern car here, not a tractor,' and led them into the new factory where his engineers had placed a virgin chassis at the beginning of the so far untested production track.

Four workmen now had to pull the chassis along to the end, while about two hundred men stood at eighty-four workstations, and put together a fully functioning motor vehicle. The result would then be taken apart and rebuilt several hundred times more until his workers could do their jobs with their eyes closed.

The factory manager had just lined everyone into position when, to Salvatore's surprise, Colonel Pancucci, dressed in full uniform and armed, stepped through the main door and saluted.

Salvatore waved for silence and hurried to greet him. Shaking hands, he said, 'Colonel Pancucci, it is a pleasure to see you. What brings you here?'

'I am sorry to break in like this, but I need you to come with me to Brescia immediately. I have gathered enough evidence to arrest D'Angelo and need you present to identify him.'

'That will be my great pleasure. Give me five minutes to run this first test build and I'll be available'

210

Salvatore returned to his factory manager and whispered, 'I must go to help this policeman. I'll watch and time this first attempted build then leave. You time two or three more practice runs for an hour then send them home. Bring them back in at nine tomorrow morning and I'll be with you all day.'

At the end of a chaotic run, he handed over his stopwatch and hurried with Pancucci to his police car, one of three waiting outside.

'You have built a beautiful road to a beautiful factory,' said Pancucci with a smile. 'But that tractor looks remarkably like a car.'

'Big secret,' laughed Salvatore. 'Say a word and I'll have you cashiered.'

Arriving at D'Angelo's building, Pancucci said 'Follow me,' and marched three of his Carabinieri and Salvatore past the new secretary and into the office.

D'Angelo looked up from two documents side by side that Salvatore saw were columns of figures. He also saw D'Angelo's face go instantly pale, probably in shock at four policemen bursting in.

He quickly opened a drawer and tried to push the papers out of sight, but Pancucci snapped, 'Leave everything where it is. Sit still and touch nothing.'

D'Angelo froze, then noticing Salvatore, jumped to his feet, shouting, 'What's that crook doing here? Get him out.'

Pancucci pulled out his pistol and pointed it at the ceiling. 'I said *sit still* so sit down *now* and don't move.'

'I am a senior government official, and this is government property. You have no right to here, especially waving a pistol about. Get off these premises immediately or I'll have you arrested.'

Pancucci nodded to his Carabinieri. All three rushed round the desk, grabbed D'Angelo and cuffed him to the right chair arm. In the shocked silence that followed, Salvatore heard the click of high heels and the outside door slam. Through the window he saw the young secretary fleeing down the road.

D'Angelo, staring at his cuffed wrists, deflated and slumped sideways. 'Why are you here? What have I done?'

Pancucci pulled an official document from an inside pocket and read, 'Francisco D'Angelo I am arresting you on suspicion of fraud, bribery and working with or membership of an illegal organisation.'

He turned to Salvatore and said, 'Signor d'Bergamasco, can you identify this man as the politician who demanded a series of bribes from you in exchange for licences relating to a factory your company is building near Salò?

'Yes, Colonello.'

'And did he threaten to make sure your factory would not be built if you refused to pay those bribes?'

'Yes, Colonello.'

D'Angelo came back to life and shouted, 'He's lying. I'm not the criminal. He is, by taking me to expensive restaurants and offering me money, a car, and a house for all the licences needed to build a factory. I turned the crook down, but somehow he managed to get them, probably from a dishonest politician in Milan. Arrest him, not me. I am innocent.'

Pancucci turned to his Carabinieri and said, 'Get him out of that chair and take him to our Bergamo Barracks.'

To D'Angelo he said 'You'll be held in a cell until tomorrow, when I will commence interrogating you. By then I am certain you will have considered carefully that it is better to cooperate than try to lie and cheat your way out of the mass of direct evidence we have against you.'

The two policemen dragged him backwards from the room, heels dragging, his face crumpled into fear and tears. Salvatore wiggled his fingers at D'Angelo in a little goodbye wave.

Pancucci smiled and said, 'The man's a coward. He'll be easy to crack. He'll probably bring down a load of others with him. This little arrest will give us a big haul. I'm sure you'll come to court and give evidence.'

'It will be a pleasure.'

Pancucci shook hands and said, 'Thanks for your help. One of my cars will return you to your tractor factory.'

Chapter 46

Romance In Venice

Anton decided to put plans for the launch of the new cars aside for two days and whisked Ginnie off to Venice.

He believed that this unique city of more than a hundred small islands, linked by canals and bridges, must be more romantic than anywhere else he had visited. And, sure enough, the amazing place captivated Ginnie.

On arrival, following a train journey of almost four hours, they sat enjoying afternoon tea alfresco at an elegant café in St Mark's Square, surrounded on three sides by the stately arcades of public buildings and on the fourth side by Basilica di San Marco's domes and arches and the soaring St. Mark's 10th century bell tower.

'The view from here is breath-taking,' murmured Ginnie, taking his hand in hers. 'I've never seen anything to match this. Certainly not in America.'

'Yes, it's amazing,' he agreed, kissing her hand. 'But wait until you see the other sights, art galleries and museums, and we explore the canals on a gondola, darling. Let's start right now by taking a ferry ride and looking at the famous bridges, the Rialto and The Bridge of Sighs.'

'Wow,' exclaimed Ginnie when they approached the Bridge of Sighs, with its windows encased by stone bars. Anton told her: 'It opened in 1603 and passes over the Rio di Palazzo to connect the newly built prison to the interrogation rooms in the Doge's Palace.'

'My goodness, Anton, you are knowledgeable, darling.'

'I've just read it in the brochure,' he admitted with a grin.

The playful push she gave him almost knocked him over. 'Hey, steady on,' he said. 'You don't realise how strong you are.'

'Don't worry, Anton. I'll try to be gentler in the bedroom tonight.'

The next day they explored the Doge's Palace, built in 1340 to house the Doge, the supreme authority of the former Republic of Venice.

They took a gondola ride, starting from the crowded Grand Canal and then gliding along some of Venice's most enchanting back canals.

As they sat back, completely relaxed, Anton put his hand in his pocket and pulled out a small box which he handed to Ginnie.

'Another ring?' she asked as she opened the box and gasped at his beautiful gift.

'This is an engagement ring,' he whispered. 'Will you marry me?'

Ginnie did not hesitate. 'Yes, Anton, my darling. I would love to be your wife.'

Within seconds they threw their arms around each other and kissed passionately, rocking the tiny boat. The gondolier whistled, laughed, and sang a love song while struggling to keep his craft steady.

On the train back to Milan, the newly engaged couple started to make plans for their wedding. 'Let's make it a quiet affair,' suggested Anton. 'We don't want Salvatore turning it into some big showbiz type of function, do we?'

'I agree,' Ginnie said, snuggling up to him.

'In that case there's no reason why we shouldn't

book a small church immediately and have the wedding as soon as possible.'

'That would be lovely,' she murmured. 'But I need to tell my father we've got engaged and let him get used to the idea of me not returning to New York. I should warn you, darling; he's very much like your brother Salvatore – he likes to be in control. It's best if I break the news gently.'

Chapter 47

D'Angelo In His Cell

Francisco D'Angelo sat in his cell in the local Police Station reflecting on the circumstances of his arrest and arrival.

That swine d'Bergamasco used an underhand trick by recruiting some sort of private eyes to spy on me and use the evidence to get me accused of crimes. The worst accusation is that I associated with criminals to extract money from honest citizens.

His lips curled at the thought of 'honest' citizens. He knew that most citizens, if they had his position of authority, would have done exactly the same. Except that damned policeman called Pancucci or something like that. He made a mental note to punish him when he got out of this situation. *I'll get him posted to Naples or somewhere so that he can find out how difficult and dangerous it is to do his job without the co-operation of the local Carabinieri.*

He laughed and said out loud to himself, 'If that d'Bergamasco thinks he's got me in a bad position, wait till he finds out what my revenge will be. He promised me a lot and then went back on his word. I have no car or income from him. He doesn't know yet what I've been doing in these little backwoods as he probably thinks of us. I have so many strings to pull that he doesn't know about yet.'

He turned his mind to his secretary: 'She turned out to be another spy. I'll make her suffer for going over to Salvatore. She'd better keep her mouth shut or she'll be finding out what my revenge will be. I don't take kindly to people going behind my back.'

His mind went on dreaming what he would like to do if he got his hands on her. She'd live to regret her actions. He became quite excited before he realised he was still in a bad position with the law.

His thoughts turned to what actions he needed to do to get out of his predicament. After going over all possible options he knew only one that would be certain to work.

He carefully considered the cunning message he needed to send. He had to seem to be asking for help but make it appear he would be doing the person a favour to help *him*.

Finally, he formulated a detailed plan that he felt sure would work and pleased with himself, knew that all he could do is wait for the right opportunity.

His cell door banged open and in walked the hated Pancucci. 'Out,' the damned man ordered.

D'Angelo played the frightened man and cowered back in his cell.

'I said out,' snapped Pancucci. 'Get out now, before we drag you out.'

Still acting, D'Angelo whimpered and shook his head.'

Pancucci turned to a policeman beside him and said, 'Cuff him,'

'There's no need for that,' Francisco whined. 'I'm not going to run anywhere am I.'

Pancucci shrugged his shoulders and waited for the officer to finish cuffing him.

D'Angelo dropped the pretence of being frightened and shouted, 'You're going to regret this; when I get out, I'll see you out of a job if it's the last thing I do.'

Pancucci grinned. 'It may be a very long time before you see fresh air again, so you'd better start thinking about how you'll survive in prison rather than making empty threats against me.'

They marched D'Angelo along a corridor into an interview room where Pancucci read out a series of charges relating to bribery, fraud, stealing public money and soliciting bribes.

'I am now going to question you about these alleged financial crimes and bribery.'

A stenographer came into the room and sat, pencil poised, ready to record the interview and the policeman removed the cuffs.

Pancucci went through the usual formula of establishing D'Angelo's full identity, home address, and workplace and the usual ritual about anything he said would be taken down and could be used in evidence.

D'Angelo answered everything in a loud clear voice until the questioning started, when he stared down at the table with a slight smile and a short shake of his head every time Pancucci spoke.

'This went on for some time until Pancucci lost his temper and shouted, 'Have you nothing to say in your defence?'

D'Angelo raised his eyes for the first time and stared at Pancucci with hatred.

'You'll have my defence in court if ever this nonsense goes that far. I'm saying nothing because I'm not guilty and I demand to go back to my cell because I have nothing to say to you.'

He pointed to the stenographer and said, 'Write down that I told the police I am innocent of all these crimes. I'll prove my innocence in court by answering every question clearly and truthfully.'

Pancucci said, 'Cuff him.'

'No,' said D'Angelo, placing his hands under the table. 'You are charging me with civil crimes. I am not a violent criminal to be treated this way, so stop waving those things about. Remember I am a fully trained lawyer and know you have no right to handcuff me. To do so is to commit a civil trespass and I will have you charged.'

Pancucci nodded at the policeman, and they returned D'Angelo to his cell by holding on to his sleeve.

Once in his cell D'Angelo said, 'I need some food and drink as is my right.'

Pancucci said nothing and left, slamming the door behind him. A short time later another policeman came in with a tray and said, 'Stand back from the door.'

D'Angelo grinned. 'Am I so dangerous you worry I might try and get out?

'Just procedure,' the officer muttered.

Francisco gestured to him, 'I have something to ask you, 'Will you take a message for me to someone important to my defence?'

The policeman shook his head, 'That's strictly against all the rules, Sir.'

'How about if I tell you the name of the person and that you will be well rewarded for your trouble? Alternatively, when he is disappointed, bad things happen to people, and we don't want that do we?'

The policeman said, 'Stand back from the door please or I shall have to call for assistance.'

D'Angelo moved away and watched the young man place the food on the table and pause for a moment, obviously thinking. He returned to the cell door and peeked into the corridor, obviously checking they were alone and whispered, 'What is his name and what is the message?'

D'Angelo grinned in triumph, and said, 'It's better you don't know his name but go to this small restaurant and tell him where I am and what has happened. That is all.'

The policeman paled at the name of the restaurant. He knew exactly who would be in there.

'All the police know of that place,' he said. 'I have a family who rely on me, please make sure nothing happens to them.'

'Just go and deliver the message and nothing will happen to anyone.'

Chapter 48

Isabella's Big Movie Premiere

Momentarily dazzled by the flashing camera bulbs, Isabella blew a kiss to the crowd whilst placing a silver Gucci stiletto on the red carpet as she stepped out of a white limousine. With perfectly coiffed dark hair, dressed in a stunning red chiffon and sequin fish tailed ensemble, which clung to the contours of her voluptuous body, the ravishing beauty heard gasps ripple through the crowd.

Though this was her first movie, Isabella knew that her leading man, acclaimed Italian actor, Giorgio Rossi, handsome in a black tuxedo with silk lapels and matching bow tie, always drew the crowds. With Leonardo Rinaldi as producer of the movie, there was guaranteed excitement, and glamour for his audience. Isabella could see and hear his admirers waving programmes and calling for autographs. The reaction of his fans to this hitherto unknown actress proved that he hadn't failed to deliver for them again.

Signore Rinaldi had suggested that Isabella arrive unaccompanied as the impact would be greater. 'Let this striking newly minted movie star bask in her own personal glory. What a momentous occasion it will be.'

Gosh, I've never experienced this before, an inconceivable buzz flowing through me from head to toe, filling every pore of my skin. Oh, it's both magnificent and extraordinary. I feel as though a cloak of splendour is being wrapped around me.

Briefly distracted as she caught sight of her proud family gathered inside the movie theatre, Isabella gave them a beaming smile then turned to wave to the crowds. Continuing to move with slow steps along the red carpet, she remained acutely aware of timing with Giorgio Rossi arriving shortly afterwards.

In the foyer of Rome's Teatro Adriano, the air charged with positive energy as family, close friends, celebrities, fellow actors, and powerful movie figures, politicians, and business leaders, spilled through the limited space of the lobby before taking their seats in front of the big screen.

Sometime later, excited chatter died down as the lights dimmed, with the only sound being the whirr of a projector as the countdown to the movie appeared on screen. FIVE, FOUR, THREE, TWO, ONE.

A white star symbolising 'Stella' movie production appeared next, followed by the film title 'I CAMBIAMENTI." The irony of the title did not escape Isabella, *Changes. So much has changed in my life in recent months, most of it good, I must admit. This is my dream come true, INCREDIBILE.*

Credits followed, names printed inside white boxes, as though cards had been placed in front of the camera, Giorgio Rossi's appeared first. A sharp intake of breath seemed to come from somewhere around Isabella until, she realised it came from herself when she saw her name printed in huge letters on the next white card. *ISABELLA D'BERGAMASCO.*

Dio Mio, it's me on the big screen, it's happened.

Minutes later, there were more gasps, not from Isabella this time but from those around her, family, friends and maybe others, as her face appeared in closeup, dominating a whole theatre for the first time. Basking in the glory of that moment, Isabella felt her cheeks burn as the blood rushed to her head with pure elation.

Why am I not critical of myself up there but when I look in the mirror, I find fault? Though I've improved, I'm not as hard on myself as in the past. It's as though I'm looking at someone new up there in the character I'm playing.

It seemed that no time at all had passed when the word 'FINE' signalled the end of the movie. The audience rose to its feet in a round of applause that filled the movie theatre in appreciation. A beaming Giorgio Rossi, the international star, took Isabella's hand and hauled her up into a big hug. Over the noise and acclaim, she managed to hear him say. 'You were fantastic, darling. This is for you, my sweet. Our future in the world of cinema. Get both arms up, project your biggest smile all over the theatre and wave at your audience with gratitude for their reaction. Blow kisses. Show that you love them, and they will love you forever. For the rest of your career.'

Beaming, both actors turned to face the gallery. The attractive actor nodded at his co-star and praised 'Bella, magnifico' in recognition of her powerful performance. Isabella had heard it as no secret he argued against taking a chance doing this movie with an unknown. But Rinaldi had been very persuasive. Thank God for his foresight. *And now this lovely man is applauding me as enthusiastically as our whole audience. What a gentleman. What a wonderful colleague. I could marry him here and now.*

The excited crowd, still clapping, whistling, and calling compliments, pulled aside, allowing Isabella and Giorgio to leave first, with handshakes and congratulations delaying their departure.

Finally entering the packed foyer, Isabella felt her heart skip a beat as a familiar face eased his way towards her.

Frank Bernstein, gosh he still has the same effect, even from a distance, just the sight of him.

'Signorina d'Bergamasco.' Frank extended his hand in greeting.

Electric shocks shot through Isabella's whole being as she took it, managing to reply, 'Isabella, please call me Isabella, we are well acquainted, I feel, and it is you who introduced me to Signor Rinaldi in the first place.'

'Isabella, how striking you look this evening,' Frank complimented her. 'Every inch the movie star. Congratulazioni on a fantastic performance. Your talent knows no bounds.'

Ooh these shivers of delight running through me, just at the sound of my name on his lips. This is almost as good as orgasm with Alberto.

Isabella felt her face flush with embarrassment, as though he had read her mind. Frank didn't appear to notice. She had been expertly made up for the evening: any blush would be conceived to have been orchestrated by pink powder.

Before she could recover enough to continue the conversation, Leonardo Rinaldi joined them. Beaming from ear to ear and clapping his hands with glee the excited producer declared 'What a star we have discovered, Frank. What a star. You will go a long way my dear. Congratulazioni.'

Agreeing wholeheartedly, Frank nodded in appreciation, then to her absolute dismay, excused himself, citing an urgent engagement which he had delayed in attending her premiere. Fixing a smile on her face, Isabella thanked him for coming, then turned back to Signor Rinaldi, continuing their conversation.

It wasn't long before Alberto took his place by Isabella's side with a big kiss. Though they hadn't arrived together, he came as her escort for the end of this special evening.

It's only fitting that I introduce Alberto to my family, but it would be best that they don't converse for too long. He might feel the necessity to share his passionate fascist views, despite me requesting him not to. I don't need their disapproval. He's only a lover after all. I'm not planning to marry him. They are aware he is my chaperone for this evening, and I'll leave it at that. Polite conversation will be sufficient. When we go for dinner later, I'll make sure he's placed between the lovely Ginnie and me. She will entertain him with American stories and no doubt involuntarily steer the subject away from politics.

Requisite handshakes and appreciative comments on Isabella's performance followed as numerous guests approached her, many she had never met before. Future movie options were inferred discreetly through short exchanges, in reply to which Isabella smiled sweetly, responding 'Grazie,' gracefully.

As the evening ended, Isabella took a deep breath and released all the pent-up tension she hadn't even been aware she'd been holding in. Just as she relaxed into an easy stance, Alberto whispered into her ear 'I have plans for you Bella, la mia stella. Tonight, I will bring you to heights you have never reached before. You will truly be a star in the sky, even more than you are on the big screen.'

Isabella felt that familiar stirring within her: not Frank Bernstein's electric shocks but exciting all the same. She smiled in reply, slowly, sensually, whispering to Alberto that she couldn't imagine a more fitting closing scene to this incredible evening.

Chapter 49

Giuseppe's Confrontations

Giuseppe came out of the guest room and stood on the bedroom hall landing, when the two-hundred-year-old grandfather clock chimed six thirty. The door to his and Francesca's bedroom opened, and he saw her. She had been crying.

'Go back to bed Francesca. I'll see to the kids. I'll do breakfast and take them to school.'

She nodded and closed the door.

After dropping off his children, it occurred to him to drive to his apartment on Seregino Road. He could call Rosalina from there and arrange to see her after work and finish their affair. However, slowing to park the car, he saw her entering the apartment block.

Good. No time like the present

Giuseppe unlocked the door to his apartment and stepped into the hallway to see Rosalina's back before she spun around, faced him, and smiled saying theatrically, 'Darling Giuseppe. What a lovely, lovely surprise.'

That smile is the one she uses to disguise her true feelings

He closed the door and asked, 'Why are you here Rosalina?'

'Oh, darling don't interrogate me. My, my that's a nasty cut you've got on your forehead. I know you'd like me to kiss it better?'

'No. Not right now.'

'We could play doctors and nurses,' said Rosalina.

Giuseppe snapped, 'No. I've come to tell you our affair ends *now*, Rosalina. I take half the blame for starting it. But we've betrayed our loved ones. I'm finishing it.'

'You can't just ditch me.'

'I just did.'

'You piece of dirt. No man dumps me,' screamed Rosalina her face a mask of pure spite.

'Lower your voice, Rosalina. It's not just about me ditching you. I mean who are the people you've been bringing back here? To my apartment. A bunch of bloody Fascists?'

Giuseppe paused, 'No. You know what? Don't bother answering. Just get out now.'

Rosalina cleared her throat, 'That suits me. It's a crummy apartment anyway. I'll ruin you. I'll spread all sorts of rumours. I'll tell your pretty, little wife everything we did in the bedroom. I'll even tell your kids. And my husband.'

'If you go near my bambini, I swear to the Almighty you will regret it,' said Giuseppe, his hands curling into fists. He took a step towards her.

Rosalina's face betrayed alarm, but she stood her ground.

Giuseppe said, 'I know you bring your Fascist friends here. Why?'

'Political discussion. Not sex. You don't have the intellect to understand. All you want me for is sex,' said Rosalina sweeping a hand across the little table to her side and deliberately pushing an antique vase off the table to smash upon the marble floor to explode noisily into a hundred pieces.

Giuseppe marched to the apartment door, snatching it open.

'Get out of here. Now.'

Rosalina's eyes widened and she snarled, 'You are a pathetic lover. I've had much better and I can get another one any time I want. And don't waste your time telling my husband. He prefers men. Exclusively. He cares not for my dalliances.'

'And don't bother telling my wife. I told her last night.'

Giuseppe opened the door with one hand, her wrist with the other and swung Rosalina into the corridor.

'When we are fully in power, we will make certain that people like you will suffer d'Bergamasco.'

'We? You mean your Fascist friends?'

Rosalina stormed from the building.

Giuseppe slammed the door behind her and stood for a moment thinking of Francesca, sure she would not abandon the luxurious life he gave her and his family and accept his sincerely offered promise that it would never happen again.

The remainder of his day passed quickly. Giuseppe continued monitoring the tender prices for the special equipment needed later for the Salò factory, satisfied that after threatening the tenderer with no future work. 'I need this specification at a lower price. If you can't agree I'll throw you out and go elsewhere in Europe.'

At the end of his working day, Giuseppe telephoned home, hoping that Francesca had thought through their current problem and decided to stay with him.

She answered and said, 'Giuseppe I'm taking the children to my friend Angelica's for the night.'

'I hope to see you tomorrow then.'

'Perhaps. And have you broken up with that woman?'

'I have.'

'Well, that's something I suppose.'

'Francesca? Francesca?' said Giuseppe, but she cut the call.

Giuseppe reflected on his wife's last words, 'Well. That's something I suppose,' and dared to think that just maybe she did not immediately think of throwing him out or demanding to annul their marriage.

Perhaps we can rebuild our life together after all, aware that realistically he may be clutching at straws.

With winter on its way Giuseppe, despite the cold, decided to leave his car and walk home. *At least if I stride along, I'll keep warm and enjoy some well overdue exercise.*

A short time into his journey he remembered a short cut through a small alley. The pavement and road were covered in ice that sparkled beneath the light of streetlamps.

Giuseppe vacated the alley, perturbed to find that the streetlamps were out, but grateful to see through an archway ahead, a small piazza illuminated by a solitary streetlamp. However, the silence and darkness of the street surrounding him made him uneasy and he picked-up his pace and aimed for the archway and the piazza.

Giuseppe saw two silhouettes appear in the archway. Behind him he heard footsteps of two men and instinctively knew he may have been expertly ambushed, both in front and to the rear.

Trapped, and knowing he could not take on four, he shouted, 'I've no money on me, but take my watch. It's a Breitling. It's worth a lot. Take it. Please.'

They ignored his plea and rushed towards him.

'Bastards,' he whispered, launching into a sprint, targeting the smaller silhouette hoping to knock him over and dash across the piazza just as he heard the footsteps behind him now louder and so close, he could hear their owner's breathing.

He smashed the heel of his right hand into the nose of the smaller silhouette, knocking him onto the piazza's ice encrusted cobbles.

Giuseppe leapt over the prone figure but skidded and crashed down onto the cobbles.

Three other silhouettes arrived and all set about raining punches and kicks at Giuseppe before dragging him through the archway, across the street to the doorway of the old bakery where the attacker Giuseppe had knocked over joined in.

Giuseppe lay on his back, every part of his body in pain. He tried vainly to focus his eyes, but they were too swollen, full of blood and tears.

'We Fascisti are the future, d'Bergamasco,' whispered one of the men, who had crouched down next to Giuseppe and placed one hand over his mouth, while the other hand slid a knife between his ribs. 'And this is for Rosalina.'

They ran off and left Giuseppe laying on the cold concrete of the old bakery step, in absolute agony, unable to move and sure that he may be dying.

Chapter 50

Novella Signs Her First Business Deal

Adriano returned to Novella's villa to show the full-size ladies' knitwear his factory had made from her doll's knitting patterns

'That's incredible Adriano, I would never have thought it possible.'

'They are amazing, I must agree. Have I convinced you enough to sign our agreement your lawyer is holding?

'Very much so, I am just waiting for him to get back to me after he's had a meeting with your papà.

'I believe they have already met and discussed matters so it should not be long. In the meantime, my pa would like to visit our factory and show you around. Would tomorrow be too soon.

'Tomorrow is perfect, shall we say ten am.

'Wonderful, I will come and pick you up. We could lunch at the restaurant in the square after
if you like, then I will drive you home.'

'I would be happy to do that. I'll be more suitably dressed for the occasion than the first time we met.'

They laughed.

Next morning Novella is ready when Adriano arrived prompt at ten. Novella is just about to climb into his car when Julia calls. 'It's Signor Russo on the line, shall I tell him you will call later?'

'No, just tell him to hold the line please Julia.'

Novella turned to Adriano, 'I must take this call, it's my lawyer.

'Of course, I'll wait here in the car.

Novella raced indoors, 'Buongiorno Signor Russo, thank you for calling. Yes, I will be available to attend your office at two-thirty this afternoon. I look forward to seeing you.'

Back in Adriano's car, she explained. 'My lawyer's able to see me this afternoon to sign the agreement. Will you still have time to bring me home or have you another engagement?

'No. I am available all afternoon. I will sit in your lawyer's waiting room for you.'

'That is kind, thank you.

Novella felt that meeting Signor Giorgio Berardi senior seemed like meeting for the first time, Adriano all over again. Their kind, calm and delightfully entertaining personalities perfectly matched. Giorgio looked every bit a financial and influential man, rugged in nature but refined in business. His loosely hanging mop of hair hung to the nape of his neck, very pleasing on the eye.

Novella felt sure she would enjoy being a part of the Berardi family company. On a tour of the factory, she glanced at the rows of women in their own workspaces, reminding her of how many hours she had sat, knitting by hand, to reproduce her dolls clothes into women's wear. Novella felt happy she would not be doing that job anymore. She would just continue designing dolls clothes and pass the patterns onto the factory to transform into women's wear.

When leaving his factory Giorgio Berardi took her hand in his and kissed her fingertips. He looked up and smiled. 'It has been a joy to meet you, my dear Novella. I look forward to when you are a part of the Berardi family knitting company. I am sure you will be very happy with the result of our work for you.

Arriving ten minutes early for her lawyer's appointment Novella and Adriano stepped into the waiting room. She felt anticipatory nerves expounding a joy unlike nothing she had ever known. She welcomed the buzzy tension. Setting out on this new venture felt so exhilarating and a leap of faith.

Stepping into Signor Russo's office, she felt her own power emerging in a brisk handshake.

'It's good to see you again Signorina d'Bergamasco, are you ready for this important change in your life?'

'Very much so Signor Russo.

'Please come into my office and take a seat.'

Novella calmly sank into the comfortable brown leather chair opposite Signor Russo. Smiling inwardly, she listened to his relaxed voice. 'I have met with Signor Berardi senior and his lawyer. Mr Berardi has been very generous in offering a good deal to secure the work with you. I am satisfied he is being fair and reasonable. I'm sure you will do very well with his company. Now, take your time reading through the documents. There is no rush. It is important you know what you are signing, and please raise any concerns with me before you sign.'

He passed the documents across his desk and then asked if she would like a coffee.

'No thank you. I want to concentrate.'

Novella, eager to understand every word, pored over the five pages for ten minutes, before saying, 'I have studied the documents very carefully Signor Russo and I'm happy with Mr Berardi's view of our joint agreement. I am ready to sign.'

'Is there anything you would like to raise with me first?'

'Nothing thank you; I am completely aware of what I am signing.'

Novella did not hesitate. Taking the pen Russo offered she signed her name. Her scrawled his signature underneath.

Their business concluded, he ushered her to the door and bowed. 'I wish you all the best in your exciting new journey Signorina. If you have any doubts as the agreement progresses, be sure to come and see me.'

'Thank you, Signor Russo, please call me Novella from now on.

'And you mia cara Signorina, please call me Carlos.'

Returning to the waiting room, Novella could not contain her delight. With a rapturous smile she saw Adriano sitting there looking thrilled at her obvious joy. He leapt from his seat, rushed across to her and without thinking planted a kiss on her lips.

Her initial surprise turned to laughter.

She grabbed his arm, and they walked out into the air together as a very happy looking couple

Chapter 51

Giuseppe in Hospital

After the attack, Francesca sat at Giuseppe's side as he lay unconscious in Bergamo's Principessa di Piemonte hospital in a private suite, tightly gripping his left hand and praying, until distracted by Colonello Pancucci entering the private suite.

Her husband occupied a bed surrounded and connected to a mass of medical equipment, including a variety of tubes and a black rubber ball inflating and deflating in time with his breathing.

'My men are in their positions,' said Pancucci 'The hospital is secure and your husband safe, Signora.'

'Thank you, Colonello.'

Pancucci saluted and left.

The night before, Francesca had received a call from the hospital at after midnight while staying at her friend Angelica's. 'How did you find me?' she asked.

'Your man next door left his house at the same time as you yesterday and followed because you drove off at such high speed to make sure you arrived safely.'

This might not have happened if I had stayed in our house last night. You wouldn't have walked home.

She released her grip on Giuseppe's hand and tenderly stroked it, whispering, 'I want you back my sweetheart. In every sense of the word.'

She placed her other hand on her oblivious husband's forehead. 'Sorry about the goblet of 1899 Masseto, my love,' she smiled, 'I do hope you were impressed with my accuracy and the quality of the wine. Hurry up and get better, my darling.'

Giuseppe regained consciousness that afternoon saying weakly as he opened his eyes, 'Francesca? It's so good to see you.'

'And it's good to see you too.'

Francesca bent to kiss his forehead but went lower and landed the kiss upon his lips.

'I'm not sure that I deserve that.'

'Nor am I Giuseppe,' said Francesca.

'What happened to me?'

'You were attacked.'

'Of course. Bastards.'

'A cop found you outside a derelict bakery,' said Francesca. 'Who do you think attacked you?'

'I've no idea.'

'Local scum I suppose.'

'Indeed. No more than that, sweetheart,' said Giuseppe all too aware of who was behind the attack but decided not to worry his dear wife.

They held hands while Giuseppe fell in and out of sleep for the remainder of the day.

Francesca eventually joined Giuseppe in sleep, oblivious to the nurse delivering the evening newspaper that she had requested earlier. She woke around 7pm and immediately saw that the attack on Giuseppe occupied the front page, with a large black headline, proclaiming 'LOCAL INDUSTRIALIST WOUNDED IN HORRIFYING ATTACK'

'Oh god,' she murmured to herself, 'Publicity about this is the last thing we want. Who knows what problems it may bring out? Especially if that woman's husband arranged the stabbing.'

Chapter 52

Giuseppe And the Bank

Still in considerable pain from being stabbed through the ribs a few weeks ago, Giuseppe entered Salvatore's office with trepidation.

'Well, what's so important that it can't wait for normal office hours?' Salvatore demanded.

Giuseppe, rubbed his hands over his head in despair, 'I don't know how to tell you this brother, but something has happened, and I don't have a solution.'

'Every problem can be solved,' Salvatore snapped. 'Now spit it out and let me get back to my evening entertainment.'

'There won't be any evening entertainment for you I'm afraid. We're facing ruin unless we act decisively and quickly.'

'What the hell are you talking about man? How on earth could we be facing ruin?'

Giuseppe raised agonised eyes to his brother. Then said the fateful words, 'That damned Banker D'Innella found out I have been sleeping with his wife and took his revenge on me.'

Salvatore frowned, 'You've been bedding his wife, you idiot? Of all the women we encounter through our business, you had to choose the banker's wife. What on earth possessed you to do that?'

Giuseppe shrugged, 'I never meant it to happen like that, it just did, I meant it to be a little dalliance but then went further until we became caught up in fantastic sex and I couldn't stop. She told me he preferred men and wouldn't care. I don't know if that's true, but the consequences are dreadful. He said he'd ruin us, and he has started now.'

'How did he find out?'

'I met her last night and told her it is all over. She screamed at me and said she'd tell everyone, including my wife. I told her I already had and after throwing things around the room, she'd forgiven me and said I could stay. She must have gone straight home and told her husband to bring revenge down on us.'

'And what has he done?'

'He's cut off all our credit. Everything. He's called in all our loans with immediate effect. They have to be paid within fourteen days with full interest. Of course, we can't pay unless we sell all that we have. And I mean *all* that we have. We'll be left with nothing. Even our houses and the factories will have to go to cover the debts.'

'You stupid idiot,' Salvatore shouted. 'When we signed over the properties as security, you said the loans would be paid off easily. That's why we did it.'

He shook his finger in his brother's face. 'This is all your doing and if we get out of this I'll see you punished. Now the best thing to do is go to another bank and get them to give us the credit we need.'

Giuseppe smiled miserably. 'You don't understand Salvatore; we can't go to another bank; he foresaw that, and he's taken the trouble to blacklist us with all of them. Not one will touch us now. I don't know what he told them, because as soon as I entered a bank they stopped me and wouldn't even consider any proposal I put forward. I've called in every favour I have and got nowhere,'

Salvatore paced back and forth while he went over this dreadful news. Then sank back into a chair, hands on his head. Finally, he looked up and said, 'What about a foreign bank? Maybe in France, or England or even America? We could offer our new project as collateral.'

Giuseppe shook his head, 'Don't you think I've tried every option I can? I've been traipsing round banks till my feet felt they were wearing out and not one will even consider us at this short notice, it takes weeks to set up loans of the size we need, and we don't have the luxury of time.'

'So, we're meant to just sit down and let some little banker ruin us because you couldn't keep that thing in your pants,'

Giuseppe looked at him in anger, 'You're no better, I've heard rumours of you having a dalliance with some woman when you were visiting Avellino. You aren't the saint you're pretending to be.'

'You go too far brother,' Salvatore snapped. 'At least my little peccadillos aren't going to ruin us.'

'Easy for you to say that, but I bet when you started you didn't know much about the woman you were seeing. What if she'd been connected to Mussolini or Cosa Nostra or someone like that?'

'Stop that right now, this conversation is going to get us nowhere, we have to get a solution and quickly. Now there is one option we can try. What about the Medici Bank, have you tried them again?'

Giuseppe's face paled, 'You said never to have any dealings with that crew, because of their reputation of being linked to Mafia money. If they get their sticky fingers into our business, we'll never get them out; and the interest rates will be more than we can afford. And also,' He looked at his brother. 'They have their own way of collecting them as well. One missed payment and you could end up with a hand or an ear missing, or worse.'

'They may be our only option for now. Go first thing tomorrow morning and see what can be arranged. For the moment we'll have to deal with this the best way we can until we get back enough revenue to pay them off once and for all. I'm almost ready to start production in the factory and as soon as we can get cars into the market we'll start getting plenty of money coming in. I'm certain they will sell well and quickly,'

Giuseppe turned to leave, but before he could, Salvatore called him back and pointed his finger at his face and said ominously. 'Never forget brother, you are responsible for this mess and even if you do forget, I never will. And for the moment, do not tell anyone of our family.'

Chapter 53

Isabella in Contemplation

Speeding along the winding Almafi coast road, Isabella felt the strong wind whip around her face, circular tinted glasses protecting her lovely eyes from the dazzling sun. Her bright red head scarf matched the red lipstick carefully applied to her mouth. Driving back to Rome after a leisurely weekend break at Alberto's family home in Ravello, she had time to process her innermost thoughts.

Our car launch is getting closer. I need to present a more glamorous facade than ever, even to my family, especially to my family. I am the face of the cars; they need me to be at my best. Of course, my absolute best.

The glamour of the movie business, though still as infectious as ever, can't fill the void that seems to be like a gaping hole inside me. Before this, everything at home seemed solid. There has always been an unacknowledged hierarchy, we all knew our places and while I'm not under any illusion I sat at the top, as Italian men tend to assume that position, I certainly didn't belong at the bottom.

I feel like I'm walking through shifting sands. Why is Novella being so cold to me? She has changed beyond belief. She's become so ambitious. It's as though my little sister has disappeared. Even my brothers are looking at her differently. Yet they appear to have more respect for her. They never had the closeness with her that she and I shared. She has always been the constant in my life, always there, especially when we lost Mama and Papà. Have I taken her for granted?

This sensation of self-admonishment felt alien to Isabella. She had never seen reason to question it before. *I have never been confident about what others see as my beauty, but I have always been assured in my actions. Now they don't appear so cut and dry.*

Isabella had questioned Anton. He had been reluctant to answer, whether because too wrapped up in his own life to notice – especially in his newly hot romance with Ginnie – or ashamed to admit that he just didn't know.

Ginnie could become a good friend to Novella, but hadn't they got off on the wrong footing by Novella expressing doubts about her intentions towards Anton, which the American heiress had, unfortunately overheard.

These worrying thoughts were replaced by others and Isabella found her concentration slip, narrowly avoiding colliding with a car coming from the opposite direction, as she rounded a bend. The near miss shocked her back into driving mode for another five minutes, after which she found her thoughts intruding once more.

Novella seemed fine when I spoke to her on the phone, though so cold and almost dismissive of anything I had to say. She appeared to have no interest in my career and when I asked about hers, I felt she didn't want to divulge too much. There were so many things I wanted to tell her that I couldn't on the phone but now I wonder if it would have been a good idea to confide in her at all.

Before now I could have shared my recent experience with my sister. The house party with Benito Mussolini briefly in attendance. I know I need to be careful as I become more well-known, but I feel a sense of belonging with Alberto's friends. The camaraderie is wonderful. Alberto was so keen for me to go to that party and I'm glad I did. His friends and acquaintances really believe in the fascist cause and are not afraid to say it. The women surprised me too. They weren't at all how I imagined, in fact quite the opposite, some loud and opinionated, though not in the men's company, but only a fraction meeker and more reserved. It must be great to have such staunch beliefs, and truly have a cause.

Mama might well have been ashamed of me. I have been so distracted by my own desires that I haven't considered what's going on around me. Though, Papa would applaud the fact that I'm tough and realising my ambitions. However, I can't help but feel that I might just be a good time girl.

Does Novella need me? Or are we beyond that? Is her resentment of me too far gone? Well so be it if that's the way she wants it. She has Anton. He'll probably do his big brother act and bring her back to common sense.

Isabella found an anger welling up inside of her and pressed her foot a little harder on the accelerator. The tyres screeched as she braked slightly when approaching a hairpin bend. Common sense prevailed and easing off the pedal, the car slowed to a safer pace and anger gave way to more ponderous thoughts.

Being at that party has given me food for thought about the family's new car factory. I realise that Salvatore is fending off a crooked politician but what about the Mafia? Where will we be if they try to step in? Perhaps it might be a good idea for me to go to more fascist parties. If I mix in those circles and get to know powerful people, it could be less likely that my family will be intimidated as I could ask the Fascists for protection. I shall write to Paolo; he is wise and impartial. Best not to mention it to the rest of the family just yet though. No doubt I'd be shot down. Once the launch is under way and we are on more comfortable ground I can sound out each of my brothers, leaving Salvatore till last. He might see reason if I have the support of the others. Let them see that I haven't been given the title of Creative Director for nothing. I'll command a whole different respect than Novella with her little tantrums.

Reluctantly leaving the beautiful glistening azure waters behind, Isabella continued her journey to Rome, deep in thought, with Novella still at the forefront of her mind.

While enjoying a glass of Château Cheval Blanc in the village square under the evening sun over last weekend, Alberto had suggested something which had both horrified and interested her.

'Amore mio, has Novella any weaknesses you could use to your advantage. Maybe not right now but keep it as a secret weapon to use later.'

Isabella's eyes had widened in astonishment at such a proposition. 'I know nothing of her personal life.'

'Ah but you could find out more by getting close to Ginnie. She is no doubt lonely in a strange country and Novella may confide in her. It makes sense, no?'

Isabella acknowledged this with a nod, considering a new aspect to her lover. *How have I not noticed the devious side to Alberto before? Well of course, he is a fascist in changing times, he would need to be devious to further himself within the movement.*

Alberto continued by saying 'If you record your conversations with Ginnie in writing, you will have what you need, carefully documented, as a safety net for the future. We must always be prepared for battle

Bella, and this is a weapon you will have in your artillery for your protection.'

Now, driving more slowly and pondering Alberto's scheme, a feeling of uneasiness crept over Isabella. Papà's dark eyes wafted into her consciousness, a look in them that she personally, had never experienced before. Contempt.

But papà. I don't need to do anything with the information, I'll only use it if it looks as though Novella is going to seriously upstage me at any point. The words were defensive as she spoke into the wind, now blowing a little fiercer, even though she had turned inland, away from the coast and again pressed her foot hard on the accelerator. The engine howled at full power speeding on through the country roads towards her destination.

Chapter 54

Launch Day Plan

On 4th October 1922, Salvatore called Anton to his office and said, 'You'll remember that a month ago you and I sat drinking too much wine and discussing the need for a dramatic launch day to show our four amazing new cars. Have you thought of that evening and come up with any plans?'

Anton laughed. 'I remember it well. We invented so many ridiculous ideas that became more absurd the more booze we drank and laughed all the way home at our stupidity. Did you drive or me?'

'Who cares? What does matter is that for the last few days I've been going over that evening in my head and think we came up with several terrific ways to present our new range of cars in a way never before seen in this or any other industry.'

'How?'

'For instance, Anton, we nearly fell from our seats laughing at one of your daftest ideas.'

'Which one?'

'That we rent the Atalanta Football Club Stadium for a week and put on a big show the like of which Bergamo has never seen.'

Anton frowned, obviously struggling to remember and sort out what he had meant.

'Think about it now in the cold light of day, and it doesn't seem so stupid.' chuckled Salvatore. 'Properly advertised and presented, we could put on a tremendous show with thousands of people attending and probably sell hundreds of our whole vehicle range in one day.'

'My god, you're right,' said Anton, his face lighting up with excitement.

'No. *You* were right. You may have been drunk, but your clever marketing mind, although pickled in alcohol, must have been working at top speed.'

'Now I remember Salvatore. I said we could present the day like a big musical play or a New Year Fair, with Isabella singing and dancing in front of her stage troupe. Oh, how we laughed, but as you just said; now, in the light of day we could make it work. Let's quickly remember all the other silly ideas we threw about and think of more.'

'You're right. Then get started with planning. Remember that Launch Day is exactly three months to the day on 14th January.'

'Yes brother. But what will Atalanta think of losing use of their stadium for a day? Will they allow it?'

'What I haven't yet mentioned is that yesterday I hired the whole place for seven days from Sunday 7th to Sunday 14th of January.'

Salvatore laughed at Anton's shock and uncharacteristic silence. 'Come on Anton,' he said. 'Speak up. What you think?'

'Bloody amazing.'

'I went to school with the owner. He thought it an incredible idea and wondered why he hadn't thought of it himself. I think he'll start selling it for other big shows.

'One thing you said, Anton, is that we should make the whole day one big musical play.'

'Did I? Let me whip out a few more ideas. We can get Isabella to bring other film people and pay them if necessary. We can invite the whole Atalanta soccer team and other famous sports people. That champion boxer, Leone Jacovacci who pretends to be American.'

Salvatore clapped his hands, 'And the whole Italian champion cycling team. Think of how many would come to see them. I'm sure we could fill that stadium with customers and their money.'

'You may be right. Keep talking and I'll make notes.'

Salvatore took a large piece of paper and set to scribbling, while Anton spouted a series of suggestions, many bringing the brothers to breathless hilarity.

Eventually he slowed and stopped. In a short silence, the two brothers looked at each other, then stood and hugged.

Anton took a deep breath.

'I think we've done it, brother.'

Salvatore said, 'So do I. Now I'll pick the best of it out and summarise in a letter to the board. Everyone must start taking their part from today.'

'Shall I go and leave you to it?'

'No. I may need your help.'

Shoulders hunched, head down, he scribbled for fifteen minutes, crossing out and rewriting until he sat up and said, 'How is this?' read out loud: -

To The Board of Motori Bergamsco

I have rented the Atalanta Football Club Stadium for seven days from Sunday 7th to Sunday 14th January 1923. There is no home game on 13th, so we have plenty of time to prepare for and rehearse the launch of our four new car models on that Sunday.

In the stadium we will erect a large rostrum to present our new range of cars in a Grand Entrance, which will be strictly rehearsed on Friday and Saturday, 12th, and 13th as though a Grand Theatre Show.

I have employed Isabella's film producer Leonardo Rinaldi to conduct the rehearsals and run the big day, and Giorgio Rossi, who starred in Isabella's film, to act as Master of Ceremonies from the big stage on Launch Day. And of course, our now famous and beloved sister and film star, Isabella, to circulate among the large crowd and, perhaps, bring her dance troupe and put on a singing and dancing show for the thousands we can expect from all over our Province.

If we fill the whole of Lombardy with colourful posters and advertising, offering food, drink and entertainment, people will come from Milan, Verona and beyond, probably even Venice, to meet with Giorgio, Isabella, and Leonardo plus any other attending film personalities they may bring to circulate and talk and promote our cars, themselves, and their films.

I plan for free food and wine to be served in large, heated marquees placed around the ground in which our four cars will be on show. On the centre of the football pitch will be an arena with at least a hundred cars for sale with Anton's staff taking orders and giving short test drives. Twenty photographers will be available to take pictures of buyers in their cars. If you have any other marketing ideas, however wild they may seem, please tell Anton to include them if he does not already have them in his notes.

I have spent several days and nights discussing these imaginative plans from Anton and congratulate him. He will now use the next three months planning and arranging the marketing and advertising of this great day.

Make sure you are available in Bergamo during this week, during which we will also be honouring our late but wonderful and beloved papà.

Chapter 55

Wedding And Marketing Plans Clash

Anton and Ginnie began planning for their wedding by visiting churches in Bergamo and chose one of the smallest, the Madonna dello Spasimo, containing the tomb of Santa Lucia.

'It's so beautiful', Ginnie said for the second time as they sat on a bench, marvelling at the historic building, the construction of which began in 1764 on the ruins of an earlier church from 1592.

They decided to have a quiet wedding and were delighted to find that the church had a date free at the end of November.

'Let's book it,' urged Anton, influenced by his romantic feelings and desire to be married to this wonderful American lady. But then his business brain took over and he added: 'Maybe I'm being too ambitious. It's less than two months away. Do you think we can fit all the preparations into the next few weeks? At the moment I'm tied up working on the marketing plan for the car Launch Day.'

Ginnie smiled. 'I'm willing to do most of the arrangements. As long as you don't leave everything to me, we can get it done.'

They kissed, hugged, and booked the date.

Leaving the church, Ginnie clutched Anton's arm and whispered, 'Everything should work out as long as Salvatore and my father don't throw up too many obstacles. Your brother will be pressurising you to work all hours on the Launch, while my father is still trying to persuade me not to rush into marriage with an Italian Stallion.'

Ginnie wrote to her father, telling him that she was deeply in love with Anton and asking him to give her away. Meanwhile, she chose a wedding dress and started preparing for her marriage, leaving Anton to concentrate on a marketing plan.

While sitting on the sofa together in Anton's flat one evening they brought each other up to date on what they had achieved so far. He told her about the five Ps and why they would be vital to achieving his objectives.

'Are you going to tell me what the five Ps are, darling, or leave me guessing?'

'They stand for product, profit margins, place, promotion and people.'

'What do they mean exactly?' she queried. 'People, for example?'

'People are our target audience. To use a pun, we need to know what drives them. And we need to motivate them to buy our cars.'

'And place?'

'That refers to considering where our customers already spend their time – that will help me decide upon the optimal marketing locations. Product and promotion speak for themselves – they involve brand perception. We'll be running two campaigns, one aimed at all car drivers, men, and women, young and old, while the second for The Town Car, will solely be directed at ladies.'

'There's so much to do, isn't there?' Ginnie sympathised. 'Where will you start?'

'I'll seek sponsorship first and then commission posters. They're cost-effective because they are relatively inexpensive to produce and can be displayed for an extended period of time. Posters are also eye-catching and can be placed in specific locations, such as on billboards, in store windows or on public transport.'

Ginnie gave him a kiss on the cheek. 'You're very clever, my darling. I didn't realise posters were so important.'

'If you think about it they're more memorable than other forms of advertising, such as adverts in newspapers which can soon be forgotten.'

Anton explained that to obtain maximum impact the wording should be short and punchy, with one set of posters declaring: MOTORI BERGAMASCO LEADS THE WAY IN STYLE, ELEGANCE, AND PERFORMANCE.

Brightly coloured images of the three new Motori Bergamasco cars would fill the rest of the space.

This would act as a taster and be followed by advertisements in newspapers and magazines giving details about The Town Car for essential daily use, The Tourer for long distance driving, and The Speedster with its extra powerful engine for young men driving the valleys and mountains.

A second poster would declare: A TOWN CAR LADIES WILL LOVE and show Isabella standing next to the new town car, specially aimed at young women about town, young mothers to take their children on picnics, and mature matrons shopping or visiting friends for coffee and conversation. Newspaper and magazine adverts would stress that our company are adding elegance to the new Town Car to ensure that ladies are given the style they deserve.

'It sounds very impressive,' his fiancée enthused.

'There will also be a third series of posters and advertisements,' he revealed. 'These will announce the launch day at the Atalanta Football Club stadium on Sunday 14th of January. The build-up to this will be a series of personal appearances by my sister Isabella, the famous actress.'

'You seem to have come up with a master plan, darling. But I thought there would be four new cars.'

'You're right,' he confirmed. 'The Gold car being designed to Novella's personal specification is top of the range and I feel it should be kept secret and revealed on Launch Day. We need to concentrate on selling the less expensive models first, but during the launch we will have sales staff taking orders for the deluxe Gold car as well. The three standard models will be presented on the football pitch and marquees, with the gold car, branded as The Novella, being our star attraction on stage after Isabella's big dance routine in a triumphant end to a triumphant day.'

Anton spent the following days frantically briefing advertising and marketing companies, newspapers, and magazines as well as booking venues where Isabella could appear to advertise the big day. He also liaised with Isabella and her stage troupe to ensure that the opening would be marked by a dazzling song and dance performance, as well as booking celebrities to attend. These included showbiz personalities from stage and screen, boxer Leone Jacovacci, the acclaimed Italian international cycling team, and the Atalanta soccer squad.

Salvatore continually demanded regular updates on progress being made, and meetings between the two brothers went on until late at night.

Amid all the frenzied activity, Anton did not realise how much he neglected Ginnie until she finally confronted him by declaring: 'We're hardly spending any time together. I see no point in me planning for a wedding to a man who ignores me.'

Her fiancé apologised profusely. 'I'm so sorry, my darling. I will make more time for us,' he declared. But within seconds the telephone rang with Rudolph Valentino's agent saying, 'He can't attend, but I have a couple of top actors who can.'

As the telephone call continued Ginnie stormed off to her room.

The next day the couple had a fraught conversation over breakfast.

'Let's be realistic,' demanded Ginnie. 'You obviously feel that our wedding can be squeezed in between all these arrangements you're making for the car launch. That's simply not acceptable. I think it's best if we postpone getting married.'

'Surely it's too late to postpone it now, darling.'

'No, it isn't. I'll just inform everyone that we will be coming up with a new date early next year – after all this is over. Meanwhile, I'll go back to New York for a couple of months.'

Anton, horrified to learn that this would result in his fiancée returning to America, protested, 'Please don't leave, darling. I need your support and encouragement.'

'I must go back to help my father run our hotels at this busy time over Christmas,' she pointed out. 'It will also give me the opportunity to win him round because he's not happy that I'm planning to marry an Italian and live in Bergamo. Don't fret, darling. I'll return in the New Year, and we can rearrange the wedding then.'

Chapter 56

Isabella - New Life

The stunning views from Isabella's hillside Bergamo penthouse paled into the background as Alberto's contorted mouth spat out the words, 'You'll just have to get rid of it, throw yourself down the stairs or something. Find one of those backstreet whores who sort these things out every day. How do I even know it's mine?'

Tears streamed from Isabella's dark eyes as she instinctively placed her hands protectively upon her belly. Having had no monthly bleed for the preceding eight weeks, a visit to the discreet family doctor earlier in the day had revealed that she is with child; likely in the first trimester of pregnancy. Though she had suspected such an outcome, nevertheless the shock had been all encompassing.

The beautiful actress, slimmer than ever but still retaining her womanly curves, had shaken from head to toe. At the same time, she experienced an overwhelming sense of protectiveness towards her unborn child. She had questioned if the perceived butterflies in her tummy were excitement, or indeed fear of what Alberto's reaction might be to her news.

Any concerns Isabella might have had about a backlash from her boyfriend were not unfounded. Nevertheless, she would never have expected this level of anger and blame.

How can he even suggest that this could be another man's child? Yet, he has revealed a nasty, jealous streak since the movie premiere. He seems to be under the illusion that there is something going on between

Giorgio Rossi and me. Such a sweet, kind man like Giorgio would never step on another man's toes. In saying that, I'm not even sure he's inclined towards women. Well, so much for the fascist party being anti-abortion. Here is Alberto, one of their leading benefactors and followers, suggesting I do the opposite. How did I get him so wrong? Have I been saved from a lot worse?

Alberto, now pacing back and forth in an agitated fashion, picked up his valigia and tossed it onto the large double bed. Crumpled cotton sheets lay static beneath the small piece of luggage, any memory of the entangled naked bodies united in passion below them such a short time before, now permanently erased.

She watched her enraged lover grabbing his clothes and belongings and throwing them into the case with furious haste.

How can I have a baby now? Aside from the fact I'm not married, nor would I want to marry the father, I have a successful movie career to consider.

Alberto's enraged voice interrupted her thoughts once more. 'Don't darken the doors of any of the parties we have been attending. You are finished in our circle. If you dare to speak of this to anyone, even hint that I have fathered your bastard, I'll make sure your name is dirt.'

Isabella felt as though she had been physically assaulted. *A bastard, that's what my child would be called... Children can be crueller than adults and my baby, he, or she, would be smeared with that awful label in Bergamo. How can I bring a fatherless child into such a cruel world?*

'My advice to you, not that you Miss High and Mighty Isabella d'Bergamasco, will listen, is to get rid of it. Subito. Right now. Today. That's your only choice.

There is no other. Your career will be in tatters if you go ahead with this pregnancy, your reputation sullied. Even your family will disown you.'

'My family would never disown me,' Isabella fired back for the first time, though a tiny seed of doubt had been planted by Alberto's cruel words.

Isabella felt the bile rise in her throat, more in defence of her unborn child than from fear of being ostracised.

'So much for your great fascist party's views on contraception and abortion. While you may not have attempted to prevent a pregnancy, you go against all you purport to believe in by suggesting I get rid of the life we have created together.'

'I don't agree with all of Mussolini's views,' Alberto raised his voice above hers. 'He is the best leader Italy could ever hope to have, but he is not always right. Besides, women line up to be bedded by him, they must take responsibility for what comes of that. So must you. Women are all the same, they try to trap men by opening their legs and offering it on a plate, expecting no consequences. Well, that won't work with me. If you choose to proceed with this pregnancy, we are finished. You won't be welcome in the Fascist circles; if you go ahead and produce your bastard, you are on your own.'

Isabella found herself openly sneering at the suggestion that the threat of him ending their relationship might be enough for her to abort her baby by whatever means. Pulling herself up from where she was seated on the high-backed balloon chair, she stood tall, as she calmly exclaimed 'Alberto, let us not be under any illusion. I do not and never have, loved you. If I've 'opened my legs' as you so crudely put it, it is because I wanted physical pleasure and nothing more. Your reaction to my news has shown your true side, which I have suspected for quite some time. You're nothing but a rich spoilt brat with nothing better to do than satisfy your own needs, which include being a benefactor to a political party whose policies you don't always agree with. It's the illusion of power that gratifies you. Your selfish, cruel, manipulative side is unattractive. Now, get out of my home. What I choose to do about my pregnancy is my choice. I WILL take responsibility for it. You won't be involved.'

Snapping the clasps of his vaglia shut, the sleeve of a white dress shirt dangling from the hastily fastened lid, Alberto muttered obscenities as he left the bedroom and marched out through the walnut wood front door, leaving it wide open as he departed in an ill-disguised rage.

Isabella felt her legs go weak and collapsed back into her chair. The blood drained from her beautiful face as the reality of her situation hit her. *What shall I do? I'm in the middle of my second movie. If I go ahead with it my pregnancy will show soon. What am I even saying? I can't get rid of it. This is a new life inside me, mama and papà's grandchild. If they were here, they'd hug me and say, 'Don't worry. We'll find a way, carissima.'*

I'll have to decide quickly. Yet I can't do this on my own. I need support from someone I trust. Someone worldly enough to guide me in the right direction.

Picking up the receiver of her brass candlestick telephone, Isabella dialled a familiar number. The soft tones of Alfina's voice opened the floodgates and Isabella sobbed her friend's name into the phone.

'What on earth has happened mi bella amica?'

Concern emanated from the young lawyer as she tried to make out what her dear friend needed to communicate. Eventually, realising that telephone operators from the local exchange might be listening in and sensing that this is something very traumatic indeed, Alfina took charge and said 'Bella, you must take deep breaths, pour yourself a brandy and I'll be with you as soon as possible.'

'Whatever the matter is,' a concerned Alfina spoke aloud to her empty office as she replaced the receiver, 'considering Isabella's rise to stardom, it's important that it is kept under wraps. Something that has reduced my ever-resilient friend to this state has to be very serious indeed.'

Some hours later, long after the sun had set, Alfina reached the beautiful hills of Bergamo. Pulling back the gate of the elevator that had ascended to the floor of Isabella's penthouse, a sense of panic crept up her throat when she observed the main door of her friend's home lying wide open and the apartment in complete darkness.

Nervous what she'd find, Alfina took slow, tentative steps through the main door continuing on through the interior, calling Isabella's name as she progressed. Her vision adjusted enough in the inky blackness to reveal the shadow of a figure lying on the large double bed in the main bedroom. On closer examination she found Isabella fully clothed, positioned on her right side. One arm placed above Isabella's head, the other across her flat stomach.

Tenderly stroking her comatose amica, Alfina lowered her voice almost to a whisper. 'Isabella,'

Her friend didn't move.

Alfina tried twice more and on the third call, Isabella stirred. A flick of the switch of the Carrara marble bedside lamp revealed those dark, red rimmed eyes opening slowly, blinking in the light, straining to focus on the face hovering above her. A slow smile spread across her full lips as she recognised her treasured friend then, a fraction of a second later, as conscious reality dawned, Isabella burst into tears.

Alfina wrapped her arms comfortingly around her darling Bella, aware of how frail her body felt. It appeared that she had lost a lot of weight recently. Afraid to hold on too tightly she pulled back and looked into Isabella's dark eyes, pools of salty tears filling them and spilling down her cheeks.

'I'm pregnant,' Isabella blurted out, as sobs wracked her body. 'I don't know what to do. Alberto wants nothing to do with it. He told me to get rid of it and said we're finished.'

Indignantly, Alfina responded 'Fascist idiota, no loss there Bella, he's only good for one thing. That man doesn't have a brain between his ears. Do you want to get rid of it?' she continued carefully.

'No, I don't think so.' Once more, Isabella placed her hands protectively upon her belly. 'But how can I have it? I have no husband. Being unmarried and pregnant would ruin my career. Alberto was quick to point that out, the arrogant sod.'

'Isabella, you are a wealthy, famous sex siren,' Alfina pointed out. 'Men fall over their feet just to get a glimpse of your beauty. It wouldn't be impossible to pay someone to marry you. It can easily be arranged.'

'Really? Truly?'

'Of course. I have connections. I would have a contract drawn up, which you and the contracted party would sign. A lump sum would be paid to him when you wed. You'd have separate lives and divorce a year after the baby is born. A citation of irreconcilable differences due to the pressure of a little one within a marriage where you have such a high-profile career would be perfectly acceptable. When the divorce is final, you would pay the lucky man another lump sum to ensure he stays within the marriage long enough for it to look real. He would have to sign a strict non-disclosure agreement of course.'

Isabella's eyes widened with incredulity as she took Alfina's suggestion. It sounded so cold, so contrived. 'But I couldn't marry ANYONE,' she cried plaintively, though her torrent of tears had now eased. 'How could I live with someone with whom I've nothing in common? It would be intolerable.'

'Who says you'd have nothing in common with him?' Alfina replied wryly. 'Leave it with me. I'll find someone compatible. Who knows you better than me? Ok, you may not be attracted to him, which would in fact, make it less complicated, but if you find common ground, what's eighteen months? You could buy a big villa here in Bergamo, have separate rooms, a nice garden for the little one to play in, a nanny; the whole happily married house.'

Isabella pulled herself upright in her bed. Alfina took charge, fluffing the pillows behind her. Taking a sip of the cold water her friend poured from the carafe on her bedside table, Isabella smiled for the first time since her pregnancy had been confirmed. There *is* hope. A sudden almost imperceptible fluttering sensation in her tummy made her stop in her tracks. *Is this her baby, making itself known now that she found herself coming to a decision?*

Turning to her beloved friend, Isabella nodded her head, smiling widely and acknowledged 'Yes, Alfina, please find me a husband, draw up a contract for whatever amount you think is feasible. I am keeping my baby.'

Chapter 57

Isabella Confides in Giorgio

Following Isabella into her dressing room during a break from filming, Giorgio Rossi asked if they could have a chat. Gesturing towards a comfortable two-seater leather sofa, the ashen faced actress acquiesced.

'I've been around the block enough times, Isabella, to know what's going on here,' Giorgio blurted out.

My god he can tell or has guessed.

'You are sick every morning when we are on set, need a break for the toilet regularly and appear to have strange food cravings. Are you pregnant?'

Isabella felt the blood drain from her face and felt she must have the look of a rabbit caught in headlights. She slumped onto the velvet cushioned stool in front of her dressing table.

'Yes Giorgio', she acknowledged, tears starting in her eyes, 'I'm in my first trimester. Alberto is the father but wants nothing more to do with me and the pregnancy. You have been such a good friend and confidante, guiding me through my career since our first movie. I really hope you're not disappointed in me. I would hate to lose you. However, I'll understand if you feel you have to distance yourself from any scandal this may cause.'

Isabella had a sudden horrifying thought.

If Giorgio has worked this out, how many others suspect?

As if reading her mind, Giorgio stood up and crossed the room. Taking her fingers in his, he led her towards the small settee and eased her petite frame into the leather upholstery.

Filling the rest of the sofa with his large, toned physique, Giorgio patted Isabella's shoulder, assuring her 'No-one else has even hinted that you might be pregnant. The fact that a stomach bug has been going around the set over the last few weeks would lead our colleagues to believe that you too have succumbed. However, as your friend, I have noticed other things. You're peaky, you've lost weight. As for the food cravings you appear to have, what can I say? Trust me Isabella if you're in trouble I'll help in any way I can.'

Bowing her head, Isabella covered her face for a few moments, taking deep breaths, before explaining the position she found herself in.

Recounting Alberto's reaction to her pregnancy in detail, she carefully omitted his inference that Giorgio could be the father and continued with Alfina's solution.

'She suggested I pay a man to marry me. This will save my baby from the torment of being illegitimate.'

'Did you agree?'

'I have no other choice.'

Isabella would have said more but looking up her words tailed off at seeing an angry frown deepening on Giorgio's fine-looking face. Mistaking it for disapproval, she began to defend her situation.

He raised a hand in protest. 'No more,' he pronounced firmly. 'I cannot listen. This is preposterous.'

Isabella felt shocked at his reaction. *I hoped he might be sympathetic; he is supposed to be my friend after all. Yet, he is a man and like many, he'll be inclined to put the blame on the woman, for allowing herself to get into this situation in the first place.*

'That fascist scoundrel,' Giorgio bellowed, 'How can he desert his beautiful woman at a time like this. To lay the blame on you is cowardly. He is responsible for siring his own child. Any man would be honoured to have you as his wife. Is he blind?'

'But we were together in that bed,' she wailed. 'I am to blame as well,' but, surprised by Giorgio's outburst in her defence, Isabella felt a wave of courage flow through her body. *Here is another good friend, defending my honour, repulsed by Alberto's behaviour, willing to help me in whatever way he can. I am blessed.*

Feeling stronger than she had in days, Isabella sat up straight and took both Giorgio's hands in her own. 'It is all in motion. In fact, I'm meeting Alfina's proposed contender tomorrow. He has already been paid to sign a non-disclosure agreement in case I decide he's not for me. My secret is safe, for now. However, I don't know how long I will be able to keep it that way.'

'Where are you seeing him?'

'I've booked a private room at La Grand Hotel in Rome. I believe he is an actor himself, not well known, still in the smaller productions. However, those acting skills will be improved as he helps to keep the charade going.'

'No doubt he sees this as a chance to get into the big league,' Giorgio spoke with ill-disguised displeasure. 'Not only will he be paid to bed the most beautiful woman on the big screen but as your husband, he will improve his chance of a career break.'

This time, Isabella put her hand up in protest. 'Who said anything about bedding me, that's not part of the agreement. We'll be married in name only.'

'Don't be naive Isabella. He will most certainly make advances on you and if he is attractive, you might find yourself embracing them. Think very carefully about all of this amica, you will be putting yourself in a vulnerable position.'

Am I imagining it, or is there a hint of jealousy in Giorgio's voice?

'I don't have any choice right now, Giorgio.' Isabella responded, shortly. 'The life of the child growing inside me is more important than fending off any future marital advances, welcome or otherwise. Though, surely that could be built into the contract.'

'I could come with you for security,' Giorgio suggested, 'Even if I wait in the lounge and see him walk through. I'm a good judge of character and could get the measure of this individual. Should I sense something untoward, I could advise you.'

Isabella smiled. 'My darling friend, you are so kind to offer but you know as well as I that you wouldn't be left alone. You're a handsome famous actor, adored by women who would be fawning over you; never mind the waiting staff attending to your every need, expressed or otherwise. You wouldn't have time to make any judgements of this recommended groom. In any case, Alfina will be with me.'

'You have a valid point. How I yearn to be anonymous again, even for a short time. Fame is so stifling.'

'I am just now beginning to suffer,' said Isabella. 'You have had many more years of it than me.'

Giorgio chuckled and said, 'At first we seek it then hate it. How lovely now to enjoy eating dinner in a restaurant; take a walk along the esplanade, for coffee or drinks with friends without being bombarded by fans.'

Rising to his feet, Giorgio leaned forward and kissed Isabella on the top of her head. 'Call me tomorrow after you have met this man and let me know your decision. I'll support whatever decision you make and be here as your friend and confidante, to help in any way I can.'

Looking up into the handsome face of her co-star Isabella replied, 'I feel very lucky to have you in my life Giorgio, thank you from the bottom of my heart.'

He started to leave.

She stopped him with a few sweet-voiced words. 'Please, just one more thing.'

He paused. 'Of course. Just ask.'

'It would mean a great deal to me if you would be godfather to my child. You display the kindness and wisdom I would have liked his father to possess and as my baby will never know his father, Alberto, or my temporary husband, you, my cherished friend, will be a constant in my little one's life. I know you will.'

Giorgio brushed a tear from his right eye and with a smile full of joy, bent to brush his lips against her fingers. 'What an absolute honour, my adorable Isabella, I would be delighted to accept that role. Thank you.'

Before closing the door, he turned to blow a light kiss, and she saw a smile across his face as bright as sunlight.

Isabella sat back at her dressing table. Slowly removing her makeup, she ruminated on their conversation with a sense of having become far closer to Giorgio than ever before.

Chapter 58

Isabella Feels Defeated

Replacing the telephone handset, Isabella turned to Giorgio and said, 'Everything is agreed. I just have to sign the papers and pay the money to the actor playing the part of my husband for the foreseeable future. He seems like a decent guy, and it won't be forever.'

She saw Giorgio frown. 'I note the sense of trepidation in your voice,' he said. 'It can't be easy, the prospect of marrying a complete stranger, even if he seems attractive and agreeable.'

'Have you found somewhere to live as a family?' he asked.

'Yes.' her beautiful dark eyes lit up her face. 'I'm buying a gorgeous villa in Bergamo, with an outdoor pool, manicured lawns, well maintained colourful flower beds and a spacious terrazze. We'll have to fence off the pool of course, to keep the little one safe.'

'I'm delighted for you Isabella, but have you told Leo yet? As the producer of this movie, he will need to be made aware of your condition so that he can reschedule your scenes before the pregnancy shows.'

'No, I haven't said anything yet,' Isabella tipped her head sideways, her smile replaced by a sheepish expression. 'I suppose I should, but in private as a secret.'

'Why?'

'I plan to announce our wedding at the big car Launch Day on the 14th of January. We'll have officially married secretly before that. We'll throw a big party the next day. I'll whisper to Leo about the wedding and my pregnancy a few days before. I just want to be sure the contract is all signed and sealed first. It shouldn't be a problem to reschedule the scenes.'

Isabella changed the subject: 'On a more exciting note, the dance troupe are all well-rehearsed for the big show on Sunday. We've been practising the routine vigorously. It should be an amazing display.'

'Are you sure you're up to it? Is it ok for the baby?'

'Absolutely, I've checked with my doctor and as I've been doing this consistently for years now, it won't be a shock to my system. I can't smoke or drink though, my body just can't seem to tolerate it. The nausea is much worse when I do.'

'Will you be able to get by without cigarettes and booze?'

'Never mind about me, Sweetie. More important is, are you prepared for your Launch Day role as compere? You'll bring the house down. The ladies will swoon over you right, left and centre, while the men drool over the cars,' giggled Isabella.

'No chance, my dear girl. The men will be drooling over *you* Signorina d'Bergamasco, the cars will be a mere distraction from your intriguing allure.'

Isabella went off into peals of laughter.

Giorgio smiled. 'It's good to hear you laugh. I've heard little of that lately.'

'That is because you are here and making me happy. I am sure every woman you meet feels the same.'

Giorgio shook his head. 'To this day I have no idea why women apparently see me as such a sex symbol. I'd be lying if I said I don't enjoy it, but that's my ego. Sometimes it's just a bit much. I yearn for a quiet life.

Even just a small amount of privacy would suffice from time to time.'

Isabella said, 'Be careful what you wish for. There are plenty of struggling actors who would kill to take your place. Ride high on the adulation. You'll be old and grey before you know it, reminiscing on these times with regret for not appreciating them.'

Sufficiently reproved, Giorgio requested 'Tell me about the cars. I've memorised the oration, detailing the interiors, horsepower etc as you drive out onto the stage, but tell me what makes the Town Car so special to *you*.'

Again, Isabella's eyes lit up, this time with her passion for Salvatore's beautifully built Town Car.

'This model is branded with my name. The word 'Isabella' will be seen all over Italy and Europe, on every city street and just seeing it passing by will deny this oppression and improve women's rights.'

'How?'

'By giving us freedom. Why are we not allowed to vote? Why were Italian women not allowed to drive until 1907? Why, even now, do our fathers, husbands, and older brothers frown upon or ban us from owning or driving motor vehicles? Can you tell me?'

'I am ashamed to say, I've never given it a thought,' replied Giorgio. 'You are making me feel awful.'

'It is right that you are ashamed. You are part of the worldwide conspiracy to keep women under the male thumb without even realising it. Salvatore's brilliance couldn't be better timed. Look at those brave English women literally and truly fighting male domination. We Italian women are supine in comparison.'

She watched Giorgio's life change in front of her eyes.

'By god, you're right,' he shouted, clapping his hands. 'You see this car as the first weapon in a silken revolution.'

'Yes,' Isabella shouted back. 'And the first of upcoming female liberation, Giorgio. How wonderful that my name and Salvatore's brilliant machine will lead the charge, allowing Italian ladies independence to travel by their own means in their own time and wherever they wish.'

Giorgio threw his arms round an ecstatic Isabella, and whispered, 'You, my sweet Isabella, along with your brother and your brilliant car will change the world and I am your first disciple.'

He pulled away and hurried towards the door.

'Where are you going?' she cried after him.

'To rewrite my Sunday script.'

Through her uncontrolled screams of laughter, Isabella heard a telephone bell.

Her house maid, Maria, entered and announced a call from her brother Salvatore. Taking the call, Isabella noted the serious tone of Salvatore's voice as he commanded, 'Isabella, please come to my home. There is something we need to discuss urgently. Be here as soon as you can.'

'I'm on my way,' she answered, a sense of dread rising from her gut at the way he spoke.

Returning to the room, Isabella apologised profusely, explaining what had happened. Giorgio took the coat Maria proffered and gently ushered Isabella out the front door towards her car. Opening the driver's door, he waited until she had seated comfortably before bending his tall frame to kiss her gently on each cheek. With an uncharacteristic tenderness, he instructed 'Drive carefully caro, there is nothing so urgent it is worth risking your personal safety for.'

Surprisingly, Salvatore himself opened the large oak front door before she could even press the bell. His wife, Gabriella, stood in the background, a look of bewilderment clouding her elfin features.

Without so much as a glance back at Gabriella, Salvatore ushered Isabella into his tastefully decorated living room. Expensive paintings hung on the wall with the commissioned centrepiece over the Bardiglio marble fireplace, depicting Mama and Papà in their finery. They looked solemn and regal, standing close together as if united in their disapproval, looking down upon this fallen woman.

'Take a seat Isabella, I have asked one of the maids to bring two brandies. I think you will need a drink when we have finished.'

'I can't stomach...' Isabella began to say, then stopped, grateful that her elder brother hadn't taken any notice.

'I'll come straight to the point, the family is heading for bankruptcy, both collectively as a company and personally in our own rights.'

Isabella couldn't stop the sigh of relief that escaped her lips. *Thank heaven this is nothing to do with my pregnancy.* However, Salvatore's expression of confusion required her to summon those acting skills once more as she blurted, 'I thought you were going to tell me that something serious had happened to one of our siblings.'

Salvatore snapped, 'Something serious *has* happened to your siblings, you silly woman. To you *and* to all of us. We are all likely to go broke. To lose everything; our business, our houses, our gilded life, all because of Giuseppe.'

Isabella swayed at the impact of his words.

'How has this transpired? Who is responsible? Do the rest of the family know?'

Salvatore growled through gritted teeth, 'Our idiot brother Giuseppe has lost our whole fortune by an act of extreme stupidity. You must say not a single word of what I am now going to tell you to anyone. Not even your brothers and sister.'

'But why me?' Isabella demanded. 'Why have you chosen me to bear a heavy secret?'

'Because, little sister, something has come to my attention through our concerned family doctor. I promise he has not, nor will not divulge your special heavy secret to anyone else. I've made sure of that.'

'You know.' Isabella bowed her head in shame.

'Yes, my beloved sister.'

Salvatore's voice softened.

'Why did you not come to me yourself with this news? I would have supported you. I gather that fascist scum has abandoned you.'

Tears spilled down Isabella's cheeks as, sobbing, she once more recounted Alberto's threats and inferences that her family would disown her.

'We'd never disown you little one, we are your flesh and blood, your famiglia. Italian families look after one another, through thick and thin. Never forget that.'

A knock on the door interrupted their conversation as a young, dark haired cameriera entered the room carrying a silver tray laid with two crystal cut glasses and matching decanter filled with brandy.

"Now let me pour you a glass, darling Isabella.' Salvatore requested kindly. 'This news will likely affect you even more than the rest of the family. I don't know what plans you have relating to your baby, but I feel you must be aware of how your financial position may change when considering your options.'

Feeling a wave of total defeat, Isabella accepted the glass of Vecchia Romagna and took a large gulp.

No matter if this makes me sick. I will be retching before the night's out. All my plans – my whole life, have gone up in smoke. God help me and the child growing inside my belly. What does the future hold for us now?'

Chapter 59

Salvatore's Kidnap

Monday 8th January 1923

'I have to rush to Naples tomorrow for a final meeting with Falcone, our architect,' Salvatore told his wife over Sunday dinner. 'I'll go down on the early train and be in Avellino for a two-hour discussion over lunch and back home by between eight and ten.'

'But darling, shouldn't you be here preparing your big Launch Day for the new cars? You'll only have five days left if you lose tomorrow.'

'It's an important meeting to discuss more buildings at the Salò factory and I spent the whole of today at the Atalanta Football stadium getting the launch preparations started. Everyone knows what to do and me missing one day won't make much difference.'

'But you'll be exhausted after such a rushed journey.'

'No. I'll sleep on the train both ways.'

'Oh, very well.'

He caught the high-speed express at six am and dozed until arrival at Naples shortly after eleven. Hopping down the train steps he looked for Falcone's driver.

Instead, a different man stepped from the crowd and said, 'Signore d'Bergamasco, I have been sent to collect you. I am sorry to say that the Falcone chauffeur is ill, so I am to drive you to Avellino.'

Hurrying to the car, Salvatore saw a familiar face passing nearby in the crowd – the woman he had spent a night with last year on his first visit to Avellino, and on his second visit when she sat in that restaurant watching him.

Beautifully dressed and wearing a fashionable white hat, she strolled by on the arm of a tall man. She did not look his way, thank god.

His driver opened the back door of a large motor car. Salvatore settled into the rear seat and asked, 'How did you recognise me?'

'Signore Falcone gave me a clear description.'

Salvatore leaned back and closed his eyes, trying not to think of the terrible financial situation Motori Bergamasco had fallen into.

My idiot brother had better get us out of it in the time left before going broke.

He closed his eyes, forced himself to relax and concentrate on the meeting with Falcone. A few kilometres after leaving Naples, the driver swerved hard across the road and skidded sharply into a petroleum selling garage.

Stamping on the brakes, he said, 'Sorry, Signore. Just noticed we need fuel.'

A young man came out and started to fill the tank. The driver sat silent, looking forward. Salvatore lay back on the soft rear seat cushions and, closed his eyes, to be startled after a few seconds by both rear doors being pulled abruptly open.

Two large men forced themselves in, squeezing hard against his shoulders, trapping him tight between them.

'Hullo Salvatore,' one said, in Italian with a foreign accent, 'We're riding with you the rest of the way.'

The other turned and grinned. 'I saw you at the station,' he said.

Salvatore recognised him as the tall fellow walking with the woman wearing a white hat.

That's how he knew me. That woman pointed me out

'Where are you taking me?'

'You won't see, old buddy,' said Foreign Accent, reaching out and pulling a black bag over Salvatore's head. 'Don't try and yank it off, or my friend Maximo will hurt you.'

'And what is your name?'

'Frank. I'm from the good old USA. Now we all know each other, we can relax.'

Salvatore cast his mind back and said, 'We've met before. I remember your voice. You gave me a history lesson on the train.'

'Correct. Our joint friend Falcone had the benefit of my wisdom too.'

'Is he part of your organisation?'

'No. Nor am I yet. But who knows? I soon may be.'

Maxim giggled.

Tucked in the black bag, Salvatore lost the feeling of time and distance, but after a while, felt the car slow down and turn right. He began to hear sounds indicating they had entered a town. 'Is this Avellino?' he asked.

Maxim slapped the side of his head. 'Shut up. No talking. No shouting unless you want to be seriously hurt.'

Salvatore gritted his teeth and wondered what would happen next.

The car slowed and stopped. Maxim dragged him out and up some steps. Salvatore stumbled and nearly fell twice. He heard doors open and close before being helped down rough stone steps into what, from the musty, dusty smell, he took to be a cellar.

Maxim snatched off the black bag and said, 'This is where you'll live until tomorrow.'

'Why am I here?'

'Somebody wants to talk with you.'

Salvatore looked around the grubby basement. In the little light filtering through narrow ground level windows, so dirty hardly any light came through, he saw a basic wooden chair and a small metal table.

'If I'm to be here until tomorrow, where do I sleep?'

'The chair, the table or the floor.'

'And where do I pee?'

Maxim pointed to a bucket in a corner.

'Don't worry it's quite private.'

He opened the door to leave.

'Hold on,' shouted Salvatore. 'What about food?'

'Bread and water. Think of it as being in jail.'

Maxim went off up the steps, chuckling to himself.

Chapter 60

Isabella Finds A Solution

Having sobbed and retched in turn, Isabella's ashen face reflected back at her from the bathroom mirror. Thank God for the small mercy that the movie set had been shut down due to numerous cast and crew succumbing to the wretched stomach bug. Memories of the enormous loss of life from the Spanish Flu were fresh in the minds of Italians and Europeans in general. No-one wanted to take any chances.

Miraculously most of the dance crew had been spared, sufficient numbers well enough to continue to rehearse their spectacular launch sequence. Isabella should have been at the Atalanta stadium today, leading the cast in practice for the 14th of January launch day. However, circumstances would not permit. Ironically because of her present situation, the show could become the ultimate performance of her career, the finale so to speak.

Who would want me now? I'm hardly a role model. A penniless unwed mother. My image will be tainted forever.

Survival mode suddenly burst through, swiping self-pity aside.

It hasn't happened yet. I may be unwed but there's still a small chance I won't be penniless. None of it matters as far as continuing with my pregnancy is concerned. I will keep the baby, whether I lose all of my money or not. I'll find a way.

Alfina had been an absolute rock. A marriage contract could not go ahead without guaranteed funds to complete the pact down the line. However, the potential groom had been paid for his silence, though not told why the planned wedding would not proceed. He would wonder what may have done wrong. Had Signorina d'Bergamasco lost the baby? This could have been the biggest break of his acting career.

Isabella had refused Giorgio's calls, feigning a full calendar. He would detect the negative emotion in her voice if they had a conversation. She had to work this out herself. However, it had proved impossible to refuse a call from her sister this morning. Her maid had communicated that Signorina Novella was quite insistent that it was a matter of urgency. Isabella's recollection of the call was hazy. She had been sick so much since.

Didn't Novella say something about Salvatore being missing? I thought I'm supposed to be the dramatic one. He's likely to have turned up by now, hopefully with a solution to our financial problems.

Isabella suddenly remembered Novella's suggestion that the family come around to her home that evening, if Salvatore hadn't turned up by then. Simultaneously, the Viennese Rococo style longcase grandfather clock that she had been gifted by Leonardo Rinaldi chimed and glancing in its direction Isabella noted the time as 12 noon.

I should freshen myself up in case they get here early, in the unlikely event that Salvatore hasn't arrived home. However, I really need to lie down for a little while.

No sooner had Isabella's head touched the soft pillows arranged neatly on her bed than the doorbell rang. Just as she reached for the bell to summon Maria and advise that she would not be receiving any visitors, the sound of a knock on the bedroom door halted her.

Quietly Isabella instructed *'Come in.'*

The door opened slowly and there, filling the walnut frame, stood Giorgio, a concerned expression reconstructing his handsome features.

'Why haven't you been at rehearsals Isabella?' he demanded, softening his tone when he saw her state of disarray. 'What is wrong? You never miss rehearsals.'

Isabella stayed silent, searching for words to conceal her dilemma. However, her dishevelled appearance, sunken eyes and tear-stained face would have belied any feasible explanation and Giorgio picked up on it straight away.

'Have you lost the baby?' he asked carefully.

'No. But my circumstances have changed dramatically since we last spoke. I am not in a financial position to go ahead with the contract of marriage to that actor. I may shortly be bankrupt and by the time I know for sure, it will be too late to proceed.'

'But how will you be bankrupt? What's happened?'

'A situation arose that means I can't ask that young man to hang around on the off chance that I *may* have the money, and if I confide that bankruptcy is a serious possibility, before it's confirmed, the news will get out and destroy the launch and any chance of the company selling cars.

'My dear Isabella, you are surely independently wealthy. Your family is rich, you share in a prosperous business. Have you perhaps made some bad investments?'

Wearily Isabella gazed at him and begged 'Please don't ask. You know me so well; you would prise it out of me.'

'But darling, if you don't tell me, how can I advise?'

'Suffice it to say I am not at liberty to discuss *anything* at the moment. The only possible positive outcome to this would be that I am not a penniless unwed mother. I *will* be a mother because I am *not* aborting my baby. I will lose my career before doing that.'

'I sympathise for you in this situation and feel immense admiration at your strength of will. But please allow me to assist in some way,' Giorgio said.

'It is impossible for you to help.'

'Beneath your beauty lies such a tenacious character, Isabella, I can see you are both physically and mentally drained. Yet, your resilience is unquestionable, you are a warrior. You will always find a way to fight on. Your baby will be protected as long as you are on this earth. I have no doubt about that.'

'Fine words mean nothing Giorgio.'

'Darling Isabella. My truest friend. There is an answer to all of this, and it is staring you in the face.

'Why don't I see it?'

'Because sweet woman, you are in despair. It is simple. I will marry you. I would be honoured to do so. I'll respect every condition you place upon the marriage, even signing a contract. No money will exchange hands and I will be there to support the little one for as long as you need me, treating the child as my own, if you will permit that of course.

Through the tears that had welled up in Isabella's eyes, she saw the pleading look on Giorgio's face; the sincerity of a close friend who wants to make everything better for her.

How can I expect him to do this? It would bind him to me for at least eighteen months when he could be having a love life of his own. Yet, it is certainly the answer to my problem and a far better prospect than marrying a stranger. It would be believable. We could romanticise the union with a story of us having fallen in love while making our first movie together. In fact, it would play like a real movie itself

'Giorgio, think very carefully. If you think of your privacy as invaded before, our marriage will make it twice as bad. We will be seen as Italy's golden couple and, amazing as that sounds, we can expect a huge amount of pressure. I don't have any choice in this matter, but for *you* to shoulder the responsibility of taking us on as husband and father would be a huge sacrifice. To make this look authentic, you would be confined to family life when you are not on set.'

Giorgio grinned, his blue eyes alight with mischief. 'I couldn't think of a better way to live my life over the next 18 months. I'll get to spend my free time in the company of my beautiful friend, eating superb food, and drinking the best possible wine together in our home. We'll sleep in separate rooms and make your bed look like it's been tossed by rampant sex, to convince the staff of our authenticity. The baby will be loved by us as true parents and when the time comes for us to divorce, I will remain in your lives as godfather so the little one will never suffer the loss of a parental figure who has been there since day one.'

Filled with hope Isabella gasped as the picture he painted filled her with hope and joy. This really might be the answer to their problems.

'When you first mentioned you were going to pay someone to save you, I wanted to offer there and then, at that very moment, but thought I would be overstepping the mark. Please tell me I haven't overstepped it now. My idea just makes perfect sense.'

Isabella gasped as the picture he painted filled her with hope and joy. This really *is* the answer to their problems.

'No, my dear Giorgio, you haven't overstepped the mark at all. It is a wonderful solution. I couldn't be happier. '

For the next two hours, the happy couple made plans to find time to purchase an engagement ring. 'A big rock,' Giorgio insisted. If we are doing this it has to be done right. I can afford it.'

Isabella threw her head back and laughed loudly, she saw the sound delighted Giorgio. He wanted all to be well in his beautiful friend's world.

'Only if you allow me to reimburse you when I am back on my feet financially.'

Waving one hand through the air in a dismissive gesture, Giorgio excitedly suggested 'Let's prepare for the wedding as soon as possible. We could announce our engagement at the Launch, as originally planned, feigning having been secretly engaged for the previous two months. We could even fool our great producer, Leo. He would be very proud of our performance if he knew we were acting. We could have a lavish reception, whether or not you are bankrupt, leaving a honeymoon until after the movie has finished. I could purchase the villa in my name, so that it could be protected from any possible bankruptcy proceedings against you.'

Isabella gave a huge sigh, releasing all of her pent-up emotion, then smiled widely at Giorgio.

'Well, my darling, aren't you going to go down on one knee?' she teased in exaggerated tones.

'When I have the ring, I will do just that,' Giorgio grinned jubilantly. 'I must go and find one suitable for a screen goddess. It will be our finest scene.'

Isabella giggled in response, giddy with the joy of the moment.

With dusk setting in Giorgio left. As the door closed behind him, more sober thoughts squeezed into Isabella's mind pushing joy to the side. *Salvatore, has he returned? Please Lord let him be safe.*

Chapter 61

Giuseppe Tries To Find Money

Monday 8th January 1923

Giuseppe went early to his office on Monday, determined to do all he could to rectify the financial disaster of his own making.

Why the hell did I start sleeping with his wife? She's not that good a lover. It must have been the excitement of having a secret affair, you idiot.

He groaned, head in hands, considering the available options now that her bastard bank manager husband had cut all finance from his own bank and backlisted Motori Bergamasco with every other bank in Italy.

His brain whirling in despair, heart thumping, Giuseppe knew that everything the family owned would be gone. *We'll be destitute, but I can't tell anyone yet. Especially the family.*

Salvatore had suggested Medici Bank despite always saying the company would never use their Mafia money, so Giuseppe made a reluctant call. Luciano Buracci, junior manager, took fewer than five minutes to leave Giuseppe despondent with all hope gone.

'Your business plan is fine. But the enterprise is too huge a risk. Ring me back in a couple of months,' said Buracci.

Giuseppe lit a cigarette. He knew the man socially and always chatted happily. But this conversation he found different. *Buracci is normally unflappable, but he seemed jumpy this time. Surely, the Medici would not listen to D'Innella. No. They must already know we're blacklisted, word of our loss of one bank, followed by an official central bank kills us dead.*

After managing to concentrate on chairing an accounts department meeting, he rang an old university friend, Alfredo Macari in London who, after exchanging pleasantries, confirmed he would not invest.

'However, Giuseppe, I'll pass on your details to a friend, Reggie Mortimer. He's the owner of Belgravia Garages, he might be interested in attending your Launch Day. I'll send him a telegraph message.'

Stubbing out his cigarette, he continued his telephone calls to those around Europe he hoped might offer financial backing. No one did. At nine thirty Monday evening he returned home, crushed by his burden of worry.

Chapter 62

Salvatore and the Don

Tuesday 9th January 2023

Salvatore had a bad night, sleeping on the grimy stone floor. He tried rolling his jacket into a pillow, but a mixture of foul-smelling dried mud and the uneven flagstones digging into his buttocks and shoulders, robbed him of rest and sleep.

Near dawn the door opened, and someone pushed a plate of inedible stale bread and a bottle of water through. He spat his first mouthful of bread out and threw the plate at the door. Extreme thirst forced him to sip some water and for a while he felt better.

In the middle of the morning the door flew open, and Maxim burst in.

'Come on,' he snarled, grabbing Salvatore's arm. 'Bring your coat and come with me. Time for your chat with our Capo.'

Dragged up the stairs, along a corridor and pushed into a beautifully furnished room, Salvatore saw a heavy man rising from a sofa, apparently to greet him. Frank sat on a deep armchair alongside but did not move, apart from a grin and a flicker of his fingers in greeting.

Maxim closed and stood by the door; hands clasped.

'Good morning, Signore d'Bergamasco,' said the Don. 'I don't think we have met before.'

'And I hope we never meet again,' snapped Salvatore, watching the man's hard face and harder eyes look him up and down, studying his wrinkled, dusty state of dress.

'Normally I would shake your hand, but perhaps this time I shall forgo the pleasure,' said the Don.

He flicked a finger at Maxim, who hurried out and back with a fresh sheet that he threw over an armchair opposite Frank.

'Apologies, but I can't allow you to ruin the furniture. Please sit down. I shall introduce myself.'

Salvatore sat, relishing the comfort, but glaring at the man across an expensive coffee table.

'I know who you are and want nothing to do with you except to let me go.'

'That may be possible if you cooperate, but first let me tell you that I am the Capo, the Don, of the Campania Ndrangheta, also known as the Mafia. Our tentacles reach far, and we have influence also throughout northern Italy.'

'All very high sounding, but you are still a simple criminal.'

The Don, with a quite charming smile, said, 'Shall I call some breakfast for you?'

'I've already eaten, thank you. Stale bread and water. Perfectly acceptable.'

Frank dipped a sly wink across the table.

The Don frowned. 'This is a serious meeting between two successful businessmen. My organisation is an interested investor in new and upcoming companies such as yours. We wish to become a fifty per cent shareholder.'

'Impossible. We are a family company. Our constitution does not permit outside investors.'

The Don completely ignored Salvatore and continued, 'Your new range of motor vehicles now advertised and promoted all over our beautiful country has caught our attention and we want to help you with finance from our considerable resources. We think your new vehicles will be very successful.'

'We need no finance.'

'Our banks tell us differently.'

'Would you accept us as an investor rather than a shareholder?'

'No.'

The Don's face and voice, hardened. 'You have no choice.'

Salvatore glared into those cold, angry eyes in silence.

'So, are we going to negotiate?'

'No.'

The Don pulled a medium sized Beretta pistol from the coffee table drawer and pressed it against the middle of Salvatore's forehead just above the eyebrows.

'One more chance. Are you going to negotiate?'

'If you are going to shoot me, get on with it.'

Salvatore saw the Don freeze.

Neither face, gun nor trigger finger moved.

After about five seconds he pulled the pistol away and handed it to Frank, saying, 'This man is too brave for me to shoot. I don't want to be the one to kill him. You do it after I've gone.'

Chapter 63

Frank Takes Salvatore North

Tuesday 9th January 1923

Frank stood by a window and watched The Don drive away.

He returned to his armchair and examined the pistol.

'Hey, it's a real beauty,' he said. 'Small but takes a 9ml slug. Designed to knock anyone over.'

He turned it towards toward Maxim and speaking as though Salvatore didn't exist, said, 'Do you want to shoot him or shall I?'

'We can't do it in here, not even in the cellar. We'll drive into the mountains and shoot him among the trees. I'll do it.'

'Fine. Let's go.'

With Maxim driving and Salvatore in the back seat tied by his wrists to Frank, they went high into the forest.

'This rope is very rough and hurting,' Salvatore told Frank. 'Can you loosen or untie it please?'

'And have you jumping out, buddy? Don't worry, it'll soon all be over.'

Maxim pulled the car into a clearing and took a large heavy calibre pistol from the glove compartment.

'Get him out and fifty metres into the woods and tie him to a tree. It'll be years before he's found.'

Frank said, 'Wait Maxim. I've had an idea for us to make a bunch of money out of this guy. We'll tell the Don we did for him, but instead we'll go north and ransom him for a million dollars to his family. They've got plenty. It'll be like asking for something from the petty cash tin.'

'No. The Don will find out. We'll both be executed.'

He dragged Salvatore roughly by his bound wrists into the treeline for about a hundred metres, undid the rope and wound it round the trunk of the slimmest tree he could find.

He stepped back a few metres and cocked his pistol. Before he could aim, Frank stepped in his line of fire.

'Listen Maxim, you bozo, we'll split the million. When in your life will you ever have half a million bucks? You're a foot soldier, for Christ's sake. You'll never be anything else. Are you ever going to be a Capo? No. Nor am I. Let's take the five hundred grand and scoot. We'll disappear. They'll never know where to.'

Frank watched Maxim frown, grappling with a new and complex idea and could almost hear the wheel of his mind grinding around, when Salvatore said, 'You're right. Take me home and I'll pay you a million in American dollars to let me go.'

Frank stepped forward and took Maxim's gun.

'Come on. Let's go north.'

Following Maxim through the woods back to the car, Frank mumbled into Salvatore's ear,

'Not really how kidnaps work. We need to demand a ransom from your distraught family, not just receive an inflated taxi fare for dropping you home.'

'If you want them to worry, don't bother. They know I can fend for myself.'

'You really are a stubborn mother, aren't you?' Frank shook his head, 'I need them to understand how the handover will work – to everyone's advantage.'

He nodded towards the back of Maxim's head weaving through the trees in front of them, 'Perhaps not quite everyone.'

Their eyes met. Frank saw Salvatore struggling to comprehend.

'We have a long journey ahead of us,' Frank tried to explain. 'Plenty of time to get to know each other.'

'Not sure I want to.'

Frank smiled and called, 'Maxim; you drive. I'll keep Salvatore company in the back.'

Salvatore stooped to climb in. 'I didn't trust you when we first met. The feedback I got from Anton following your brief encounter has only endorsed my first impressions.'

Frank chuckled and said, 'Hold your wrists out so I can tie us together. We don't want you jumping out at the first opportunity.'

The engine kicked into life. 'Keep to the back roads, Maxim,' Frank instructed, 'The carabinieri may be already patrolling the main highways looking for us.'

Climbing higher on the narrow mountain road, Frank felt the temperature dropping, and he watched a light fog begin to form.

To Salvatore he said, 'I know that you and your brothers distinguished yourselves in the Alpine Battalions during the war.'

Salvatore turned, surprise on his face. 'How do you know?'

Frank now had Salvatore's full attention.

'Something we never talk about. I also volunteered. But through connections, I avoided the front; served in Military Intelligence. By its very nature everything I did needed to be covert. No written records. Even so, my contribution to our mutual victory was no less valid.'

'Your point?' asked Salvatore curtly.

'A vow of silence whether taken by choice or coercion can still conceal both good and evil.'

Light rain began to fall, and visibility dropped, making road conditions treacherous.

There followed a long period of strained silence as they drove through what appeared to be an opaque tunnel of low cloud. The tarmac surface disappeared to be replaced by little more than a rutted dirt mountain track with no habitation; just the occasional glimpse of trees lining the route.

Frank let slip his facade of absolute confidence. 'At the next town, Maxim, find the post office so we can use their telephone. We need to alert the family to the situation.'

'Why not by telegraph?'

'No. We can't leave a paper trail. I will call.'

'Better I do,' said Maxim, being uncharacteristically assertive, 'Your Italian's crap, and your accent a give-away.'

Frank saw that, like many mountain villages, Isernia still reflected the layout of an ancient Roman town, with its wide central thoroughfare and side streets at right angles. Driving down the main street in the gathering dusk of early evening, Maxim said, 'We've arrived at the right time, with the bars and restaurants already starting to fill up. The telegraph and postal office will be relatively quiet.'

He rolled to a stop alongside the small ufficio postale and began to get out.

Speaking to Maxim, Frank made sure Salvatore felt the Beretta pistol pressed against his ribs.

Frank produced a slip of paper from his pocket and handed it to Maxim, 'Call this factory private line Salvatore just gave me. Giuseppe will answer. Keep it brief. Tell him we want one million American dollars, in cash, available in twenty-four hours. We'll call again with details of the handover. Then hang up. Don't take any questions; just shut up and leave.'

Maxim slammed the car door behind him, clearly annoyed at being expected to take orders from a foreigner. He entered the building, booked a call, and entered the booth nearest the external window. Frank saw him pick up the speaker horn from the wall mounted apparatus.

Frank relaxed his grip and murmured, 'I'm not going to shoot you; no matter what. Even if you make a dash for it. But be careful of that bastard Maxim. He would pop you instantly, even in broad daylight, in a crowded street. And everyone would all swear blind they saw nothing.'

Chapter 64

Giuseppe Receives Bad News

Tuesday 9th January 1923

Giuseppe arrived at his desk before dawn Tuesday morning and worked until noon sending telegraphs to prospective investors but without success. It seemed that the whole world of banking, including India and Turkey, knew of or had heard whispers about a continent-wide blacklist of his company.

He carried on until early evening when Salvatore's wife Gabriella called to say, 'My husband should have returned from Avellino by ten last night, but he hasn't turned up. Do you know where he may be?'

'Haven't heard anything. Possibly he became caught up in a late dinner with Falcone or had more to talk about and missed the train. I'll call Avellino and check.'

'And I'll try the family to see if he stayed the night to avoid disturbing me' said Gabriella.'

Falcone sounded guarded. 'He never arrived. I assumed he'd cancelled and forgotten to tell me because of your big day on Sunday.'

'Do you have any idea where he might be?'

After a slight pause, Falcone, said 'None. He didn't come here. I can tell you nothing,' and cut the call.

Almost instantly Giuseppe's private line began to buzz. His whole body twitched in alarm and excitement. Only he and Salvatore knew this number: *Why am I alarmed. Is it Salvatore? But it can't be. He's disappeared.'*

He froze at the sound of a harsh voice spitting out incredible demands.

'Don't question us d'Bergamasco. A million dollars, American. Ready in twenty-four hours. Do it. Or he dies. We'll call tomorrow.'

Taking a deep, nervous breath he snapped, 'Anyone of common sense would know it can take days to get that amount of money, for god's sake.'

The caller switched off.

Giuseppe stared at the silent telephone, shaking in his hand., trying to work out what had just happened, and what to do.

He struggled to light a cigarette and process in his mind what had been told.

He rang Colonello Pancucci who listened without comment, before saying, 'I'll come straight away. Is anyone with you?'

'No. I'm alone in my office.'

'Lock the door until I arrive.'

Pancucci walked in with a young policeman he introduced as, 'Detective Genaro Puglia.' Both were dressed in plain clothes.

He sat down and said, 'Tell me all you know.'

'Not much,' said Giuseppe, and told them about Salvatore's quick trip to Avellino and his disappearance.

'Falcone is your architect?'

'Yes.'

'Does he usually meet your brother from the train?'

'Yes.'

'This time he didn't.'

'How do you know?'

'Our Napoli colleagues both uniformed and plain clothes, keep a continual close watch on the Stazioni Centrale. Your brother entered an automobile with Napoli registration that never reached Avellino. That must be how the kidnap occurred.'

He looked at Puglia, who nodded. 'All taken as a statement,' he said, and handed the paper to Giuseppe to sign.

Pancucci said, 'I'll call in the morning, by then I may have more information. Tell your co-directors nothing of this incident until I have explained. No hint must get out. You act as normally as possible except to tell them they must not speak or make any noise about Salvatore not returning from Avellino if the subject is raised.'

When Pancucci and Puglia left, Giuseppe felt comforted by their calm and professional manner, wondering, *How the hell did they discover the kidnap car so quickly?*

Chapter 65

Frank's Safe House

Evening: Tuesday 9th January 1923

Frank watched Maxim hurry from the post office to the rear door of the car, holding the key ring in his outstretched hand.

'You'll need these to unlock the steering wheel,' he said.

'You want me to drive?'

'Do you know how?'

'Of course.'

Frank slowly eased out of the car, took the key, and moved to the driver's door. Maxim squeezed into the back seat alongside Salvatore, his larger calibre gun clearly evident.

The already strained atmosphere became worse, as they drove from the town into the bleak forest darkness in total silence for half an hour before Frank said, 'We can't drive all night. For one thing we'll need petroleum.'

'There's a full can in the rear,' said Maxim, quick to shut down Frank's concerns.

'There's a filling station at L'Aquila,' said Frank 'I've driven this route before.'

Maxim became agitated. 'Then we should change course now. The Don may have people following us already. If we stop, they'll catch us.'

'Seriously? I've had enough of your paranoia, 'You really think that is even remotely possible?'

Frank caught Maxim's genuine concern in the rear-view mirror. He may be getting jittery enough to just shoot Salvatore and to hell with the ransom. 'We're all tired. We need a break. There's a safe house in San Cipriano; we can be there in less than 30 minutes.'

'Whose safe house?'

Maxim's voice rose several levels of fear soaring close to a squeak, 'Family?'

'Mine.' This put an instant stop to the overt conversation, but he guessed, Maxim's inner fright remained.

Frank allowed time for the man to settle before explaining, 'During the war the British set up a Casualty Evacuation Chain that stretched from the Venetian plains through Genoa to Marseilles, a great idea if the Italians could hold the northern frontline. Me being a belt and braces kind of guy, I set up my own safe house Chain that went south, reaching the ports of Bari on the East and Naples on the west, and safe passage to wherever the war couldn't reach.'

'Is that registered anywhere in the military archives?' asked Salvatore.

'Certainly not.'

Maxim still showed unease when Frank pulled up at a small timber house in a secluded copse just outside the village of San Cipriano. Frank opened the unlocked door, saying 'Follow me. It's safe on the inside.'

He breezed into the hallway, flicking on the lights, revealing the key inserted in the lock, which he employed to great effect as soon as the others were in.

The place looked immaculate, with the beds made and the kitchen well stocked as though the maid had left only minutes before.

'I pay a woman from the village to ensure that the place is ready for me at any time.'

This unsettled Maxim again. 'How safe is that?'

Frank stared into his face, cold, hard, determined, 'What's the penalty for crossing the Don?'

He needed to say no more.

'Come,' he said to Salvatore, his hands now tied behind his back.

Salvatore followed Frank as he paced the panelled hallway, stopping and reaching behind a perfect replica of Ruben's painting, 'Daniel in the Lion's Den.'

He smiled at the barely audible click when a door swung open. Frank stood aside and gestured for Salvatore to enter. 'The cellar. Please.'

Like the rest of the house this subterranean, windowless room, furnished in style with its own en-suite facilities and small kitchen fully stocked with provisions, whilst also being totally impenetrable.

Wednesday 10th January 1923

Maxim insisted on accompanying Frank when he drove into L'Aquila, confident Salvatore couldn't possibly escape from his Lion's Den. Frank kept his own demeanour deliberately contrived to deepen the man's suspicions and question what they were attempting to do.

Maxim paused before following Frank into the postal office, 'We could just leave him there.'

'To die?', Frank barely skipped a beat, 'You callous bastard.'

'Your maid would find him.'

'How would you explain to the Don that the man you were ordered to kill in Avellino, is found dead on the streets of a remote village in central Italy?'

Frank didn't wait for a response. He disappeared into the post and telecommunications building.

Maxim hurried in to be beside him. Frank picked up the speaker horn and thrust it into his hand.

Raising it to his ear, Maxim rebuilt his courage enough to speak when a harsh, unexpectedly aggressive voice, loud enough for them both to hear, bellowed, 'We need proof that Salvatore is alive before parting with one American cent. Give me that proof – *then* we can negotiate.'

Maxim turned, gesturing, and mouthing to Frank, 'They want to know he's alive. What now?'

Without missing a beat Frank grabbed the speaker horn and snapped, 'Of course. 7pm tomorrow.'

He hung up.

Chapter 66

Frank Sets Up The Handover

Evening: Wednesday 10th January 1923

Frank noted that the house seemed still deathly quiet when he and Maxim returned.

'Another twenty-four hours stuck in here – why so long?' Maxim queried, 'We could just give them the proof Salvatore's still alive now.'

'We could,' said Frank remaining surprisingly calm, and annoyingly unperturbed. 'They would still need time to gather that amount of cash without raising suspicions. A bit here, a bit there. No-one would connect the dots until we're long gone.'

He saw his reply only served to gnaw further at Maxim's raw nerves, 'The longer we stay here, the more likely we are to be discovered.'

'More so, on the open road,' Frank attempted to allay Maxim's fears. 'As long as the door is locked, the maid won't attempt to enter.'

'But she will know we're here.'

'Someone's here.' Frank snapped. 'She won't ever ask or tell who. Now, get pissed while I check on Salvatore.'

He appeared not to have moved since Frank last saw him, with no overt signs that Salvatore had made any attempt to escape. Which would have been futile anyway.

'You need anything?'

'Apart from the obvious?'

Frank took a seat.

For what seemed an eternity neither man spoke. They stared at each other in silence as though trying to connect by telepathy; to get into each other's head; to discover how they ticked, whether in time or completely out of synch. In those few minutes of calm, Frank felt a curious bond building between them and wondered if Salvatore felt the same.

Frank finally broke the almost companionable stillness by asking, 'What did your father do during the War?'

'How is that in any way relevant?'

'Just curious. My father: my adoptive American father, not my biological father, continued to make money out of the situation.'

He saw Salvatore think for a moment before giving anything away. 'With Bergamo probably the closest safe haven before the battle lines, he had a contract to service military vehicles.'

'The same then.'

Salvatore almost smiled, managed to hold his face stiff. 'And your biological father?'

Frank shrugged, 'Probably the same too, I just never knew him.'

'Your mother spoke about him?'

'Not so much with my adoptive father still alive; but, getting older she had this desire that I should know him, seek him out, let him know that she never stopped loving him. Too late now. That's somehow sad for both of us.'

'So, you know who he is? Or was?'

Frank looked him in the eye and nodded.

Thursday 11th January 1923

Frank led Maxim and Salvatore from the safe house shortly before six p.m. on Thursday; almost forty-eight hours since Salvatore's confrontation with his captor.

He could see Maxim on the verge of a breakdown, almost certainly making him even more unstable and unpredictable, a thought confirmed by Maxim saying in a quivering voice, 'If I don't report to the Don soon, he'll know something's up; he'll send someone after me.'

Frank made a point of double locking the front door and slipping the key in his pocket, before gesturing Maxim to get into the driver's seat and Salvatore to the rear.

Only when they were seated and the motor was running did Maxim and Frank exchange eye contact in the mirror, 'The Don is not the Capo di Capo, Maxim, not the Head. There is always someone higher. Now, just drive.'

Giuseppe would by now have been waiting for the call for almost an hour when they arrived outside the postal office in L'Aquila.

He would have to wait a while longer.

Maxim had the door open ready to alight when Frank clamped a firm hand on his shoulder. Speaking softly but sure that Salvatore could hear, he said, 'Before we make the call, you must contact the civic cemetery in Cremona. Here's the information you need to give them,' he slipped Maxim a piece of folded paper. 'It is important that they follow these instructions precisely. This is where the switch will be made.'

Whilst he listened, Maxim unfolded the paper and read. Before leaving, he looked at Salvatore as if it might be for the last time.

With Maxim out of earshot Frank turned to Salvatore, 'We have one chance to be free of the Don.'

He spoke with an earnest tone in his voice to prevent Salvatore from even considering a bid for freedom. 'You've seen how Maxim lives in permanent fear. For now, it is important that the Don believes he acted totally on his own, no accomplices, no superior orders, just driven by greed. And that, will do for him.'

Maxim stood stiff and still in the phone booth waiting for the call to the family to be answered. Frank and Salvatore squeezed in beside him.

Frank looked at his watch before taking up the speaker horn.

Chapter 67

Giuseppe Brings In The Police

Thursday 11th January 1923

Giuseppe waited in the reception hall. When Pancucci and Puglia arrived in full uniform, he led them to his office and pointed at three chairs. 'Those two are for you. I'll sit on your right by the telephone apparatus we will be using. It is the private number they called me on. Salvatore will have given it to them.'

He pointed to the upright telephone.

Puglia glanced around the room and moved swiftly to collect the paper and pencils, leaving the tabletop bare.

'No notes must be taken,' said Pancucci. 'Inspector Puglia will keep an official record of every spoken word and prepare it as an official document.'

Puglia moved to the telephone. From his bag he produced a small conical speaker, attached one end to an ear trumpet and the other he strapped to the telephone earpiece and lay them with care on the desk, facing Giuseppe, saying, 'The line is now open. Whoever calls this number will be immediately connected. Please call now from your normal apparatus, and say something,' he instructed Giuseppe, whose voice came out quiet and tinny, but clear.

Puglia gave Pancucci a thumbs up.

At six o'clock the family filed silently in.

Pancucci stood. 'We have reason to believe your brother Salvatore is being held by the Southern Italy Mafia for ransom. We are in contact with them and this evening awaiting a call agreeing where we meet to exchange the money. We do not intend to pay for your brother's release. We plan to rescue him when we know their handover point. I have called you here to listen to where they tell us. It is essential you remain completely silent when we speak with them, and equally essential, say nothing to each other or to anyone else after their contact this evening. The captors have a network of informers everywhere and the slightest hint, even to wives or husbands, may allow the news out. If this happens, your brother will die and be buried without trace, never to be found.'

Giuseppe felt his face freeze in shock and saw his two sisters throw hands over their mouths to suppress horrified gasps.

Pancucci said, 'We now wait in complete silence for their call to prove they have your brother, and he is alive.'

At six minutes past seven, the phone buzzed. Giuseppe took a deep breath, placed his lips close to the table and spoke into the earpiece.

'Where's Salvatore?' he asked.

'He's here,' a slightly, garbled voice replied.

'Salvatore?'

'Giuseppe? It's me. I can hardly hear you. Anyone else with you?'

'They're all here. The whole family. You alright? Are you hurt? Injured?'

'I'm fine.'

The voice not so garbled this time came through snapping an obvious instruction to Giuseppe, 'No conversation. Just deliver the message.'

'Midday tomorrow beside our fallen comrades in Cremona.'

The line went dead.

Pancucci said, 'Good. Now we can set up our ambush in the Cremona cemetery.'

Anton, pointing at the telephone, called, 'I think I know that voice.'

Giuseppe said, 'How? The kidnapper disguised it.'

'Not properly the second time. I've heard it before, but I can't remember where.'

'If you do, let me know. Puglia and I, with Signore Giuseppe, are now going to Cremona for tomorrow's midday appointment. to deliver the ransom.'

Chapter 68

The Handover

3am: Friday 12th January 1923

At dead of night, Frank ushered Maxim and Salvatore from the safe house and hung back long enough to insert the key into the internal lock, before slamming the door behind him. Taking the rear seat alongside Salvatore and securing his hands, he could sense Maxim's unhappy mood.

Maxim shook his head, 'We should have left yesterday; not now.'

'We have a seven, maybe eight-hour exhausting drive.'

'Six, if you stop bitching,' Frank snapped.

Maxim glared at him in the rear-view mirror. 'You can do your stint too.'

'Sure. The final leg.' Frank settled down for a snooze.

The sunrise woke him shortly after 7:30. He could see that Salvatore hadn't slept. Frank studied his rock-solid countenance. *This man is not easily rattled.*

Frank understood from the last few days together that Salvatore could clearly control himself and almost certainly those around him.

He tapped Salvatore's leg to gain his attention and asked, 'Are you aware of the law of primogeniture?'

Salvatore turned his head to Frank, 'It's not a law, it's more an honoured tradition among monarchies.'

Frank agreed with a slight nod of the head. 'Still observed in most Italian families. The eldest son inherits the greater proportion.'

'Our father entrusted me with running the business well before he passed.'

'And Giuseppe, your older brother, he is happy with that?'

'Happy or not, that was papà's last Will.'

'Of course. And there may have been a precedent.'

'How could there be? Papà was an only child.'

'You know that for sure?'

'He fled Avellino at a time of turmoil, and never returned.'

'Fled, implies running from something or someone.'

Frank, trying to gauge how far he could push Salvatore to evoke a defensive reaction, chose to pause the evolving unsettling conversation.

At mid-morning Frank returned to the subject. 'You trust Giuseppe to get the money?'

Salvatore ignored the question.

'With you out of the way, he would be boss.'

Salvatore said nothing.

The car juddered to a halt. Maxim swung round to confront Frank, 'Your turn.'

No-one spoke during the remainder of the journey. With Frank still behind the wheel, they turned off the busier main road onto the almost deserted Via Cimitero leading to the Civic Cemetery. He drove slowly around the perimeter, shooting his eyes left and right to scan every side street.

Frank could sense that Maxim felt also very alive to every slightest movement. A cat darting across the street. A lone person hurrying into their house. A group of school children skipping alongside the rail tracks towards the main station, laughing and chiding each other. All the while with his pistol pushed into Salvatore's body.

On their third circumnavigation, satisfied that there were no police or military vehicles parked nearby, Frank drove into the cemetery, heading for the Commonwealth Graves.

Frank detected Maxim nervous and shaking, no doubt thinking the area too quiet. There were a few mourners dotted around, tending graves, replacing floral tributes. Despite a small number of ornate mausoleums, there were very few places that could conceal an armed reception committee.

Frank parked, stuffed his beretta beneath the seat and stepped out in silence. His eyes trained to detect the slightest abnormality, he opened the rear door, grabbed Salvatore's arm, and guided him out.

Maxim, his gun openly on display and still shaking, followed them through the regimental lines of British war graves towards a newly opened burial area. Only Frank remained unmoved as they came alongside a freshly dug grave, a headstone already securely embedded in the earth.

The engraved inscription read, 'Here Lies Salvatore d'Bergamasco - Born 1886 - Departed this World January 13th, 2023.'

'That's tomorrow,' Salvatore muttered, also unmoved.

'Then maybe you will live to fight another day,' Frank responded and turned his attention to Maxim, and gestured. 'Over there. You pick up the money and leave him here.'

Frank pointed to the grave diggers discarded shovels and a large tool bag just beyond the mounds of recently excavated soil.

Frank still held Salvatore's arm when Maxim approached the anticipated hoard, pulled open the bag only to find bundles of shredded paper. 'What the f'....'

Frank, now in absolute command, facing down the most incompetent Mafia enforcer. 'Didn't you question how your lady so quickly identified our friend here?'

He fingered Salvatore, now an open target to Maxim.

'What?' Frank saw Maxim thrown into confusion, 'It's not important - we've been duped.'

He violently shook the worthless contents of the tool bag onto the ground.

'She slept with him. On his first night in Avellino. In her hotel...'

Frank knew he had signed Salvatore's death warrant.

Maxim opened fire, allowing Frank just enough time to step in front of Salvatore and take the full blast of three successive shots.

Chapter 69

Salvatore Escapes Death

Midday: Friday 12th January 1923

Salvatore felt Frank's large hand shove him off balance and backwards into the grave.

Falling six feet and landing with a thump onto freshly dug earth, he realised he had been saved from being killed by Maxim's large pistol. A second later the full weight of Frank's body crashed onto him, to lay inert and heavy, leaving Salvatore unable to move.

He heard more gunfire, and a cloud of bullets whistle safely past his refuge, followed by the sound of heavy boots racing over the turf. For a moment he thought he must back in The War, and thanked God for this trench.

Three uniformed police appeared and called down, 'Are you wounded?'

Salvatore forced himself back from the War and managed to reply, 'No, but I can't breathe with this man on top of me.'

Two policemen climbed down and lifted Frank's limp body roughly to the surface and returned to take Salvatore out of the grave by wrapping him in a blanket. Although shaking with shock, he managed to sit up and lean against his own gravestone and looked at Frank lying flat, mouth open, eyes fluttering, bleeding from three wounds in his chest, being examined by a couple of white coated doctors.

A few yards away, he saw Maxim lying dead with blood seeping from so many wounds, he must have been hit by at least a dozen heavy bullets.

About twenty black-suited mourners stood around a large hearse, smoking, chatting, and looking at him. He smiled and waved a thumbs-up. They cheered and clapped.

A voice said, 'Signore d'Bergamasco, how do you feel?'

Salvatore turned and said, 'Just about alive.'

Colonello Pancucci gave a sympathetic smile. 'And also, lucky. One of your kidnappers saved you from being shot.'

'Will he survive too?'

'You'll find out for yourself. You're driving with him to the Bergamasco hospital. The doctors say he will live and is talking. Try and find out as much as possible about him while travelling together.'

Two stretcher bearers came and carried Frank to an ambulance near the gate.

Salvatore used his gravestone to haul himself upright.

'Can you walk?' asked Pancucci.

'I'll try. Can a couple of your men bring my death announcement please? I need it for the garden.'

Assisted by a nurse, he climbed into the ambulance and sat on the bunk opposite Frank, who opened his eyes, groaned, and grinned.

'How do you feel?' he asked

'Better than you, I think. Why did you kidnap me?'

'I didn't. Maxi kidnapped you...' His eyes fluttered and closed for a moment. He groaned and mumbled, 'Being shot hurts quite a lot,' then taking a deep breath, carried on... 'I knew the Don wanted you dead and came along for the ride to save your life. And I managed.'

'You'll have to convince both the police and me of that.'

316

'Apart from locking you up, I did nothing wrong. And the Don made sure Maxim would shoot you.'

'Why didn't Don do it when he had the gun on me?'

'Dons don't shoot people. That gives you a death sentence if you're caught. That's why I didn't carry that gun to your grave. I wiped it clean and left it in the car, unloaded, with no evidence it had ever been fired. That's our secret.'

'How did you survive three bullets from Maxim?'

Groaning at having to move, Frank opened his shirt. From under three once white medical pads blood still seeped onto a thick shiny silk waistcoat.

'Look. I had this made in New York. It probably cost more than two of your cars. It should be bulletproof, but that bastard Maxim carried a big cannon with heavy slugs. Two broke through and splintered some ribs. One went further and damaged me inside, but I'm still here so my vest worked.'

Frank's eyes rolled up and he passed into a deep coma, not even moving when rolled onto a trolley and carried to a private ward in Bergamo hospital.

'He saved my life and I want to be in here with him when he wakes up,' Salvatore insisted.

The doctors shrugged and agreed to set up a second bed. A policeman came with three nurses who undressed Frank, cleaned, and dressed his three bullet wounds, and placed his fouled clothes into a secure bag they handed to the policeman.

During the night four hospital orderlies trolleyed Frank, still unconscious, from the room, 'For an operation,' and returned him just before dawn.

Near noon Salvatore, dozing on his bed, heard Frank mumble, 'Hell's teeth I'm still hurting,'

Stiff and sore, he moved as fast as possible to Frank's bedside and looked down at his ill and pale face. 'How do you feel?' he asked.

'How do you think? I've been shot three times and cut about for hours. How would you feel?'

A pretty young nurse came in with soup for Frank and helped him drink it from a big spoon. She returned with a light spaghetti lunch for Salvatore and handed a small muslin bag to Frank, saying, 'The police returned the things from your pockets.'

To Salvatore she whispered, 'We asked your wife to come and visit you. I'll take you to the visiting room when I've cleared these lunch things.'

Frank handed the small bag to Salvatore.

'Can you get my wallet out? I think one of the bullets went through it. Yes, it did. Look. Right through. And through something I want to show you.'

He pulled a creased old picture from the wallet and kissed it before passing it to Salvatore, with tears in his eyes.

Salvatore found himself looking at a treasured old photograph, a bullet hole neatly planted in the centre, yet leaving the face all too clear to recognise.

'That's my papa,' he said shocked and surprised.

'He's *our* papà,' Frank groaned, holding out a hand to shake. 'We're brothers.'

Chapter 70

Changing Times

Novella is bowled over by a telephone call from the famous Alzano Ambivere, owner of the Fashion Auditorium in Milan, the day before Launch Day.

'Buongiorno Signorina Novella, I do hope you don't mind me calling you by your first name, but I feel I already know you having met with my good friend Adriano Beradi who gave me these photographs of both you and your work here in front of me. I am very impressed and have several proposals I would like to offer you that cannot be discussed over the telephone.'

Novella is ecstatic. *Adriana has come up trumps in helping me again*

'Shall we arrange a day to meet?' she excitedly answers.

'Very much so. I appreciate the short notice, but hope you are free to come to my studio this morning so we can talk business. My Chauffeur can pick you up in one hour and return you home when we finish our business.'

Although Novella still had to prepare for tomorrow, she could not deny herself this chance call. *How can I refuse? This is an opportunity that will help accelerate my career onto a wider audience once people know I have connections with the famous Designer and Entrepreneur Alzano Ambivere.*

'Yes, Signor I can find the time, I look forward to meeting you.'

'I am sure you are very busy and have plenty to do for your big car Launch tomorrow that I will be attending along with several friends.'

*He is even bringing friends along to the Launch,
maybe to buy a car. I just
have to say yes*

Without hesitation she agreed

'Wonderful, I am so pleased you have found the time from your own busy schedule for me. Now, what I would like you to do is bring a variety of six garments for day and evening wear to show me. Is that possible?'

'Of course. I look forward to meeting you Signor.'

'Perfect, and by the way, have you ever thought of modelling your colourful and stylish clothes for Catalogues? Studying these pictures of you showing your designs, I see you have the perfect figure and face for the fashion market of today. Voluptuous figures are now out of vogue, whilst slender is in. Please, do give it some thought on the way over. I look forward to meeting you, my dear Novella.

Novella gulped with delight as another opportune moment is presented to her. She never envisaged herself as a model and yet hearing it from the Fashion Maestro of Milan, he must be right.

Who am I to argue or doubt? What exciting times we are in and how wonderful the family business is about to blossom on the motoring market after tomorrow and shy little me the chance of becoming a model

Novella laughed as she stared at herself in her long Chippendale mirror. *Who would have thought,* m*y face and figure could become my greatest fortune yet*

After a delicious lunch of Lobster Thermidor and pasta salad Novella modelled her clothes, parading along the catwalk whilst the joyous Alzano is snapping photographs and quietly whispering, 'Brava, Novella.'

Her catwalk presentation ended with delighted applause from Alzano. 'Oh, my dear Novella, you have everything it takes to be a model. I suggest we create a Catalogue of your designs. Would you like that?' Please say yes to my proposal,' he implored. 'I promise what I am asking will not interfere with anything else you do.'

'I would like that very much, thank you, but tell me, what do I have to do to play my part?'

'You must provide the garments; do you have enough stock?'

'I most certainly do, as Adriano can confirm.'

'Good, Then that makes it easy for me to buy these garments from you.'

'Will you really?'

'Yes, I insist.'

'May I add, I don't know whether this would interest you, but I also have designed a mixed collection of ladies knitwear that the Berardi company are making for me, such as knitted dresses, coats, jackets, Bolero's, and jumpers to name a few.'

'Well Novella, you are full of surprises. I am most interested. We can definitely use them for autumn, winter, and spring catalogues, and possibly, some for summer.'

'A good idea, and may I ask, what you are exactly asking from me in the form of contracts. My business Lawyer will want to know as I leave all the details for him to deal with.'

'You are quite right to ask. I can see a good business head on your elegant, slender frame. Once we agree on the final details, we will sign an agreement with our Lawyers present, which, for obvious reasons, cannot be done today. Who is your Lawyer? Is he local to you or is he here in Milan?'

'His name is Carlos Russo, and he has his office in Bergamo.'

'I know him well. This is meant to be. I'll contact him and send him our papers and suggestions. He will come back to me and we can start discussion.'

Novella smiled. *Another believer*

'This is the proposed deal,' Alzano continued. 'We will share all profits 50/50 from the Catalogue sales to be circulated around Europe, Britain, Ireland and to America where I am well known. As a personal gift to you for being so gracious, I will throw in free use of my catwalk when we have our four main shows throughout the year, exhibiting the Winter, Spring, Summer, and Autumn collections. And you can use the platform to stage any private shows you may wish to have. Are you happy with that.'

'How exciting, you are more than generous. Will that be in writing?' she joked, giggling.

He smiled at her timing. 'I will make it my priority to have it in print and signed and will give you a key to the door should I be out of the country at any time. Anything else you wish to ask before we round up our meeting?'

'One more thing, what are you going to do with the garments you are keeping?'

'I always buy new fashions for my wife Ellenelsie. She will be delighted with these beautiful clothes, and seeing the way you held your posture on the catwalk has been the icing on the cake for me. Thank you for being you, my new friend and business partner.'

Alzano reaches out for the bottle of pink champagne, and fills the flute halfway, handing it to Novella to seal their deals.

'A toast to our new Catalogue, my dear Novella. You will be the face on every front cover and every page.'

'What a surprise to have two wonderful things named after me.'

'What is the other one, pray tell me. We may be able to use it.'

'One of our new cars is named after me. A sports car, branded as The Novella Sport.'

Alzano spontaneously grabbed Novella and kissed her brow.

'Of course, the Car Launch tomorrow. The surprises get better and better with you Novella. We could present the car on the front cover of the Catalogue. Present you both as phallic symbols uniting the feminine and masculine personalities together.'

'How would you do that?'

'You change into one of your saucy, provocative, and desirable shoulder-less evening gowns, leaning toward the car. It will send lusty husbands wild.'

'Do you really think so?'

'Of course. You are opening their unconscious minds to the changing world. We are seeing the development of powerful women today, such as yourself, so naturally feminine, yet focused and determined to be noticed as more than a mere housewife and man's slave.'

'I see what you mean.'

'What colour is the car?'

'Gold.'

'Goodness me, you are so full of great ideas.'

'You are very kind.'

'When it comes to business Novella, our aim is for gold. We want no-one to forget you or your car. The catalogue will help. What an extraordinary meeting we are having. I cannot remember the last time I have been this excited. How many different cars is your company offering at the launch?'

'Four, why?'

'We will use them all. You and the gold car on the cover page of the catalogue and the other cars we will flaunt with you on the inside pages. Wonderful, just wonderful, I have already captured the visions in my mind. I can't wait to get started.'

'Oh Alzano, my family will be so pleased.'

'More important to me Novella, are *you* pleased?'

'More than words can say.'

'What perfect auspicious timing this has been for me, you, and your car manufacturing company. I will make sure the Catalogue promotes you personally on three fronts, as a Fashion Designer, a Model, and a Colour Co-ordinator for your family business.'

'Thank you so much.'

'A fantastic selling scoop. The sight of you with a gold Sports car will sell hundreds of thousands of catalogues and entice our readers to become really interested in both the men's and lady's cars you are selling.'

'I've just remembered something to tell you, Alzano. My brother Salvatore has just promoted me.'

'What for, have you done something even more special?'

'I have, I designed the chassis for the Gold and Speedster Sports Cars, so please add Chassis Designer to my list of achievements.'

'How amazing. How brilliant you are.'

'My brother Salvatore is the car designer. I suggested one idea and he said: Very good, go ahead and do it.'

Alzano clapped again. 'Your brother saw what I am seeing and discovering.'

'You are very kind.'

'Now you must be off. Let me write you a cheque for these wonderful creations you so kindly allowed me to buy. We have worked enough for today. I shall call my chauffeur to take you home. I look forward to seeing you tomorrow at your important day.

Novella holds up her hand, 'Please, forget the cheque; they are a gift, from one friend to another.'

Chapter 71

Isabella Waits for News

Rehearsals were going well, despite all the turmoil that flowed in the underbelly of preparations. With only family members aware of the enormous financial implications the family faced, an air of optimism and celebration energised all involved in the build-up to the big day as they worked with fervour. The stage had been erected first, allowing the dancers to go through their routines within the confines of the space allotted. The choreographer spent time shouting orders at the chorus, while Isabella had a break.

Gazing at the breath-taking beautifully cut diamond ring, with the light sparkling off the facets on her right ring finger, Isabella paced up and down her small makeshift dressing room, desperate for a cigarette, though fully aware of how sick it would make her.

How can I feel anything but fear for Salvatore's life at this moment in time? It seems vulgar to be displaying such extravagance when he may be in mortal danger.

Dio. The Mafia. It couldn't be worse.

Numerous questions riffled through her troubled mind.

Has Salvatore been released yet? Is he safe? Are the kidnappers still at large? Oh, he must be terrified. My darling brother who has been so understanding and supportive. Per favore Dio, keep him safe, bring him home to us alive and well. Per favore. Per favore

Needing some sort of distraction, Isabella slipped the sparkling ring from her slim digit and carefully placed it back in its box inside her tanned leather Gucci handbag.

I can keep it safely hidden for the next few days until our engagement is announced at the Launch, if there is a Launch.

Recalling how, late last night, true to his word, Giorgio had gone down on one knee, proposing in dramatic fashion, Isabella felt saddened at the memory. The look of confusion that had crossed his face as she had only nodded and thanked him broke his heart. No squeal of joy, not even a smile. Isabella had quickly explained it away with a lie. That in itself induced a feeling of nausea, nothing to do with her pregnancy.

False attestations of physical discomfort had evoked immediate concern and that precious man insisted that Isabella lie down and rest. Hours of fussing over her followed until Giorgio was confident that his dear friend had no danger of miscarrying.

Please Lord don't let that wicked lie have tempted fate.

How can I confide in Giorgio what is going on in the family when we have been explicitly ordered not to share the information with anyone, even our spouses? It wouldn't make a difference if we were already married. I still couldn't tell him. He must consider me so moody, no doubt believing he has solved all my problems. He has indeed given me the greatest gift of all, the chance to bring my child into this world without the burden of illegitimacy whilst also saving my career.

None of the d'Bergamasco family members were aware of Isabella's plans with Giorgio, not even Novella. All was to be revealed at the launch. This should have been such an exciting time, joyful, positive on every level. Now a huge shadow was yet again hanging over not only her, but all of the d'Bergamasco siblings.

Distraction now futile, Isabella's thoughts returned to Salvatore's plight.

A million dollars It might as well be a billion. Just as well the police have no intention of allowing us to pay the ransom. With a slight shiver, Isabella recollected the heated rows between herself and her siblings after the call from the kidnappers last night. Once Colonello Pancucci and Detective Puglia had left and the family's initial shock been processed, a blend of emotions swirled together to become a catalyst for anarchy.

Resentment and anger at Giuseppe because of his sexual indiscretion landing the family in such financial strife had boiled over. Tempers flared. Heated Italian blood fired through their collective veins, each finding blame in another, citing historical screw ups, recent recklessness, and current differences.

All hell had broken loose at one point, tears spilt, even by her brothers. Yet when the rage and mistrust had been spent, in true Italian style the siblings hugged one another in grief and fear for the unknown fate of their loved one.

The kidnappers explicitly requested that we not involve the police at the peril of Salvatore's life. Besides, so many of them are corrupt. Yet what could we have done? There is no hope of raising the money for the ransom. Not when we're on the verge of bankruptcy.

Giuseppe had suggested that they go about business as usual, carry on preparing for the launch as he considered that was what Salvatore would want. He had appeared to be beside himself with worry, though he expressed great faith in Pancucci. 'I see him as calm and totally honest, surrounded by a similar, personally hand-picked group of men,' he said.

How can we carry on as if nothing is happening? Our brother might be dead. When the kidnappers find the ransom has not been paid, they might kill him on the spot. The Mafia are known to be ruthless. I can't even stay at home by the phone. I've missed enough rehearsals this week and if the show must go on, it will be performed to perfection.

A knock on the cheap wooden door caused Isabella to jump.

'Signorina d'Bergamasco,' a timid sounding voice, barely audible sounded through the door.

Assuming a call to go back on stage, Isabella responded, 'I'll be there in just a moment.'

'Ermmm, I have a telegram for you Signorina,' the voice raised a little louder.

Pulling open the door with dread, Isabella practically snatched the envelope from the poor young boy's hand. Recovering herself just in time, she thanked him profusely before he scampered away.

With trembling hands, Isabella tore open the envelope.

Salvatore is alive. Being cared for in Bergamo hospital. Minor injuries. One kidnapper dead, the other injured. Keep going with rehearsals.

All energy seeped from her body. Isabella collapsed into the Chiavari side chair positioned close by.

This feeling is indescribable, not mere relief, but euphoria tempered with a divine comfort.

Falling to her knees, Isabella clasped her petite hands together and looking upwards, whispered 'Grazie Dio. Grazie mille, Dio.

Chapter 72

Frank's Launch day

I did confess that I felt a strong attraction to Isabella from the moment we first met. Not sexually, but something stronger. Of course, I didn't know then that we were blood related. I tried to explain this to her earlier today, in some cack-handed way that seemed to cause offence.

The unexpected arrival of the Don flanked by two soldiers crushed Frank's train of thought.

Smiling, the Don placed a bottle of spirits on the bedside cabinet. 'For your health.'

'Cutty Sark?'

'To remind you of home – although the bootleg variety shipped through Canada might have been watered down. Like a lot of things in transit, they become tainted.'

'That's a bit deep for you.'

'I sent our dear late Maxi to buy it. Always loyal, but never the brightest.'

Frank felt palpable tension develop in the room.

'During one of your heart-to-hearts with your brother, Maxi found a way to contact me. I went along with the plan. I had one of my own people placed amongst the police mourners at the Cremona Cemetery.'

Frank smiled and remained silent. *If he expects me to respond, he'll be disappointed*

The Don became ever more cryptic, switching subject without a beat, 'I lived in the same town as your papà, in '76, when your family banished your mama to America, and he absconded – just disappeared.'

Frank gave undivided attention to what may come next. 'We were very close,' continued the Don. 'Had been all our lives. We came through the ranks together. Protected each other. Covered for each other.'

Frank realised this is an uncharacteristic outpouring of the Don's blackened soul, 'His leaving devastated me. I felt distraught, angry, rejected, and betrayed. The whole gamut of emotions ran through me. I felt tormented for years. Having him registered as one of the landowners I thought might flush him out – but no. He remained hidden. Possibly dead.'

'And my mother?'

'Our extended Cosa Nostra kept an eye on her.'

He moved towards the bedside observing Frank closely, 'You don't look so bad, Francesco. I guess you could walk out of here at any moment of your choosing.'

'I'm here for observation.' Frank asserted, 'I believe that's the medical term.'

Lowering himself on the bed, not quite on top of Frank's legs, but close enough to pin him in, the Don managed another disarming smile.

'When you visited Avellino, and quizzed the old lady it opened those old wounds.'

'Do you want to talk about it?' asked Frank.

'Maybe another day – once Cosa Nostra here have fully embraced you.'

He jumped up, as if an entire weight had suddenly been lifted from his body. His soldiers reacted instinctively, opening the door, and standing back to let the Don depart.

He paused in the doorway, and turned, his eyes piercing into Frank's, 'You still owe me a kill.'

Chapter 73

Isabella's Launch Day

Negotiating the excited crowd at the Atalanta Stadium, Isabella's heavy disguise worked well as she made her way to the main marquee. A blonde wig, headscarf and three-quarter length mink fur coat disguised her figure. Visiting Frank Bernstein in Bergamo hospital earlier that morning, at Salvatore's request, had necessitated this charade. Feeling a little uncomfortable about her brother's request, she had nevertheless acquiesced.

Isabella's attraction to Frank hadn't waned. Her heart skipped a beat the moment she laid eyes upon him.

He looks so vulnerable, lying in a hospital bed. How I want to gently stroke the hair back from his tanned face, kiss him on his downturned mouth and make everything better. There's something so familiar about those beautiful blue eyes. I feel like I've always known him.

A firm hand, now placed on her shoulder, interrupted Isabella's thoughts. The accompanying familiar male voice exclaimed 'Isabella, I'd know those ankles anywhere.' Turning swiftly sideways, shock registered on her pale face as she glanced at the full wide mouth that had once evoked such longing in her loins.

'Alberto, what a surprise,' she managed, failing to disguise her insincerity. 'I really must hurry; I'm expected by Giorgio Rossi to run over the last-minute preparations for the show this evening.'

'Giorgio Rossi,' Alberto sneered. 'Of course, you're rushing to him. I'll bet he's been sniffing around you since we split up.'

'We didn't split up Alberto,' Isabella held her head high as she reminded her nasty ex-lover, 'You insulted me in the most disgusting way possible and left me to take sole responsibility for the child we created together.'

Feeling a tight grip on her arm, Isabella looked down at Alberto's large right hand clasping hers in an attempt to prevent her departure.

'Wait,' he growled. 'Tell me, did you get rid of the little bastard?'

'You have no right to ask me anything about the pregnancy, Alberto. All you need to know is that the problem has gone.'

Smug satisfaction registered on Alberto's face, and he loosened his grip. Isabella took her chance and scurried away. Glancing back briefly when at a safe distance, she saw him still standing in the same spot, looking back at her with a strange expression.

What did I ever see in him? Lust is a blinding force.

Relief spread through Isabella as she reached the marquee and caught sight of Giorgio commanding the attention of those around him with his charismatic personality. Popping briefly in behind a partition screen to remove the blonde wig and have her hair touched up by her personal coiffeur, she walked across to Giorgio, a smile fixed on her carefully made-up face. He made his excuses, disentangling himself from the claws of an attractive, wealthy widow and immediately noted Isabella's distress.

'It's Alberto, he's here' Isabella babbled, anxiously, clearly still rattled. 'He recognised me, even with my disguise. He accosted me outside.'

Giorgio placed a hand on her arm in a gesture of reassurance. 'He won't get into this marquee, it's by invitation only. I'll get security to remove him from the stadium.'

'No,' Isabella replied firmly. 'Please don't. He would make a scene and that's the last thing I need.'

'So be it,' Giorgio relented,' but come and take a seat, out of sight of guests. The shock has unsettled you. I'll get you a glass of water.'

Isabella disregarded his advice. 'I need to mingle, rave about the Town Car, all of its wonderful features and how it could shape women's futures. I could drop into the conversation how lots of professional women have ordered them.'

'Have they?' queried Giorgio.

'I have no idea,' Isabella smiled, 'but acting skills are a huge bonus when it comes to being Creative Director of the company. If a small number of people see the Town Car is very popular with female professionals, it will become more sought after.'

'Clever Signorina,' Giorgio approved with a grin, 'just pace yourself, save your energy for the dance routines tonight.'

Isabella negotiated a path towards Alfina, politely engaging in conversations en route. Her closest friend, appeared to be in animated conversation with two of her peers, both single ladies excited to be joined by a hugely successful movie star, as stunning in real life as on the big screen.

'Now let me tell you about our Town Car,' Isabella began as soon as they had got the niceties out of the way. She realised the two lawyers were far more interested to hear about her life on set but too polite to say. Before they knew it, both were eating out of Isabella's hand, excusing themselves briefly when she had finished describing the car. 'We really must see this exciting new vehicle for ourselves.'

Isabella pointed to where it stood in the centre of the Marquee. 'Do you want me to come with you?'

'No, we'll be fine,'

Alfina smiled, as they hurried off, a little tipsy. 'At last, darling Isabella. We finally have some time alone together and you're looking so much better, mio Bella. What a wonderful man Giorgio is to step into the breach. You'll be the envy of every woman on the planet,' Alfina gushed.

Isabella didn't reply. Her mind had inadvertently revisited the scene at the hospital that morning.

Frank had looked surprised and pleased when Isabella entered his room after a tentative knock. Immediately expressing her gratitude for him saving Salvatore's life, she had admitted 'I really didn't understand all of it, but I know I speak for our family when I say we are eternally grateful for our brother's safe return. It's such a pity that you're not well enough to join us at the launch today. You could have been our guest of honour.'

Frank smiled knowingly. She felt as if he could see right through her, into her mind, her thoughts, the fusion of mystical and confusing emotions his presence evoked.

'It's so good of you to come, Isabella,' he replied. 'I asked Salvatore to send you. There are things we need to discuss.'

'Are you ok?' Alfina's voice brought Isabella back to the present. 'You seem like you're in a bit of daze.'

'Oh, forgive me, I have a lot on my mind, there's so much to do between our routine tonight, the announcement of our engagement and of course, preparations for the wedding.'

A sudden dart of pain in her belly startled Isabella, though it disappeared as quickly as it had come.

'Perhaps I should rest for a while,' she suggested to Alfina, who had missed the moment, distracted by a handsome gentleman who smiled at her while walking by.

'I'll go to my dressing room, there's a sofa there.'

Alfina agreed but just as Isabella moved towards the exit, she was stopped by an eager buyer, with the funds to match. Quite obviously just as interested in Isabella as the motor cars, the man in question kept her standing for longer than she would have preferred.

Over an hour later, Isabella lay on the uncomfortable cheap sofa in her makeshift dressing room, nevertheless grateful for the horizontal position. Giorgio popped in on and off, regaling her with tales of tiddly ladies proposing all sorts.

In those moments alone Isabella allowed her mind to return once more to the events of that morning. She bristled now at a particular memory.

Frank had been insistent that she pull up a chair close to his bed.

'There are things we need to discuss, Isabella, information I feel is important to you and indeed your brothers and sister; facts you need to be in possession of.'

What on earth could this virtual stranger, familiar and attractive though he appears, have to tell our family?

'Salvatore is already aware of what I'm about to tell you,' Frank continued. 'However, I feel you need to know before the rest of the family because, forgive me for being blunt, I sense that you would like there to be more between you and I than friendship.'

'I don't know where you have got that impression,' Isabella had interrupted him indignantly, her cheeks burning with embarrassment.

'If I'm barking up the wrong tree, I apologise. Let me say that I consider you a beautiful, sexy, engaging woman. However, anything more than friendship between us is not possible.'

A frown furrowed Isabella's brow, at a loss to comprehend Frank's protestation.

'There is no easy way to say this, Isabella, but I have to tell you that I am your brother.'

'*What?*' Isabella gasped, disbelief sweeping across her face. 'But how? I don't understand. You can't be my brother, our brother.'

Frank told her, 'Our papà, when aged 19, fell in love with a beautiful young girl of 17 in Avellino. Before he came to Bergamo, he fathered me and named me Francesco. When my grandmother took my mama to America to avoid scandal, when I was born, she anglicised my name to Frank to fit in.'

'I can't listen to any more of this,' Isabella retorted, standing up from the chair, humiliation and disbelief sweeping over her.

He ignored her and said, 'To put it correctly, I'm actually your half-brother. Talk to Salvatore if you find it difficult to believe. He'll fill in the blanks.'

'I wish you a full recovery, Mr Bernstein,' Isabella pronounced firmly, 'But I really must return to the launch.'

'Please don't go yet.'

'Goodbye,' she snapped and swept from the room.

The mink coat had felt suffocating. Perspiration glistened on her brow. She couldn't risk removing the damned thing for fear of being recognised.

Now, resting in her dressing room Isabella pondered that conversation. *It feels like a dream, though it was very real. I'll speak to Salvatore after the launch. There's no time before then; it's not something I can deal with right now, if indeed there is any truth at all in Frank's allegation.*

A doubting inner voice taunted indiscriminately. 'Now you know why those beautiful blue eyes were so familiar, they're Papà's eyes.'

The twinge in her lower abdomen returned, eliciting a gasp, then fading as quickly as it had come. Placing both hands protectively across her tummy, Isabella soothed her unborn child. 'Be safe in there, little one, we have a way to go. I promise I'll rest after tonight's show.' As if in answer to her reassurance, a little flutter flew across her abdomen. Smiling, she stood up and walked across the small room to her dressing table. *It's likely just muscle spasms, I've read how that can happen when the womb is expanding.*

A short while later, having adorned a bandeau brassiere to disguise her swelling breasts, Isabella appeared in a knee length turquoise blue sequined dress, tassels teasing the top of her calves. She stood in the wings of the large stage area, low heeled, T-strapped silver shoes fastened comfortably. The matching silver bandeau headband fitted around her short, bobbed dark hair, glistened under the spotlights. The sound of the Bergamo orchestra echoed through the stadium as a chorus of dancers, all dressed in silver costumes, styled similarly to hers, began their first routine, the Charleston. Crowds watched in delight, their feet moving to the beat of the music.

The dancers parted in well-rehearsed style, allowing Isabella to make her grand entrance. The groove and bounce of her step work flawless, she moved to the music in exact time with her peers. Cleverly choreographed to include sensational solos, Isabella stole the show. Rapturous applause filled the stadium as the dance routines continued. Isabella's fans clasped their hands together with glee, star struck by the beautiful, talented Isabella d'Bergamasco.

As the show came to an end, Isabella bowed, smiling as she accepted a bouquet of flowers proffered by Leonardo Rinaldi. Laying them on the stage in front of her, accompanied by the many blossoms thrown by fans, Isabella stepped back. Clasping the hands of the chorus girls either side of her, she and her ensemble bowed together with beaming smiles. Isabella glanced down to the front of the audience. *There they are, my wonderful family, all together, safe, and happy. They look so proud. Salvatore is positively beaming.*

Backstage, Isabella's personal dresser rushed to wipe her brow. There was more to be done. She couldn't rest yet. The cars were to be driven out onto the stage in sequence and Isabella had to change once more. Giorgio glanced her way, looking slightly concerned but she nodded confirmation of all being well. Confident that the show could go on, he stepped back out onto the stage to prepare his big car introduction.

A quick change of clothes later, her hair touched up by the coiffeur, Isabella emerged from her dressing room, ready to drive her 'Isabella' branded Town Car onto stage from behind a large shining silk curtain.

She presented a vision in silver satin with a diamante beaded headband, and the same T-strap silver shoes and saw that Giorgio couldn't suppress a gasp of appreciation as she appeared backstage. Her gown dazzled and clung to every curve, no evidence of her pregnancy apparent.

'The ring,' Giorgio whispered into her ear. 'Now is the time to wear it. I'll announce our engagement as soon as the cars are presented.'

With a wave of her hand, in ill-disguised weariness, Isabella replied, 'Could you get it from my handbag, Giorgio? I don't want to move just now.'

'Of course.' Giorgio sped off, returning with the sparkling ring, which he slipped onto Isabella's ring finger. She looked up into his darling face, feeling so grateful for his friendship. *He is the hero of the hour, and nobody knows it.*

From the corner of her eye, Isabella noticed a stagehand giggling, nudging another. *They must have spotted the ring. The whole cast and crew will know before we make our announcement. No matter. It is to be a surprise for the audience, part of the show, the epitome of all make believe.*

Isabella hugged her brothers and sister in turn before taking her place in The Town Car, delighted at her name 'Isabella" in silver script, gracing the machine front on the grille, rear on the boot and on the bonnet a round plaque, encircling the Angel of Bergamo. She ran her hands over the smooth burnt orange painted doors, admiring the interior peach upholstery adorned with two graceful white lilies, the emblem of Italy, on each rear seat cushion.

Full of pride and admiration for her clever sister, Novella, and brother Salvatore for decorating and designing such an elegant machine, she swung in behind the steering wheel to be immediately stricken by an agonising cramp assaulting her lower belly, followed by a rush of nausea.

She broke into a sweat, gritting her teeth immobilised at the sharp passage of pain. *Not long to go. Must just get through this final act, then I can go home and rest.*

Isabella started the engine and moved to her position in a staggered line of three cars, halting to the left and slightly ahead of Salvatore in the Tourer and Anton slightly behind in the Speedster.

A trumpet fanfare began, building up excitement and anticipation. Red velvet curtains opened to reveal Isabella moving slowly onto stage.

The audience rose in a frenzy of clapping and cheering, while young men whistled and howled at the stunning beauty of Isabella, floodlights flashing off her amazing silver dress and brilliantly decorated car.

Giorgio stood to the side, commentating, and describing The Town Car's values and promoting it to young women of all ages.

'Be free,' he crooned in that lovely deep voice. 'Travel in comfort and fashion. The sophisticated modern lady is Driven By Desire to lead the way in style, and elegance in a Town Car of distinction and performance.

Isabella climbed gracefully from the car to strike a sexy pose, her right hand resting on the door, left hand perched on a perfectly thrust out hip, slim neck, held in a graceful swanlike curve.

Next came Salvatore, proudly presenting the Tourer, with a toot of the horn. Parking beside Isabella, he made a show of jumping out with agility, waving to the throng, and opening doors to show the inside space, his actions corresponding with Giorgio's commentary.

Finally, Anton revved his Speedster engine to a dramatic howl and swept out to take his place on the far side of the line. Leaping from the vehicle, he made a handsome sight, in driving clothes, a peaked hat, and goggles, arms waving above his head and strutting around his Speedster with his chest out. Manly fashion. Our typical dear flamboyant Anton.

No sooner had the rapturous applause died down than the lights dimmed, and the orchestra began a drum roll, followed by another trumpet fanfare. Isabella gasped with the audience as the stage lights disappeared, leaving a moment of absolute darkness, before a powerful single spotlight aimed directly on Novella picked her out gradually driving her cleverly designed, spectacular Gold Sport into the centre of the line-up. placing both she and her two creations firmly in the limelight of this grand finale.

Isabella applauded Novella climbing gracefully out, beaming brighter than the lights themselves, looking fantastic in one of her own elegant white knitted dresses scattered all over in shimmering gold sequins flashing bright golden rays across the stage. She too stood beside her fabulous design waving a silk handkerchief at the crowds and bowing in a formal manner.

This is her well-deserved moment. My little sister is the star of this show. How far she has come from the shy, silent little girl.

Tears of pride slid down Isabella's cheeks. Unable to wipe them away, she let them roll.

Giorgio chose his moment, just as the applause died down and the main stage lights returned, Isabella felt sad at intruding on Novella's great moment, but with time of the essence it had to be done.

Her dear Giorgio started his next big important announcement.

'Ladies and Gentlemen, before we end this incredible evening, there is something I, no, *we*, would like to share with you.'

Reaching out his left hand towards Isabella, he beckoned her to come and stand beside him.

'Signorina Isabella d'Bergamasco has done me the great honour of accepting my proposal of marriage.'

Screams erupted as the crowds cheered with appreciation. Ladies in the crowd burst into tears. Salvatore rushed over to congratulate them both, shaking Giorgio's hand rigorously, giving Isabella an almighty hug. Anton patted Giorgio on the back and kissed Isabella on both cheeks. Giuseppe grabbed both of them in a bear hug declaring, 'About time. You're made for each other.' Novella graciously embraced Isabella and brushed Giorgio's hand with a delicate touch of her lips, obviously wishing only the best for her sister.

I feel genuinely thrilled at this moment, how strange. It's almost as if it my engagement were the real thing.

An abrupt grip of searing pain, stronger than any previous ones, caused Isabella to stagger and nearly fall. She clutched Giorgio's arm.

He looked down and must have noticed her agonised expression. Almost carrying her, feet dragging to the dressing room and laying her down, he said, 'Oh my god. You are bleeding rather badly, my darling. We must hurry you to hospital.'

The ambulance bell rang loud, racing through the cold evening air to Bergamo hospital.

Isabella felt Giorgio holding her hand and wiping the tears rolling down her cheeks.

'Dio, please don't let me lose my precious child,' she wailed.

'You'll be in safe hands with the best care, my dearest darling,' Giorgio whispered, leaning down to kiss tears away.

True to his word, the doctors were awaiting her arrival, whisking Isabella through to a private ward, examining her with gentle professional touch. They saw only Signorina d'Bergamasco. Fame and stardom played no part in this moment. Here lay a patient who needed reassurance and the best possible care they could provide, no matter what fame, fortune, or their personal judgements of pregnancy outside wedlock might be.

Later, Isabella's pale face crumpled again into tears. The bleeding had abated though she knew a threat of miscarriage remained. Grabbing Giorgio's hand, she whispered, 'If I lose my child, I won't hold you to your proposal. Your life is your own. I will announce that I have broken the engagement, so it won't affect your popularity. You are such a true friend, Giorgio, I will love you always.'

'Hush now darling Bella,' Giorgio whispered back. 'You may not lose your little one. You have been very stressed. Alberto's shock appearance wouldn't have helped things. You heard what the doctor said, you need bed rest. I won't see you bankrupt; I will support you. With your blessing, our wedding *will* go ahead.

Isabella and Giorgio exchanged a look which spoke volumes. Neither voiced them. She laid one hand on her belly, then with the other, took his. Two sets of eyes met, seeing each other as if for the first time.

Chapter 74

Giuseppe's Launch Day

Saturday evening. 'Thank God that's over,' said Giuseppe. He poured Francesca and himself a large whisky and collapsed onto the sofa beside her.

'You miserable so and so, Giuseppe. I loved the rehearsals. All that showbiz glamour. It's fun. The stadium looks like Hollywood. Anton has done a tremendous job.'

'I suppose so,' said Giuseppe. His dark mood worsened, wondering how the company would pay for the Launch, let alone Salvatore's long-term expansion project.

God if only the family knew we have no money. We're broke. And it's all my fault. Keep calm. Don't let on. Not yet. Something miraculous might happen.

He downed his whisky in a gulp and poured another.

'Cheer up darling,' whispered Francesca. 'I know you don't like meeting the public, but I'll be at your side tomorrow.'

'Yes. Thanks, my love. I'm not that good with people,' said Giuseppe, allowing himself a brief smile and thinking, *Bloody Anton. He's deployed Francesca to shadow me in case I put off any prospective customers.*

On Sunday morning. Giuseppe felt surprised to find himself in better spirits than the previous day. *Perhaps it's because I'm fed-up by our wretched money situation. Maybe I'm excited about going back to the Atalanta Stadium. I've only been to one match this season. Or maybe I love driving this fabulous car.*

346

Gliding along, he shouted out through the open window 'Well done to you, my brother. This thing is gorgeous to drive', as he and Francesca glided through the streets of Bergamo in the sleek, purring sky-blue luxury Tourer.

He parked the car beside a The Town Car in one of the heated marquees, set up to feed hot food to the public and show the cars.

'Is that car for sale?' asked Francesca.

'That's why we're here, my darling. To sell as many as we can.'

'It's beautiful with all those colours and decorated with flowers. I'll buy one before we go home.'

'But you can't drive, darling'

'I'll learn.'

'But you have no money.'

'But you have.'

Still full of guilt about his affair, he succumbed and said, 'Very well darling. I'll buy you one and have it delivered home after Isabella's show.'

Francesca turned, enveloping him in a huge hug, whispering, 'I knew you would.'

Over her shoulder he noticed an elderly man in an ankle length fur coat and white peaked cap with a much younger woman staring intently at him. *Why? I don't know yo*u.

Giuseppe stared back. The man turned and moved away through the crowd.

Francesca pushed Guiseppe away. 'Come on, let's enjoy a quick coffee before we and venture outside to mingle with your public.'

'There seem to be more fans here than when Atalanta are playing,' Giuseppe said to a passing stranger who laughed and agreed.

'This way Giuseppe,' said Francesca pushing him through the crowd and reminding him of a Russian princess with her fur hat, long black overcoat, and high heeled boots.

'Where are we going?

'I'm looking for the mayor. I'm going to sell him a car.'

'Don't be ridiculous. You're not a sales lady.'

'Just you watch.'

Giuseppe watched, amazed. Francesca deliberately opened her overcoat to reveal her full figure in all its glory, before luring the man into a green Tourer and selling it to him in under three minutes while Giuseppe merely completed the sales sheets. Their teamwork harvested three further sales within the hour.

'We're rather good at this aren't we darling?' shouted Francesca pulling Giuseppe along with her as she sought the attention of Bergamo's MP. Giuseppe followed like an obedient puppy, carrying the sales sheets, and stood mute while the politician bought a red Tourer, showing little interest in the car, while examining Francesca's breasts through a pair of small round-lensed spectacles perched low on his nose.

'His car colour goes with his politics,' she giggled.

However, Giuseppe did not listen because he again saw the man with the ankle length fur coat and white peaked cap, and his woman. This time, the fellow deliberately waved to catch his attention before a tide of people swallowed him and his young lady. They disappeared, leaving Giuseppe even more puzzled.

Giuseppe and Francesca attempted another two sales with no success before Anton steered Giuseppe into one of the marquees and loaded him with a batch of shiny, colourful brochures to distribute, and led

Francesca away. After handing out all the brochures Giuseppe saw a man dressed in a rich black cloak and made his move, maneuvering the man towards the vivid gold Sports Novella Sport.

'Fancy this stunning machine, Sir?' asked Giuseppe, only for the man to politely protest and open his cloak to reveal the red satin surplice. 'I am of the church, young man. Cardinal Allegri. I have come to simply bless the Launch of your wonderful machines at your wife, Francesca's request.'

Embarrassed, Giuseppe apologized, bowed, and retreated into the crowd, receiving the Cardinal's graceful blessing as he went.

Giuseppe, not to be put off approached a burly looking woman who rebuffed his entreaties to view a Town Car by explaining, 'I work here darling. I'm just a member of the crew who assembled the marquees.'

Giuseppe considered giving up and grabbing a brandy, when he saw a tall business type hovering by a Tourer and about to turn away, haughtily shouting to the woman next him, 'it's far too small.'

Giuseppe hurried over. He guessed the problem and gave up on salesmanship niceties. 'Just watch will you,' he said to the man while motioning Ricardo Bisola, the Atlanta giant goalkeeper.

'Get in Ricardo and let me do the talking,' he whispered, before turning to the businessman saying: 'See? You can adjust the wheel, pedals, seat, gear stick even elevate the lining on the ceiling a little. Look. Ricardo fits and he's far bigger and taller than you. Do you want the car or not?'

'Put like that. Yes, I want it.' said the tall man.

Astounded and proud of his sale, Giuseppe rewarded himself and Ricardo with a quick brandy in one of the marquees in the company of Ricardo and the entire Atalanta team, until Francesca found him and dragged him out into the throng, 'Idiot we've still got hours to go.'

'But Francesca love, I made a sale. I wanted to celebrate.'

'I made three my dear. Look, there's Stefano Signori. Let's try him.'

'No. He's a fascist.'

'Fascists buy cars too, you fool. So, fascists are customers. Especially fascists with money and he's a top dog. If you're not going to help me then take these brochures and give them away.'

She shoved the pile of paper into Giuseppe's arms before weaving through the crowd to be at the politician's side just as Giuseppe heard an English voice speak from behind him.

'Are you Mr. Giuseppe Bergamasco?'

'That's me,' replied Giuseppe, in his cultured English. He turned, to face the man with the fur coat, white peaked cap, and the much younger woman.

'I'm Reggie Mortimer of Belgravia Garages in London. Alfredo Macari's friend.'

For a moment Giuseppe struggled with an accent he took to be London patois.

'Yes. Alfredo mentioned you might turn up,' said Giuseppe.

Reggie shook hands and said, 'Your cars are absolutely stunning old chap. Perfect in every way. I'll order immediately. I need ten Tourers to begin with. I've got all the import, export licenses. And ten Speedsters for the younger lads. Possibly more. It's one o'clock. Come on. Let's have some dinner and talk business.'

At lunch Reggie, introduced his seventh wife. 'Yes, seventh,' he repeated at Giuseppe's raised eyebrow.

'Money brings women,' he laughed 'And some of them run off with it.'

'Have you seen our Town Car?' asked Giuseppe. 'Designed especially for young brides, to use around the city.'

'Yes,' said his seventh wife in an entirely different accent to Reggie's. 'I want you to buy me one, Reginald. It looks so beautiful with all those colour and flowers and things.'

Reggie laughed and rolled his eyes and laughing again. 'Oh Giuseppe. These posh birds. They want to be the first in any new fashion.'

Daring to joke, Giuseppe said, 'Perhaps you ought to buy ten, Reggie, one each for the other seven and three to sell.'

Reggie's wife glared at Giuseppe, probably for mention the previous seven wives, but her husband grinned and stuck an elbow Giuseppe's ribs. 'Oh, you're a real card.'

Turning to his wife he blew a kiss. 'Ok, my darling. I'll buy ten. One for you and nine for you to sell to your tippy-toe girlfriends clipping around London on their high heels. You'll frighten the sparrows buzzing around like a squadron of painted pigeons.'

She squealed in delight, clapping her manicured hands and nodding thanks to Giuseppe.

Reggie signed the order, saying, 'Ship them all, soon and poss.'

Leaning forward, he whispered, 'I planned to buy five of that model in a month or so, but now I know she'll get rid of nine in a flash, on to a good thing. All my mates have new young wives and will do anything to keep the nookie coming.'

After waving them off in their Rolls Royce, Giuseppe determined to look at his English thesaurus for *chaps* and *lads* and *posh birds* and *nookie* and other words he may need to sell cars in London.

He found Francesca who kissed him on the cheek and slipped her arm through his, on hearing of his sales success. 'Brilliant darling. Come on, let's do a few more before our luck runs out.'

The couple laughed and joked with would-be customers and sold a further four cars before Giuseppe's mood changed when he saw the look on Enzo's face as his colleague from the factory ran to him and whispered, 'Padrone. The police are here. They are looking for you.'

'What? Why?'

'It's your bank manager, Giorgio Iannella and his wife. They have been murdered.'

Chapter 75

D'Angelo's Launch Day

Francisco D'Angelo woke on the morning of the launch day determined to get his way with D'Bergamasco. He dressed with care and tried and get a message to the Capo and find out the situation but couldn't contact him.

He made his way to the Atalanta Stadium where the d'Bergamasco launch of their new cars would take place. On arrival, he sneaked in by merging with a large group of obviously wealthy people in case the family d'Bergamasco had taken precautions to keep him out.

It soon became clear that no strict security measures were in place, leaving him free to roam at will. He could see that the family had made it a grand affair with no expense being spared in the pursuit of selling the brand.

He saw many personalities from the world of showbusiness and sport wandering around examining and buying cars. As he wandered around, he saw the figure of his arch enemy Salvatore and, without thinking, charged over to confront him. D'Bergamasco turned in surprise and sneered, 'How the hell did you get out of jail?'

'Never mind that. I've got friends in many high places,' Francisco snapped. 'Now are you going to keep your word and give me a car for allowing you to build your factory? You're getting off lightly if I walk away with only a car.'

Salvatore yelled back: 'Get away from me you slimy dishonest bastard. I'm giving you nothing. Now get out before I have you thrown out.'

A blind rage came over D'Angelo. He drew back a fist to strike d'Bergamasco in the face when a pair of strong arms grabbed him from behind and held him back. A loud voice snarled, 'I am Anton, and we have the police here. You are not welcome, so I'm asking you to leave, Signor D'Angelo or we'll have you arrested again, this time for threatening behaviour.'

Francisco realised he had no position of power here, and a couple of d'Bergamasco employees turned up to grab his arms. He didn't struggle, but his devious mind came into action with a plan to add interest to new demands he would make in the future.

'They slipped that illegal factory past me by changing it from producing agricultural tractors to manufacturing luxury cars without permission. I'll stop them getting with tricks like that again. Just let them wait till they see what I have in store for any expansion. That dammed family will be laughing on the other side of their faces then.'

He glared into Salvatore's face and allowed himself to be pushed out of the Stadium gate, his head already devising schemes to make their future life a misery.

Chapter 76

Novella's Launch Day

Driving along the road to the Atalanta Football Stadium Novella felt eyes on her and her beautiful Gold car while passing strangers out walking glanced at her and the car.

Approaching the Stadium entrance, she is thrilled to see so many people at the gates. She waved, as she offloaded her soft top roof, to give people a view of the car's interior, and hoping it will help buyers recognise her throughout the day.

'Good morning, good morning, thank you for coming to see our new designed cars. If anyone needs assistance, you will find me circulating the Arena or in the Marquee. Wishing you all an enjoyable day.'

Inside the Marquee, Novella smelt the coffee aroma drifting through the air and made her way toward the bar before the crowds appeared, pondering on the day ahead. *I've nothing else to do all day except walk about and talk, unlike Isabella, who will be singing and dancing. I'm not a car salesperson papà. Do help me find the words to convince people to order my hand made car today please.*

Music filled the air from the sounds of the orchestra playing in the background as people streamed into the Marquee, staying with keen interest, and placing orders for cars. Surprisingly relieved, Novella is finding it quite easy to charm people into buying the new look vehicles.

She gave a smile to the heavens. *This is your day papà. Enjoy it to the full. I am your proud devoted servant keeping your memory alive.*

One man spent several minutes staring, before approaching Novella. He smiled and introduced himself. 'My name is Leonardo Rinaldi. I have to say I am torn between this beautiful Gold Car and the Speeder Sports. They are both so attractive and irresistible.'

'I'm glad you like them.'

'I'll just spend a little more time deciding, but I will be back when I have made my mind up.' He smiled then turned his eye back to the car.

As promised, he returned an hour later, looking thrilled with his decision. 'I've made up my mind. I'm going to have them both,' he chuckled. 'Please take my order for this beautiful Gold and the cheque for the Speedster. Now tell me, am I right in thinking you are Isabella's younger sister?'

'Yes, I am.'

'Mm, charming, pleased to meet you, have you ever thought of acting? I'd be happy to give you a screen test and audition. Here is my private number, please, take my card.'

Novella is taken aback with surprise as she takes the film producers card.

Isabella will not be very happy with me if I upstaged her on the screen, best to keep well away from provoking her moods.

'Thank you, I'm flattered, but really, acting doesn't interest me, though I do sing and play the piano, but that's as far as it goes musically. Isabella is the gifted one when it comes to acting. I am a fashion designer.'

Leonardo looked down his nose, obviously misliking what he heard. 'Shame, a real shame, though I am sure acting will be in your whole family if one star is born. It just needs to be eased out. Call me if you change your mind. I'm a friend of the family now, so you will see me from time to time, and you never know what the future may hold.'

Novella smiles, and bubbles up inside as she watches Leonardo Rinaldi leave the marquee. Throughout the morning, she is kept busy charming the public into placing orders until lunch time, when to her relief, there came a lull as people's interests were more on their bellies, than on cars.

Relieved to have a break, she ate a welcome plate of warm tuna pasta then decided it is time to take a breath of air and see who else she can attract to buy cars. She saw a group of women surrounding the Town Car, so waltzed over to have a chat.

'Hello ladies, I'm pleased to see you admiring our most popular Town Car that is on sale especially for us women of the fairer sex. I do hope you like my artistic designs that decorate the car. They help to make us seen and get noticed when driving on the roads, don't you think.'

'You're right,' said one of the women. We want to be seen, when going shopping and driving our children about, don't we ladies? '

Nods of approval broke out amongst the group.

'Are you married with children?' one younger lady asked.'

'No not yet, but when I do marry, I will definitely have a Town car. What about you?'

'I fancy something like that black sports. It's exciting to look at. I bet it's an exciting drive.'

'I haven't test driven the Speeder Sports yet, but I do have my own handmade Gold Sports that is worth a look in that Marquee over there. This model is made to order so you'll have a short wait. There's an order book to write your name and details should you decide on the Gold.'

'Can I buy on hire purchase? I am single and earn a good income, so I am in the position to buy.'

'Of course, whichever one you choose, talk to that salesman over there, he will give you all the details you need.'

"Thank you, I'll go there now.' She looked at her friends. 'Do you want to come and look with me Vittoria?'

Novella glanced at the two young ladies heading toward the Marquee when her friends Daisy, Isola and Emilia chase after them, Isola calling out, 'We will be interested to know about hire purchase too.'

Novella then turned to the other married women and coaxed them into buying Town cars before leaving them to carry on their nattering.

'Thank you, ladies. I'm sure you will be very happy with your choice of car.'

She made her way to a man sitting relaxed in a Speedster Sport.

'Good afternoon, sir, you look comfortable, can I tempt you to buy this car?'

'You most certainly can,' smiled Alvize Renzo. 'This car is intoxicatingly divine, and I just adore black, it shows a seductive air of mystery about it, perfect for me.' he drawled.

'I'm glad you think so.'

'Come, beautiful Signorina, sit in the passenger seat beside me and let's talk business.' With a deal done, Novella made several more sales with the Tourer, Town Car and Speedster and got right into the swing of selling car after car. Bursting with joy by the exhilarating buzz of tempting people from all walks of life and mixing with many famous names.

I will learn from this day's experience when selling my fashions. A gentle persuasive chat goes a long way

Her mouth, dry from so much talking, Novella desperately needed a coffee and made her way back to the Marquee.

A large group of both men and women had gathered in one corner of the long bar, sipping wine. She could see Alzano had brought a lot of celebrities from the world of fashion with him. With coffee in hand, she joined them. 'Here she is everyone, the new face of the Novella Catalogue, but today we will not distract her with fashion, for Novella is here solely to talk about cars, as I am. Let me be the first of my friends to place an order. I choose this amazing Gold Car. It's has me written all over it.'

'Same here,' came several other voices, until one man said, 'I love it. Maybe next season I'll buy it when I am bored with the black one I've already bought. But I also want the Tourer today. What a beauty.'

'What about the Town Car?' came another voice. 'I thought you always liked to buy everything in three's.'

'What's the point, I have no wife or children,' He laughed.

The joviality carried on until the selling drew to a halt.

With a planned date to meet up with Alzano to conclude the first part of their new business deal in a month confirmed, Novella hugged and waved goodbye to him and her new friends.

The Marquee now emptied of people, ready to see the show. She followed, as the crowd drifted toward the stage, soaking up its electrifying atmosphere.

Her own day, had been a fantastic success, more than she could ever have imagined. *I hope it's been as successful for the family as it has been for me.*

Novella stood with her family watching in awe at the lively and tantalising dance show. Looking up at

Isabella she wondered if her sister is okay as she didn't look her radiant self, even with her makeup on. *maybe It has been too long a day for her and maybe I also look a little wiped out too, though I feel quite wonderful, and full of energy.*

As soon as Isabella and her dancers took their final bow, and Salvatore made his presence known, Novella knew she must change her clothes, drive to the rear of the stage, and wait with her siblings' cars behind the curtain until she is introduced to the audience to round off the finale.

It will be me and my Gold Car driving into the spotlight at the end of the show. Yes. Just for a few minutes, I'll steal the show from Isabella. I must saviour this moment, no matter how brief. She's been in the limelight the whole day. She's had her face splattered across every billboard far and wide for weeks. Now it's my turn to enjoy my own success because dear sweet Salvatore has made sure I'm not left out. The Gold car is my Design Chassis, and the Clothes I will be wearing are my own Creations. I must change into my white alluring figure hugging knitted dress covered with gold glittering sequins, that I designed especially for this day. My whole collections will be remembered when the new Fashion Catalogue comes out in the Spring with me and my Gold Car dominating the cover and every page.

I am so excited. I must make my family proud and show them how much I have grown and overcome my shyness. This is my moment to show off; to test the theory of what Isabella's producer Leonardo Rinaldi believes – that acting abilities can run in a family. I need to put on the performance of my life. And it's the same for dear Salvatore who needs to show no sign to the public of his recent terrible kidnap ordeal

The applause for Isabella now over, Novella is ready to make her mark. She stands on her car seat parked in the centre of the stage, just behind the curtain, the other cars positioned either side of her. The clapping begins. She is trembling with joy, waiting for the famous Italian actor Giorgio Rossi's voice to call out her name, welcoming her into the limelight.

'Ladies and Gentlemen, please now welcome Novella d'Bergamasco and her amazing handmade Gold Sports car.'

A drum roll begins. The crowd chanting her name, "*Novella, Novella, Novella.*" The curtain draws back. The orchestra begins to play. She is staring into the darkness until a single bright spotlight shines on her and her car. She is thrilled by the erupting sound of screaming, whistling, and clapping, as flood lights flash from all directions.

She throws out her open arms until the clapping subsides and she catches her breath. Showing her appreciation, she throws the audience warm kisses as they continued their applause.

Novella climbed from the car and joined her family lining up for a final bow.

Novella takes one last look into the immediate sea of faces and couldn't believe her eyes. Her heart skipped a beat, then skipped another and another. Not daring to move her gaze for fear of losing sight of the dark wavy hair with its exciting and pleasurable little curl that had stirred something deep within her, what seemed a lifetime ago, but her heart had never forgotten. But the young man is going nowhere, for he has seen her, and she could tell by his warm captivating smile he is very happy.

He pushed through the crowd and climbed onto the stage and ran to give her a huge hug.

Oh, Luca my love, you are here at last

Destiny had spoken, the night belonged to the young sweethearts. As Novella lovingly gazed into Luca's eyes he pulled a precious gold and diamond ring from his finger that he had bought the very day upon their first meeting, waiting for the right time to place it on her finger. That day has arrived, her heart full of rapturous joy, she knew they could never lose each other again. 'My heart is yours forever my adorable Novella.'

A new dawn had begun for the young lovers.

Chapter 77

Anton's Launch Day

With the Car Launch day in January drawing nearer, Anton found himself working flat out from early morning to late at night.

The list of things for him to arrange and check seemed endless – the venue, licencing, ticketing, vendors, performers, stages, technical production, security, toilets and many more!

Recruiting and coordinating on-site sales staff and caterers, providing sufficient food and drink were high on his list, along with ensuring that around four hundred cars would arrive at the Atalanta football ground on time.

But he found time to exchange telegraphs with Ginnie, in America to spend Christmas and the New Year with her father. Her last message told him: 'I'm sure you will make the Launch Day a big success, darling. Then you can turn your attention to the small matter of marrying me.'

She followed up with a second message expressing deep love and telling how much she missed him and saying, 'Your big day will soon be over in Bergamo so nothing to keep you there. Come to New York for a couple of months rest. I miss and love you so much and want us to be together. We could even get married here away from your family who don't accept me. Please say yes.'

'I'll think about it,' he replied, and the next day telegraphed 'Yes.'

In the few days before the Launch, he found her idea becoming more attractive every time it came to mind and began to consider a plan that may change his life.

Anton arrived at the Atalanta Football Stadium at 6:30am on Launch Day and immediately checked if the three cars being displayed for sale were in each marquee. He had decided that the deluxe Novella Gold car, designed to his sister's specifications, should be on show in a special enclosure in addition to being presented on stage at the grand finale.

Keep calm, he told himself as he hurried around the ground having discussions with caterers and sales staff before the event opened to the public at 10am.

He then greeted early arriving guests and thought he had everything going smoothly until he heard a commotion outside one of the marquees.

Rushing to where he could hear the disruption, Anton felt horrified to see a full-scale row taking place between Salvatore and his enemy, the corrupt politician Francisco D'Angelo in full view of several guests.

It quickly became clear to him that D'Angelo had demanded a free car for allowing the building of their Salò factory to go ahead. The large-set, sullen looking man shouted: 'You're getting off lightly if I walk away with only a car.'

Salvatore swore at him and yelled: 'I'm giving you nothing, you dishonest bastard. Now get out before I have you thrown out.'

A clearly furious D'Angelo looked about to hit his brother. Anton dragged him back and said: 'I'm asking you to leave, Signore D'Angelo.'

After an uneasy silence the disgruntled politician turned on his heel and marched towards the exit.

'Are you alright?' Anton asked.

'Yes, I'm fine. The bloody man had the nerve to turn up here demanding I give him a top of the range car.'

'Well, now you can calm down, Salvatore. The last thing you need is any further stress following what you've been through.'

Turning to the guests standing nearby, he added; 'I'm sorry for any embarrassment caused just now.'

Anton felt relieved he could now concentrate on trying to ensure that the rest of the day went without a hitch.

He succeeded until the late afternoon when the lighting and sound system failed just before the time Isabella's stage show should start.

Anton ran to join the engineer checking what had gone wrong. The workman pointed out a mains cable had been severed.

'How long will it take to fix?' Anton demanded as Salvatore joined them.

'Give me half an hour and I'll have it repaired,' answered the harassed engineer.

'Do you think it's been cut deliberately?'

'Looks like it.'

'This must have been that bastard D'Angelo or one of his thugs. He'll pay for this,' Salvatore snarled.

Fortunately, both sound and lighting were restored before darkness descended, enabling the song and dance show to go ahead to great applause.

Anton had no time to sit back and enjoy the spectacle due to interruptions in dealing with a stream of questions and requests from staff and performers.

As a result, Anton saw only part of the fabulous song and dance performance by Isabella and her troupe and unfortunately missed the introduction of sports stars, including the Atalanta football players and the Italian international cycling team. And he never stood still long enough during the whole day to chat with the half a dozen or so famous film star friends carefully chosen and invited by Isabella.

Giuseppe, in a state of breathless excitement, rushed from the crowd and told him, 'Four rich customers bought a Novella Gold Sport from me. Every single one of them and my London friend bought thirty cars,' and hurried away to find and tell Salvatore before Anton could shake hands and congratulate him.

But Anton was ready to take part in the spectacular finale, driving a Speedster on stage together with Isabella in a Town Car and Salvatore in a Tourer.

There followed the presentation of the brilliant Novella Gold sparkling under the stage floodlights, driven on by his clever younger sister to loud applause. How happy and triumphant she looked. He clapped and cheered with the large throng, and shouted, 'Brava, Novella, Brava, Brava, Brava.'

Most of all he felt great delight at being told by Giuseppe that car sales may exceed all expectations by the end of the event.

What excited Anton even more, is the thought of being with Ginnie again, "I'll be waiting on the dockside" she'd telegraphed"

Anton realised he must no longer avoid telling Salvatore he would not be returning from America. *To safeguard my Motori Bergamasco inheritance I'll ask him to make me our United States representative and stay on the board, and hope that Comet Cars also have a job or I may sacked by both.*

Before leaving for home when the final few guests were emptying the now dark Stadium, he went to find his brother.

Chapter 78

Salvatore's Launch Day

At 7am, Salvatore lifted cup of bitter breakfast espresso to his lips and groaned at the strain on his battered arm, ribs, and spine.

To his wife, he said, 'Such a small cup, but my back muscles and arm feel the weight.'

'But didn't you fall two metres into your grave, darling?'

'True. And Frank crashed on top of me after being shot.'

'You're lucky It will take a few weeks for the bruises to go, but he saved your life.'

Salvatore peered through the window at his gravestone leaning against a tree, the inscription just readable in the early dawn gloom.

'I'll have to find a place for that damned thing.'

'Somewhere out of sight, my love.'

At 7:30 Salvatore set out for the Atalanta Stadium, hoping that Anton had managed to get the complex Launch Day all set up. *He's not the best organiser. I should have been here. I shouldn't have gone to Naples.*

Approaching the hospital turning, he decided to leave Frank to rest. *After all, he's had three bullets and an operation to contend with. I'll leave him to rest and see him this evening on the way home.*

Leaving his car and walking on stiff legs through the gate, where Anton ran forward and hugged him, saying, 'Oh I'm happy to see you alive and well.'

'Oh, for god's sake,' groaned Salvatore pushing him away. 'Thanks for the welcome, but I fell six feet into a grave and a big man fell on top of me. I pain

367

everywhere. Take it that I am just about alive, but not sure yet about well.'

'But you can still Joke.'

'That wasn't a joke. I ache all over. Come on. Show me around, but slowly please.

Relieved to see that Anton had excelled himself, after an hour Salvatore let him go and sat in a warm Marquee to eat a small plate of excellent pasta before leaving to have another check around.

Customers seemed to be crowding round and buying cars from every Marquee, from the football pitch, in the show-and-drive area on the football pitch, and even where cars were held outside to be brought in and sold. The Stadium became so crowded that when he met his friend the Atalanta Club owner Salvatore said, 'Seems we have all of Milan and most of Lombardy here.'

'You're right. Lucky the ground is frozen solid, or I wouldn't have a football pitch for next Saturday.'

Salvatore shook hands with film stars, the entire Italy international cycling team and a massive world champion boxer pretending to be American.

In the mid-morning his mortal enemy, the crooked politician, D'Angelo, pushed his way from the throng. Thrusting his face into Salvatore's, swearing and shouting, 'This man's a criminal. He's cheated me. He owes me a car.'

'What are you doing here?' Salvatore shouted back. 'You're supposed to be in jail. I'm giving you nothing. Now get out before I have you thrown out.'

D'Angelo pulled back a fist, but before he could strike a blow, Anton burst from the crowd and growled, 'I'm asking you to leave Signore D'Angelo.' The politician pushed Salvatore away and marched towards the gate.

'Are you ok?' asked Anton, brushing dust from Salvatore's jacket.

'Aching like hell from falling into and climbing out of a grave, but I'll tell you about that later. Take me somewhere to sit down and have a drink.'

Anton led him to the VIP Marquee. Salvatore downed two brandies before Pancucci appeared and whispered 'The Don is here. He's bought a car. If I find him I'll have him arrested. We know that your friend D'Angelo told him you'd be getting off that train in Naples, so is accessory to your kidnap. If I get the Don I'll get D'Angelo too.'

'How did he get out of jail?' asked Salvatore.

'Bribed a judge,' said Pancucci. 'Nothing I could do to keep him in.'

Salvatore stayed long enough to rest, before taking his place in Isabella's fantastic show and the cars presentation. When hugging her goodbye, she whispered, 'I went the hospital to see Frank this morning. He told me the oddest thing. He says he's our brother. Angry at him saying such a stupid thing I got up and stormed out.'

'Take no notice,' said Salvatore. 'Remember he'd been shot by three bullets and had a painful operation. He would probably have been hallucination and with the drugs talking. Don't make him look foolish by telling the others.'

'I won't. Imagine him being our brother. How ridiculous.'

Salvatore drove to the hospital. Frank looked slightly better, sitting sipping whisky. He smiled and asked, 'How did the day go? Did you sell plenty of automobiles?'

'They seemed to be going well. How do you feel?'

'Bad, but a bit better. I had two visitors today to cheer me up, the Don and our sister Isabella. It didn't go well with either.'

'Isabella told me. I said you must be hallucinating and affected by the operation drugs and not to tell anyone.'

'Why?

'Remember,' said Salvatore. 'This is our big day. That news will cause too much shock and confusion. I'll call them to my house for dinner tomorrow and tell them after several glasses of wine.'

'That'll help oil their shock and ease the news.'

'I hope so. Anyway, what did the Don have to say?'

'Well, he brought me this whisky. Want some? And he told me the history of our papà and my birth. Interesting story. I'll tell you all when I'm out of here at another family dinner at your house.'

He handed Salvatore half a glass of Cutty Sark. 'Careful, it's got quite a kick. Now tell me more about how your day went.'

'It looks as we sold a lot more cars than expected.'

'So why are you looking so down brother? What's your problem?'

'We're bankrupt. Our bank manager discovered that stupid Giuseppe had been stuffing his wife and closed all our accounts.'

'Then find another bank.'

'He's had us blacklisted throughout Europe.'

'How much do you need?'

Salvatore told him.

Frank whistled. 'Hey, brother. That's quite a pile. But I can help.'

'How?'

'I know papà's rule that only family can join in and run the company. Well, what is more family than a long-lost brother?'

'But how can you help?'

'I'm a multi billionaire and your brother. I'll do the finance; you make the cars. How's that for a deal?'

Printed in Great Britain
by Amazon